SOLDIE
THE
RETURNING

SOLDIER FROM THE WARS RETURNING

CHARLES CARRINGTON

Pen & Sword
MILITARY

First published in Great Britain in 1965 by
Hutchinson & Co (Publishers) Limited

Republished in 2006 and again in this format in 2015 by
PEN & SWORD MILITARY
An imprint of
Pen & Sword Books Ltd
47 Church Street
Barnsley
South Yorkshire
S70 2AS

Copyright © C E Carrington, 1965, 2006 and 2015

ISBN 978 1 47384 1 840

The right of C E Carrington to be identified as Author of this
work has been asserted by him in accordance with the
Copyright, Designs and Patents Act 1988.

A CIP catalogue record for this book is
available from the British Library.

Printed and bound in England by
CPI Group (UK) Ltd, Croydon, CR0 4YY

Pen & Sword Books Ltd incorporates the Imprints of Aviation, Atlas,
Family History, Fiction, Maritime, Military, Discovery, Politics, History,
Archaeology, Select, Wharncliffe Local History, Wharncliffe True Crime,
Military Classics, Wharncliffe Transport, Leo Cooper, The Praetorian Press,
Remember When, Seaforth Publishing and Frontline Publishing.

For a complete list of Pen & Sword titles please contact
PEN & SWORD BOOKS LIMITED
47 Church Street, Barnsley, South Yorkshire, S70 2AS, England
E-mail: enquiries@pen-and-sword.co.uk
Website: www.pen-and-sword.co.uk

Contents

Acknowledgments

I am obliged to my friends: Mr. Herbert Van Thal for instigating me to write this book, Mr. John Terraine for correcting some of the grosser errors and for allowing me the use of two maps which originally appeared in his own books, Dr. Noble Frankland (and his colleagues at the Imperial War Museum), and Commander Charles Drage, R.N., for many stimulating discussions about what it felt like to be young in 1914.

Thanks are also due to George Allen & Unwin Ltd., for allowing me to quote from *The Supreme Command 1914–1918* by Lord Hankey (1961).

'WE TALKED OF WAR'

JOHNSON: 'Every man thinks meanly of himself for not having been a soldier, or not having been at sea.

Were Socrates and Charles the Twelfth of Sweden both present in any company and Socrates were to say, 'Follow me and hear a lecture on philosophy'; and Charles, laying his hand on his sword, were to say, 'Follow me and dethrone the Czar'; a man would be ashamed to follow Socrates. The impression is universal; yet it is strange. But the profession of soldiers and sailors has the dignity of danger. Mankind reverences those who have got over fear, which is so general a weakness.'

SIR WILLIAM SCOTT: 'But is not courage mechanical, and to be acquired?'

JOHNSON: 'Why yes, Sir, in a collective sense. Soldiers consider themselves only as parts of a great machine'.

(Boswell's *Life of Johnson*, 10th August 1778)

Preface

I do not wish to add to the number of histories of the First World War. The narrative on which I have strung my reminiscences is conventional not in the sense that I have copied the popular writers but in the sense that my point of view is shared, more or less, by a large number of old soldiers with whom I have discussed the experiences of our youth, so frequently, over so many years. We do not, of course, agree in our judgments about individual actions, and would have been donkeys indeed if we had not formed strong personal opinions from our own knowledge of public events. I claim, only, that mine is an authentic record. This, so far as I can recall my past, is how it struck me at the time and I shall venture an assumption that other veterans will agree with, at least, a considerable part of my comment. If a learned student should say that I am wrong about this or that historical incident which research workers have elucidated and have shown to be different from what I suppose, my rejoinder will be to say: 'Very well. You may be right. But this is what we thought about it in those days.' I offer a case-study of the First World War as it appeared to a young soldier who had no inside knowledge, and no contact with the inner circles of the governing class.

One of my qualifications for speaking is that I saw the First World War from below, as a combatant soldier in a line regiment; and the Second World War from above, as a staff officer. Though I achieved neither distinction nor high promotion, it was then my privilege to meet several of the Commanders-in-Chief, to know a great many secrets—and some scandals—and to live in the fringes of the world where policy was made, among personages who regarded Divisional Commanders and such as rather small fry. On the whole, as I have grown older, I find myself willing to accept the general incompetence of human beings, and I no longer expect a superman to emerge with a solution for every unforeseen problem. I am inclined to think that the

First War commanders did pretty well, according to their lights, and the tendency to blame them for the crimes and follies of a whole generation now seems to be disingenuous.

Long memories, though they present the images of what happened fifty years ago more vividly than the events of yesterday, are treacherous, and such efforts as I have made to check my references have revealed to me what Shakespeare meant when he wrote of old men remembering 'with advantages'. To my chagrin I have been obliged to reject one or two anecdotes on which I have been dining-out for forty or fifty years, and I here make public apology for an episode that I have allowed myself to recount in Chapter 14. After searching my home letters and scraps of diary, and after consulting *Hansard*, I am unable to substantiate my claim to have been present at the Frederick Maurice debate in the House of Commons. I was in London about that date; I did visit the gallery of the House; I saw the scene I have described; and I followed the manpower controversy with keen attention; but I do not now think it likely that I could have heard the debate on 9th May 1918. This, I think, is a build-up of several memories jumbled together, and still worth something as a contemporary impression. I make the critics a present of this confession.

What allowance the reader will make for tricks of memory I leave to his judgment, assuring him that very much of my material has been drawn from contemporary letters and diaries, and from early drafts of the book which I published in 1929 under a pseudonym (*A Subaltern's War*, by 'Charles Edmonds'). Most of it was written ten years earlier and much more was written than was published. It is thus anterior to the pacifist reaction of the nineteen-thirties and is untainted by the influence of the later writers who invented the powerful image of 'disenchantment' or 'disillusion'. I go back to an earlier stage in the history of ideas.

I have thought that it might be stimulating to middle-aged readers who tend to form their notions of the First World War upon their memories of the Second if I made occasional comparisons between the two.

C. E. CARRINGTON

I

Before the War

SOLDIERING, on the whole, is a young man's trade. The first appeal for recruits in 1914 called for able-bodied men between the ages of nineteen and thirty, that is to say men who in 1964 are between the ages of sixty-nine and eighty years. In 1914 there was no such thing as national registration, so that recruits could easily falsify their ages, as I did among thousands of others. Kitchener's Army contained many boys of seventeen, many men of forty. When conscription came a check was kept on ages, but later the shortage of recruits led to a cruel call-up of older and of younger men. In the desperate French campaign of 1918 thousands of conscripts, under nineteen years old, were sent to fight abroad in spite of pledges given, so that many men born in 1900 and now no more than sixty-five years old saw active service in the First World War. How many of the combatants of 1914–18 still survive in Britain? Not less than 300,000, I estimate, and most of them under seventy. How many served in both world wars? This is a more difficult question to answer, not only for lack of statistics, but because the two wars were so different in character.

The First World War hardly came to Britain. German naval raids on coastal towns, in the first few weeks of the war, did a little damage and inflicted casualties on a scale that would have been thought negligible twenty years later. Air-raids on London, alarming because unfamiliar, were never powerful enough to interrupt the life of the city. Over large parts of the country, during the greater part of the war, there was little change in the social pattern. High prices and high wages, a difficulty in buying food, shocking as they seemed, brought about no fundamental change, and rationing—very efficiently administered—came in only for the last few months, to be instantly abandoned when the war was over. But over the nation there hung the dark cloud of the casualty

13

lists. The young able-bodied men were away at the front and of those who reached the fighting line about a quarter never came back and another quarter came back maimed. In the First World War you were either a combatant or you were not, that is speaking of Britain and the British. Those behind the line suffered some deprivation, but for the most part neither hardship nor danger; those in the line were under suspended sentence of death. The people at home with their anxieties they could do nothing to assuage, their sympathies they could do little to express, were often unhappier than the soldiers at the front, mostly volunteers, who were sustained by a dogged unreasoning pride. Between the two groups, combatants and non-combatants, there lay a psychological barrier which perhaps grew more impenetrable with time, until, after ten years' silence, some inhibition was lifted and a flow of self-conscious revelation came from the fighting men in every combatant country. Nothing is stranger in the history of the First World War than the sudden outburst of soldiers' autobiographies which reached its climax in 1929 and 1930. Until then a dumb protest, now a phase of exhibitionism.

Nothing like this happened in the Second World War, since, before it began, everyone expected the worst. There was no call for volunteers to improvise a new system, no distinction between combatant and non-combatant. Within ten minutes of the Declaration of War the air-raid sirens were telling the people of London that they were in the fighting line. No one supposed that it was the duty of every able-bodied man to fight in France while the women and the weaklings kept the home fires burning. For the first half of the war the main strength of the Army was at home in the comparative comfort of training camps and enjoying periodical week-end leave. Often the soldier going home from his safe country quarters found his wife, booted and helmeted, dealing with air-raid incidents under fire. There was no barrier between soldier and civilian and no psychological trauma to be healed after the war was over, accordingly no flood of revelation ten years later. The Second War did not reproduce the morbid states of the First, because the load was shared.

I do not in the least imply that there was less heroism, and sacrifice, even that there was less bloodshed, in the Second World War than in the First. I rather think there was more individual heroism, and for the reason that the battles, except in Russia, were not mass-battles. In 1916 everyone who was able-bodied had to go through the mill and it would be a great mistake to suppose that every man in Kitchener's Army was a hero. A modicum of physical courage is common enough and, helped by discipline and *esprit de corps*, the majority of men can muster up enough to face fire at least once. This is the theory of the nation-in-arms, the strategy of using massed battalions, which dominated military thinking on the continent of Europe from 1792 to 1918. The British Army conformed in the First World War though this kind of mass-murder was contrary to our tradition; we had rather specialized, ever since Crécy and Agincourt, in shooting down the massed battalions with a small highly trained corps of professional soldiers. However, 1916 was the moment for mass-attacks, according to the best military opinions (on which I have more to say later). 1940 was very different. Technical advance in weapons, tanks, and aircraft had placed the firepower in the hands of specialists so that the fighting was no longer done by crowds of riflemen in line or column but by small highly skilled groups—mighty men of valour—bomber crews and tank crews and gun-teams, while the masses were deployed behind in the ancillary services. The teeth of a modern army are more formidable than they were in 1916 but the tail is much longer. The number of soldiers who fired a shot at the enemy in the Second World War must be much smaller than the number in the First, because the Second War was fought by champions. I have heard Sir Brian Horrocks say on the radio that in the forefront of the battle you always seemed to meet the same few faces. Not so in the First War, when everyone was there, or so large a majority that the fighting soldiers had a hearty contempt for everyone not a fighting soldier. Men in uniform back at the base were expected to be a little ashamed of themselves and to make excuses. I dare say there are men in their sixties now reading these lines who have never quite rid themselves of an apologetic air for not having been 'in the trenches', even if they were doing other work of the greatest importance. I never noticed a hint of this sensitivity in the nineteen-forties, when any stay-at-home could produce his 'bomb story'. In 1916 you were no one unless you had a 'trench story', though it was unlikely that you would waste it on a civilian audience.

At the front of the battle the dangers and the losses were no less severe in the Second World War. Leading units in action had casualties as great as those at the Somme or Passchendaele but the number of men deployed along the front was much less, and so, accordingly, were the total casualties.

(2)

If there were to be a war who would be the enemy? In the nineteenth century it would have been either France or Russia, perhaps both. As recently as 1898 we had been on the brink of war with France, and the French had openly encouraged the Boers against us in South Africa. About the turn of the century there was a change of policy and there was also a change of heart. My brothers and I were, as children, pro-French and anti-German, whereas I think my parents found it difficult to reconcile themselves to the *Entente Cordiale* of 1904, since in their youth they had been pro-German and anti-French. As for the Russian bear, it was always a bogey in the dark background. The Crimean War was remembered as our last great European war and in Edwardian days there were still Crimean veterans in Chelsea Hospital and in the service clubs. Russian infiltration on the North-West frontier of India was the subject of innumerable novels and melodramas and when the Japanese fought and beat the Russians, though it did not touch us deeply, we were on the Japanese side. Everyone knew that Russian warships had fired at British trawlers on the Dogger Bank in 1905, supposing them to be Japanese, and we boys rather regretted that the Channel Fleet had not blown the Russians out of the water before the Japanese did.

But Russia, very weak after the war and the Revolution of 1905, faded out of the picture as the German Empire and the Kaiser began to dominate the scene. At the Morocco crisis of 1911 there was no doubt that we were lined up with France against German aggression, and, though I knew nothing of such political niceties as a schoolboy, Lloyd George's speech at the Mansion House implied that the well-informed political classes had taken the same step.

No one outside the establishment knew in 1911 that staff plans were being prepared for a British Expeditionary Force to operate in France against a hypothetical German invasion. The British public was not thinking of the invasion of France but of the invasion of England. If Germany had been content to become the strongest military power in continental Europe it would have been difficult to inflame British opinion, since we did not care about the German Army but about the German Navy. For a hundred years the Royal Navy had policed the seas of the world in order to preserve peace for a world-wide empire. The German Navy, which had no such mission and no such empire to defend, could exist only to challenge British supremacy and therefore was a menace, or so the situation looked in the reign of King Edward. As long ago as 1871, an anonymous book, *Battle of Dorking*, describing a German invasion of England had been widely read, and the successive naval building programmes of 1898, 1900, and 1906 had each set off a new wave of alarm. Invasions became a favourite subject for science fiction with astonishing roles allotted to the newly invented aeroplane. Captain Frank Shaw, in the popular boys' weekly *Chums*, ran serials on this fascinating theme. Griffith's *World Peril of 1910*, published in 1908 and now quite forgotten, was a best-seller; the *Englishman's Home*, describing resistance by a family caught unawares, was so a popular play in 1909 as to beat all records by running at three London theatres simultaneously; the *Riddle of the Sands* (1903), a spy story of the German preparations for invading Britain, was something more, a classic thriller. Spy scares broke out, some German spies were arrested, and the comic writers made great use of the German peril:

> 'I was playing golf the day
> That the Germans landed.
> All our troops had run away,
> All our ships were stranded;
> And the thought of England's shame
> Very nearly spoiled my game.'

Only the fervid imagination of H. G. Wells in *The War in The Air* (1908) combined science fiction with the forebodings of war to prophecy the downfall of a civilization.

How seriously were these alarms taken, or meant to be taken? We must look back into a sober conventional society which had not known war, except by proxy and at a distance, for a hundred years, nor revolution for two hundred years, the society in which old Sir William Harcourt had said to the young Winston Churchill: 'My experience is that nothing ever happens.' Scare-mongers did not get under the skin of the stolid British people. The diplomats, as we may now read from their published memoirs, were growing anxious, as Europe—for no valid reason—began to arrange itself in two armed groups. On the other hand, liberal intellectuals tended to write the danger down. The Cabinet Minister charged with preparations for land warfare, Haldane, was a student of German thought and an admirer of German technique. While working to provide his own country with an efficient army he strove no less for friendship with the German nation. Several Cabinet Ministers were pacifists at a time when that creed implied that wars were neither necessary nor probable. Norman Angell's *Great Illusion* (1910) convinced the thinking part of the nation that war would not pay and suggested to many that such good men of business as the Germans would never be so foolish as to start a war. Organized labour was inclined to take the line that international action by the trade unions could checkmate the militarist governments. And the potent force of inertia supported those who thought that the best way to prevent war was to deny the possibility of it.

Asquith's Government (1908-15) was perhaps the most talented administration that has ever ruled this country and in the critical years the key positions were held by Lloyd George as Chancellor of the Exchequer, Grey as Foreign Secretary, Churchill at the Admiralty, and Haldane at the War Office. Of the Navy I shall not have much to say except that the young Churchill and his old colleague 'Jacky' Fisher, the First Sea Lord, provided Britain with a battle fleet that kept two paces ahead of the Germans. The change from coal-fired to oil-fired ships gave them a margin of speed (at the cost of making the Navy dependent on Persian Gulf oil) and the advance from twelve-inch to fifteen-inch guns for the main armament gave a margin of striking power. Naval rivalry between Britain and Germany, rather outside my subject, was also a rivalry between the two old admirals, Fisher and Tirpitz, neither of whom succeeded in persuading his government to adopt a bold aggressive strategy, though each created a navy that was the pride of the nation. While few British liberals or internationally minded socialists in Britain decried or despised the Royal Navy, the Army, ever since Cromwell, had lain under suspicion. While the Navy could count on its parliamentary vote, never lacked ratings, had its own dockyards, ordered its ships, and munitions, the Army was kept on a tight string. Rigorously reduced at the end of every war, closely scrutinized, it had no funds for development, no plan for expansion in wartime, no organization for enlarging the supply of munitions. Well did the soldiers know that every penny must be fought for, and that the Treasury was their determined opponent.

(3)

It requires an effort now to realize how distinct had been the life of the Army from that of the civilian world in the nineteenth century. The officers were an aristocratic caste, still linked with the Court rather than with the political administration, and the rank and file were recruits from the unemployed. Wellington's saying that his soldiers were the scum of the earth was still true of the Army of the eighteen-eighties. But, taking in men of very poor quality, a good regiment could make them the salt of the earth. Between the reorganization of 1881 and the War of 1914 there had been a reformation in the British Army, credited by the soldiers to one commander, Roberts of Kandahar, who had spent his long life promoting the soldiers' welfare by building up their self-respect. What had occasionally been done by a talented colonel in a good regiment became common form, so that the regular army that went to France in 1914 was a different body from the drunken, reckless ne'er-do-wells described in the early stories of Rudyard Kipling.

The British Army, since the eighteenth century, was repeatedly torn by an internal struggle between the officers who had served in the overseas empire—in India or Africa—and the officers at home whose professional interests were in European campaigns. Even Wolfe, while conquering Canada, complained of his distaste for the colonies, and longed for a command in Germany. Wellington could not establish his reputation until several victories in Spain had proved that he was something more than a 'sepoy general'. The disasters of the Crimean War were largely due to the fact that 'European' officers with no recent fighting experience got all the commands, to the exclusion of the 'Indian' officers. In reorganizing and re-equipping the Army (always on the cheap) and planning for the next war, during the reign of Edward VII, we find the old, inevitable, division between colonial experience and continental probability. During the eighteen-nineties when the students were the future world-war generals, the Army Staff College at Camberley was under the influence of a brilliant teacher, Colonel

Henderson, the biographer of Stonewall Jackson. The First War generals were Henderson's young men, and their doctrine was based largely on the lessons of the American Civil War, a 'colonial' campaign on the largest scale. At the same time Henderson did not neglect the wars of Europe and the rival view was that the next great war would more resemble the Franco-Prussian War of 1870 with its short intense battles and massive strokes. Who could say? One of the silliest gibes made by civilians against soldiers is that they always try to fight the last war. What else can they do? No general should gamble with men's lives on a speculation; he can only start with the equipment actually to hand and should use it in the way that experience has shown to be best.

In 1899 the British Army had a rehearsal for continental war which was to give them a tactical advantage over French and Germans. Soldiering in modern times is a strange profession and very different from sailoring When an admiral takes a fleet to sea in time of peace he is carrying heavy responsibility and incurring some risk. What he does is what he would have to do in wartime and men's lives depend on his efficiency, so that the change from peace to war for a sailor is merely a heightening of intensity. A battle fleet exercises influence by its presence and rarely fires its guns. Many a naval officer, Lord Fisher for one, has a long and distinguished sea-going career without ever seeing a fleet action. There have been soldiers, too, who have spent their lives in barracks without smelling powder, but we cannot judge their quality. A sailor is judged by sailing, but a soldier by fighting. In time of peace his training has an element of make-believe and his worth is not known until he comes under fire. In 1914, with the exception of two or three old generals—Hindenburg, aged sixty-seven, Mackensen, aged sixty-five, Von Kluck, aged over sixty, veterans of the War of 1870, there was hardly a soldier in the German Army who had even been in battle. All the more credit, then, to the efficiency with which the German commanders applied the forty-year-old lessons of the Franco-Prussian War to the same campaign fought with new weapons. But their forecasting failed and might not have failed if they had seen as many colonial campaigns during those forty years as the British or the French. Like the British, the French had their 'colonial' generals and their 'continental' generals. Joffre, the generalissimo in 1914, was a colonial, the conqueror of Timbuktu. Gallieni, who struck the decisive blow in the Battle of the Marne, was an African general; the leader of the continental school was Foch, an instructor from the Staff College. The victories of Napoleon and the lessons to be learned from the French failure in 1870 were his guides, and until 1914 he was never under fire.

Roberts and Kitchener, colonial generals and not graduates of the Staff College, had fought and won the Boer War, to which we must give a moment's attention. More than 250,000 volunteers from Britain and the Dominions served in South Africa against the Boers between 1899 and 1902. That is to say they had learned at least one lesson of soldiering which was unknown to the German Army—what it feels like to be shot at and shot over. Much nonsense has been written about the Boer War. The British Army made a bad beginning because they misjudged the nature of the campaign. In one week three widely separated columns, hundreds of miles apart and acting independently, were defeated by concealed Boer riflemen. No one could have foreseen this as no one had ever before been confronted with such a task. This was the first campaign in which soldiers used magazine rifles with smokeless powder. These three defeats were a sore blow to British pride and armchair critics at home blamed the generals. It is important to notice that the soldiers on the spot thought otherwise, and Buller, after his defeats at Colenso and Spion Kop, did not altogether lose the confidence of his men. When I was a young soldier in 1914 the old Regulars still spoke of Buller as their favourite general. A bad general, but a popular general, he was not ruthless enough. Buller seemed to have all the qualities and the experience that should have made a Commander-in-Chief until they were tried in action. He had won the V.C. as a young officer; he had done well in several campaigns; he had served in the War Office; he had commanded at Aldershot, and now he was ripe for high command overseas. But in battle, heavy casualties unnerved him, he plunged into the fighting line to make personal courage serve for cool direction, and tamely called the battle off when another effort might have brought victory. A young staff officer named Douglas Haig was a sharp critic of Buller's method. See how Haig, fifteen years later, applied the lesson he had learned from Buller's failure of nerve, brought about by being too much involved.

After the initial defeats in South Africa, old Roberts, aged sixty-eight, was sent out to take command with Kitchener, aged fifty, as his deputy and chief of staff. They quickly, cheaply, and efficiently defeated the Boer armies and occupied the two Afrikaner republics. This straightforward campaign of 1900 quite restored the morale of the British Army, if indeed it had been shaken by the defeats of 1899. The cavalry commander under Roberts was Sir John French, aged forty-eight, who did extremely well. He won the first victory of the war, over Cronje, the most celebrated Boer general, by piercing the centre of his line with a whole division of cavalry at the charge. Their losses were negligible, and neither French nor his staff officer, Douglas Haig, forgot that day. The later phase of the Boer War need not detain us. The world was astonished at the persistency of the Boer guerilla campaign, the first of many which since have defied the efforts of regular armies.

There was much to be learned from the Boer War and the Army studied its lesson, perhaps too thoroughly. As a rehearsal for Armageddon it was invaluable, especially in those branches of soldiering that the romantic writers don't dwell upon. Equipment, transport, commissariat, ammunition supply, sanitation, field hospitals, staff duties were so well tried out that the British Army, twelve years later, was the best provided in the world (not excluding the American Army). A great many clever young officers and N.C.O.s had also been 'screened' by the hard test of active service. Every war must begin with its Bullers, its generals who look like battle-winners, and in every war the testing time comes when the first battle is not what was expected. Every war has its surprises, and it is rare for the generals in the first campaign to survive to the last. At the end of every war there is a professional corps of well-tested young majors and colonels who are inclined to be critical of their seniors and opinionated about what they will do when their turn comes to command. But the next war will be different, again, and will produce its own Bullers. Some young officers marked out by their success in commanding columns on the Veldt were Haig, Plumer, Smith-Dorrien, Byng, Allenby, all in their early forties at that time. It was assumed that they would get commands in the next war, under Sir John French.

Among the many books published in Edwardian days forecasting the character of a future war there was one which was much discussed by professional soldiers and which may be seen to have affected the art of generalship in the First World War. Its title was *The Green Curve, and Other Stories* (1909), and its author was a young officer named Swinton who used the pseudonym of 'Ole Luk-oie'. Some years later this ingenious and imaginative soldier was one of the inventors of the tank. The stories, based upon experiences in the Boer War and the Russo-Japanese War, sometimes descriptive and sometimes fanciful, pointed the way to the deadly warfare of the future when battles would range over the same ground for many days, when the distinction between combatant and civilian would vanish, and when the general must be a technician rather than a swashbuckling hero. *The Green Curve*, the story which gave its title to the book, was concerned with 'logistics', a branch of the science of war which was to dominate the battlefield—perhaps it always had—though not yet known by that name. A general commanding a beleaguered city took the advice of a mathematician who presented him with a series of graphs setting out the periods during which the garrison and the civilian population could survive on calculated scales of food supply. Instead of making heroic gestures the general applied himself to the study of curves on squared paper, but by a wrong calculation he based his plans upon the curve drawn in purple ink rather than the curve drawn in green ink, thus consigning himself to defeat and his country to ruin. To us, the interest in this simple story lies in the fact that, only fifty years ago, the notion of basing policy upon statistics was new and astonishing, until we remind ourselves that statistics itself is a modern science. Indeed the earliest use of the word 'graph' quoted by the *Oxford Dictionary* is as recent as 1878.

Another of these stories, *The Point of View*, which I remember as a subject of discussion when I was a young soldier, throws a sharp light on the generalship of those days. The story gives three accounts of the same battle: the first is by a group of dogged but exhausted soldiers who for days have been fighting over the same shell-torn entrenchments, with a sort of resigned fury because they well understand that they are being sacrificed to create a diversion while the decisive blow is struck elsewhere; the second picture is of the staff officer at headquarters sifting through whole files of messages from the battle-front and methodically recording the progress of the fight by sticking pins into a map, until suddenly he realizes that one message recounts the destruction of his own regiment and the death of his comrades; the third picture is of the Commanding General who, at the crisis of the battle, has gone fishing. Why not? He has made his dispositions and issued his orders and, until reports come in, he can exercise no further influence.

Late in the day, cool, rested, and relaxed, he returns to take charge and to exploit his gains, having carefully secluded himself from the confusion and distress which a detailed view of some corner of the battlefield must have shown him. The fighting soldier's point of view, the staff officer's point of view, the general's point of view, are thus distinguished.

Scientific warfare coolly conducted by commanders from positions where they could take a detached view was the accepted doctrine in all the 1914 armies. The principle was expressly stated in the Field Service Regulations of 1910, the little red book which Haig had authorized as Director of Military Training at the War Office and which every officer was supposed to study. Beautifully lucid and practical, the Field Service Regulations was a model textbook so far as it went, until contingencies appeared which it had not foreseen and did not provide for. The section on reconnaissance is significant. Every junior commander, it insisted, must reconnoitre his own front, a personal responsibility that went as high as the major-generals who commanded divisions. But since the Commander-in-Chief could not possibly reconnoitre the whole front it would be better for him to train his officers to give accurate reports and to rely on them. If he went to look for himself at some particular sector he would be unduly influenced to give it his special attention at the cost of some other sector, which he had not seen and which might be more vital.

The argument, convincing at first sight, explained the antipathy between the troops and their commanders which was so striking a feature of the First World War. Not only did this system weaken the trust of the Army in its leaders, since they were unseen and unknown, it also tended to delude the higher command. Operational staffs could do no more than 'paint the picture', that is they constructed an ideal panorama of what the battle should be, if it were in fact as tidy as the marked maps in the operations room. But battles are never tidy.

The main tactical lesson of the Boer War had been the decisive strength of aimed rifle-fire by troops sited in good defensive positions. Thereafter the British Army devoted itself to shooting practice, under the nice old-fashioned name of 'musketry', and distinguished itself in the next war by shooting straighter and faster than any other army. The Boer War had not been a 'colonial' campaign in the sense that the British were fighting half-armed barbarians. It had been a cause of chagrin that the Boers had the more up-to-date artillery, bought from France and Germany, and it was in the handling of field artillery that the most interesting experiments were made in the next few years. The French produced the most successful field-gun, their celebrated seventy-five millimetre; the British decided for a rather heavier gun, the eighteen-pounder, to replace their Boer War fifteen-pounders, but an artillery replacement was an expensive luxury for an army on the cheap, and supplies of the new gun were still scarce in 1914.

What were the lessons of the South African War about the new machine-guns, then generally known by their inventor's name as Maxims? The machine-guns in use were clumsy, too large to be man-handled for more than short distances, and were water-cooled, with delicate mechanism that often jammed under the rough conditions of the battlefield; and when water failed they soon seized up. If on the other hand they fired sweetly they rapidly used up their ammunition. Transport, water-supply, and ammunition-supply made the machine-gun a troublesome uncertain weapon. Rapid fire by trained riflemen was more reliable, and remained so until the unexpected trench warfare of 1915 gave the machine-gun its opportunity to dominate the battle-field. Nevertheless, the Army had recognised the machine-gun as the weapon of the future and had approached the Treasury for an increased allotment of money to provide machine-guns. It was when their re-quirement was flatly rejected in 1907 that the generals decided upon the alternative of making British soldiers the best riflemen in the world. The lightweight air-cooled automatic, carried and fired by a single soldier, had not yet appeared.

The controversial question in the science of warfare was the future of cavalry. The general staffs in France and Germany were convinced that massed cavalry, fighting mounted and using the *arme blanche*, would dominate the early and the later stages of a modern continental war. Only cavalry could find out the enemy's movements and pin him down; only cavalry could exploit the situation when the enemy's line was pierced. While the Germans were of one mind about cavalry there were two opinions in the British Army. The 'colonial' school accepted the necessity of retaining the regiments of horse but would have armed them with rifles and used them as mounted infantry who rode to the battle but fought on foot, the regular practice in the later stages of the Boer War. Though Delarey, the most successful Boer general in the last year of the war, was all for mounted charges. The 'continental' school regarded the use of mounted infantry as a concession to the wide spaces and rapid movement of a colonial campaign. In the close country of Europe with troops thick on the ground, they supposed, horse regiments would still be used for reconnaissance and for exploiting success, by shock action. The confident assurance that cavalry was not yet obsolete was too widespread to be dismissed as stupidity. We shall see in fact that the British cavalry did fight several conventional campaigns in the 1914 War and did better than French or German cavalry but there is in this controversy an emotional element. What is the explanation of that glamour which for so many centuries has attached to the mounted swordsman, to the cavalry charge, even though so many of the celebrated cavalry charges have failed? The reluctance of skilled professional soldiers to admit that the day of the mounted swordsman was over had its counterpart in the delight with which the public heard the news—rarely indeed—that the cavalry had broken through. It was not an obsession confined to old-fashioned generals.

We are here confronted with a social phenomenon of far greater significance. The first years of the twentieth century which saw so many changes in the life of man saw the end of the 3,000-year-old partnership between the warrior and the war-horse. Since the Shepherd Kings conquered Egypt with horsed chariots, since 'horse-taming Hector' fought at Troy, chivalry, the prowess of the knight and his steed, had been the school of manhood. Every aspiring champion was a horseman, and social pre-eminence, athletic success, rank and wealth, were seen in terms of horsemanship. Labour and transportation depended on horsepower; travel and social intercourse went by riding or driving, and the governing class in any society was the class that had horses at its disposal. The aristocrat was the cavalier, the horseman; and this notion which the human race had accepted for a hundred generations was not easily displaced. If I were to venture a general comment on the leaders in the First World War, pointing out with the hindsight of fifty years later what now seems plain and what they overlooked, I should fix upon mechanical transport. War is the forcing house of inventions and we may notice that the aeroplane which before the war was a powered box-kite of stick and string was an effective flying machine by 1918. The caterpillar tractor, an experimental fad before the war, had become the formidable tank by the end of it. Radio telegraphy developed in the war years into radio telephony, but mechanized transport did not much evolve. By 1914 the London buses had already become motor-buses, the hansom cabs were rapidly giving way to taxi-cabs. Morris had put his first light car on the market, you could buy a motor-cycle for twenty-five pounds. The internal-combustion engine should have ousted the horse from military service, but it did not do so.

The science of war as taught at the staff colleges was still in the railway age. The American Civil War had been the first in which strategy turned upon railway communications, and the Franco-Prussian War the first in which railways had been built for strategic objectives. By 1914 the German state railway system had been completed to carry troops to the frontiers, a strong hint of the German aggressive intention. Large-scale war was based upon supply by rail and the routine ran that an army could not operate—without improvising a special organization—more than twenty miles from its railhead, the limit of range of horse transport.

All the armies were organized by divisions, that is to say fighting groups of 15,000 to 20,000 men, composed of all arms and provided with administrative services to enable them to fight a detached campaign. The establishment of a British infantry division in 1914, not much different from a French or German division, was substantially a horse-drawn organization. The thirteen infantry battalions had no mechanical transport. The colonels and senior officers had riding horses; the baggage wagons and field kitchens were horsed, and mechanization went no further than a few push-bicycles for orderlies. At brigade headquarters the officers were mounted on horses but modernity broke in with a section of despatch-riders on motor-cycles. The Divisional Commander, a major-general, had a motor-car, and even a company of fifty motor-lorries for the service of his 20,000 men. The field-guns were horse-drawn, as were the ammunition columns; the supply columns that carried the daily rations from railhead were horse-drawn, but the field-ambulance wagons were light motor-trucks. In the harum-scarum days of 1914 some improvised armoured cars were used in Flanders, but not again. It was thought a great thing when some London buses were brought to Ypres to transport troops behind the line, and greater when General Gallieni despatched a brigade of French infantry to the Battle of the Marne in Paris taxis. Then, not much more happened of this sort. A vigorous programme of mechanical transportation for the armies might have solved the problem of mobility—but no one seems to have thought of it. When the B.E.F. went to France in 1914 there were no more than 200 motor-cars, 100 motor-cycles, and 800 motor-lorries for the 160,000 men and these were mostly civilian vehicles hastily requisitioned. Four years later there were forty times as many motor-vehicles for an army ten times as great, but still the armies marched and their supplies plodded in horse-drawn wagons at two and a half miles an hour.

Horse-drawn or mule-drawn! Englishmen nowadays scarcely know a mule by sight. The horse, chiefly maintained for sport or pleasure, is still with us; the mule no longer. As the war progressed, conditions grew tougher so that the stubborn hardy mule largely replaced that high-spirited and timid creature, the horse. The man and the mule seem to be the only animals stupid enough to stand up to shell-fire.

(4)

All general staffs have planning sections which study the action to be taken if there should be a war, and though the autumn manœuvres may be fought between 'Redland' and 'Blueland' serious soldiers know that the scheme relates to a real situation which is likely to occur. If the war which the planners have in mind is to be fought in association with an ally, at what point does the factor called 'collusion' arise? Had the Germans any right to claim, in 1911, that the *Entente* powers were plotting to encircle them? It was plain that Britain and France were drawing together, that Britain and Germany were drawing apart, but it was also plain that professional talk in the German services was all concerned with neutralizing or defeating the Royal Navy so as to invade France the easier, while professional talk in the British and French services was all about defence against invasion, a weighty consideration when we come to assessing war guilt. To be sure there was 'Jacky' Fisher, talking wildly of the necessity for a preventive war. As no one else was in favour of applying the Nelson touch by 'copenhagening' the German Fleet, the complete rejection of his proposal becomes evidence of British innocence. The German Army, on the other hand, had a rich old tradition of making treacherous assaults on weaker neighbours, and was preparing another. The French Staff had received secret intelligence of the Schlieffen Plan on which German strategy was based from 1906 onwards, but either they did not believe in it or were not afraid of it. Their own plan, Number XVII of 1912, paid little attention to the dangers of a powerful flanking blow through Belgium but proposed to meet the German invaders by a brisk counter offensive all along the frontier. '*Tout le monde à la bataille!*' While the precise plans were secret everyone interested in military affairs was aware of the probabilities. The British public, however, was distracted by alarms over a German invasion of their island, which seems in fact never to have been high in the list of German plans.

Balfour's Committee of Imperial Defence was formed in 1905 soon after the *Entente Cordiale* agreements, and in the same year the first staff talks were held between British and French staff officers. Though at this stage there was no commitment, the continued 'collusion' at various levels between French and British led to strategic moves which made Britain's co-operation with France, in any war which might occur, almost inevitable. To the student today the horrifying feature of 1914 is the gradual loss of control by the politicians as the military machines began to revolve. First steps in 'mobilization'—it was a new word to us then—gained momentum until the armies could not be held back from lurching into war.

While Haldane was at the War Office, 1905–12, and Churchill at the Admiralty, 1911–15, both Army and Navy were organized for the action that might be necessary in a new Franco-German war. To take the Navy first, though the move came later in time, Haldane's un-successful attempt to negotiate a standstill in the armaments race with Germany was followed by a re-grouping of our battle fleets. The Mediterranean, so long the field of British seapower, was given over to the French Navy, while our home force, the historic Channel Fleet, was moved into the North Sea. From this moment, 1912, there was a commitment in honour if not in diplomatic form to prevent the Germans from operating against the Channel coast of France. By this time the Army had also been re-grouped. The Aldershot garrison became the First Army Corps, and the other regular troops in Britain a Second Army Corps, with a definite role of fighting on the left flank of the French Army.

The reorganization under Haldane had four branches: first was the preparation of the regular army in Britain as a continental expeditionary force; secondly, the conversion of the old volunteer regiments, the 'Saturday afternoon soldiers' into a trained and equipped Territorial Army fit to take over the task of home defence when the regulars had gone abroad; thirdly, the bringing into the system of the territorial armies of the self-governing colonies whose contingents of volunteers had given so good an account of themselves in the Boer War. The fourth branch was the formation of Senior Officers' Training Corps at universities and Junior Officers' Training Corps at public and grammar schools, without which the armies of 1914 could not have been created. No money at all was allowed by the Treasury for this drastic reconstruction which was achieved by vigorous economy at a time when the Army Estimates were being reduced. Haldane needed military assistants and Douglas Haig, the young staff officer who had given the most practical evidence before Lord Esher's inquest into army reform, became his right-hand man. It was a strange partnership between the scholarly lawyer and the fashionable rich cavalry officer, but both were Scots endowed with a fund of seriousness and a stern Calvinistic sense of duty. Haig was at the War Office from 1906 to 1909 and was largely responsible for planning the expeditionary force; then after a spell in India, which he disliked, he was promoted in 1911 over the heads of many others to the Aldershot Command, the spearhead of the Army. This was an unobtrusive administrative career of which the public heard little. They heard even less of the secret planning for a campaign on the French frontier, in which the protagonists were two academic soldiers: Henry Wilson, who commanded the Staff College at Camberley from 1907 to 1910 and then became Director of Military Operations at the War Office, and Ferdinand Foch, his opposite number at the *Ecole de Guerre* in France. A close friendship grew up between the two who shared secrets and enjoyed a world of private jokes. Though Foch was superior in rank and in intellectual ability, Wilson, who had fought at Spion Kop, was the more practical soldier. While Foch solved problems on paper, Wilson cycled up every road in Belgium by which the Germans could come. Wilson was the more accurate of the two in his appreciation of the way the war would begin. Wilson, more than any other man, was responsible for the submission of the British commanders to French doctrine. A respect for French professionalism and for the intellectual prowess of the French higher command became very general in the British Army where intellectual ability was not a common quality. A willingness to accept French doctrine, strange indeed to the student of history, was general in the First World War and not extinct at the beginning of the Second. On both occasions it cost us dear.

(5)

The Boer War was twelve years past when the crisis of 1914 appeared, so that not many people recalled the names of the commanders who had made their mark in South Africa. There were perhaps no more than four or five generals who enjoyed a wide popularity and whose exploits were known to everyone in Britain. First, of course, Lord Roberts, the favourite of the whole nation, 'Bobs', who had given his long life to India, had fought in many wars, and by precept and example had raised the moral character of the British soldier and the repute of the Army. Already an old man when he took command in South Africa, he was past eighty when the First World War broke out. He had long foreseen its coming having ventured the prophecy—it is said—as early as 1908 that it would come in 1914, would be a long war, and would be won by Colonel Foch, and had stumped the country in vain to arouse public opinion in favour of national military service. With all his popularity he could not convert the British from their inveterate dislike of militarism, yet he had contributed indirectly to the enthusiasm—such as it was—for Haldane's Territorial Force, though he did not approve of the voluntary principle, and, in addition, he had inspired a strong movement for rifle-shooting as a sport. The rifle had won the Boer War and was going to win the yet unforeseen battles of Mons and Ypres. Even at the age of eighty-two Roberts was called to Asquith's first War Council in 1914 and unerringly put his finger on the weak spot in the strategic plan. It was too late for him to make his influence felt in that direction and, a few weeks later, the old hero died in France, while on a visit to the battle-front.

Next to Roberts came the formidable figure of Kitchener of Khartoum (just 'K. of K.' or even just 'K.'). Admired, respected, trusted but not loved, Kitchener has been unfortunate in his biographers; the official life by Sir George Arthur is no more than an official life; several other controversial works are partisan defences of this or that policy, written too soon on inadequate evidence; and the recent life by Sir Philip Magnus is largely composed of superficial tittle-tattle. In our age two Englishmen, and two only, have towered above their contemporaries by 'plain heroic magnitude of mind': Kitchener in the First World War and Churchill in the Second. The two were colleagues in 1914, and Churchill has paid generous tribute to the steadfast qualities and honourable dealings of the old field marshal, who had disliked him when he was a brash impudent young political soldier, and who stood by him when he fell from favour in 1915. Churchill at forty-two, taking the blame for failure in the Dardanelles, was one of the best-hated men in London; Kitchener at sixty-five had so solid a reputation that in the eyes of the public he could do no wrong.

While Churchill, so extraverted and so articulate, has made himself known to the whole world, revealing faults that were endearing as well as talents that were astonishing, Kitchener, fifty years after his death, is still an enigma, that heroic type of the nineteenth century which the psycho-analysing twentieth century is unwilling to accept— the 'strong silent man'. He made no concessions in public, so that the dichotomy between his personal and his official life remains unhealed. The Kitchener of Sir Philip Magnus is a figure of mythology, not a human being. How can we explain the historic fact that this outsider, who had spent his whole life abroad, and had no social gifts, reversed the trend of our national life in one week, winning the entire confidence of the nation, convincing Asquith's highly talented administration and overruling Whitehall, by a sheer display of personality. It is the most astonishing revolution in English history, and no adequate account of it has been written.[1] All the biographers of Kitchener dilate at length on the political quarrels in which he found himself entangled, whereas not one of them devotes as much as ten pages to that astonishing achievement, the creation of Kitchener's Army.

Kitchener, though of pure English stock, knew almost nothing of England. Born in the far west of Ireland, where his soldier father lived for the sake of economy, he was educated in Switzerland. A truant from the Royal Military Academy at Woolwich, he fought in the Franco-German War and never forgot the lessons of defeat. A slim, tall, handsome young officer, an aesthete and an Anglo-Catholic, uninterested in girls, he fled from regimental duty and from English society to the Middle East, where his life was spent. From 1874 until

1. V. W. Germains, *The Kitchener Armies* (Peter Davies, London, 1930), provides a useful chronological summary.

1914 he never knew a Christmas in England. Topography, military intelligence, secret service, desert warfare made up his whole external life in those regions of the decaying Turkish Empire which were passing under British control, and he was a Turkish general before he was a British general. Of his private life we know little except that he was the second of several brothers who admitted his superior talent, his father was an eccentric martinet, and his mother died when he was a boy. Did he remain a Christian? We can only say that he remained a dedicated man with a stern sense of duty. A man of taste, certainly; while he read few books he was a keen, indeed a rapacious, collector of works of art with an eye to the chance of loot on his campaigns. Though temperate in his habits, he enjoyed luxury and pomp. Absolute power corrupted him, encouraging his arrogance, ruthlessness, and contempt for irresponsible critics. No apologetic can make of Kitchener a pleasing personality, yet his own staff, his 'boys', were devoted to him and whole nations accepted his leadership. Nowadays when reticence is out of fashion, it may be necessary to allude to the rumour that Kitchener, in whose adult life no woman played a part, was a homosexual. I mention the subject only to dismiss it. If he had been guilty of sexual misconduct, some hint of it would have come to light in 1915, when his enemies conspired against him so viciously; but no such hint was dropped.

Kitchener rushed into fame in 1898 as the conqueror of the Sudan and the avenger of Gordon. His image was created by the war correspondent G. W. Steevens, who described him as the 'Sudan machine', a paragon of cool efficiency and economy, unswayed by emotion or sentiment. It was not out of character that critics accused him of callousness and even cruelty to the conquered Sudanese and he made no excuses for attempting to discredit the Mahdist cult by desecrating the Mahdi's tomb. It was just as typical that his first administrative reform was to found the Gordon College at Khartoum with money from British subscribers. The Sudan was to become the model province of the Empire after he had killed the Khalifa and his emirs, and had humoured the French out of Fashoda and away from the Nile Valley. He lived to plan the Gezira scheme for co-operative cotton-growing, the best of its kind in the continent of Africa. He had an unshakeable faith in the future of the British Empire and an unswerving loyalty to the Crown.

C

Kitchener was not pleased to be called away as deputy to Roberts in the Boer War and was most displeased to be left in South Africa, after Roberts's departure, to wind up the guerilla campaign. He did it, as he did every task, disdainfully, with immense thoroughness, never sharing the load of responsibility, making all decisions, keeping all secrets under his own hat. In the last stages of the Boer War we can see Kitchener's method at its most characteristic. A master of improvisation, fertile in expedients, attentive to every detail, he controlled as many as fifty or sixty columns of troops without relying on intermediate formations. He was never at a loss and so prodigious was his capacity for work he was never behindhand. But the dictator who scorched the earth of South Africa and interned the people without a qualm was enlightened in his politics, always opposing the extremism of the civil authorities. Milner, the civilian High Commissioner, demanded unconditional surrender and colonial rule; Kitchener, the soldier, persuaded the Boer generals to capitulate on terms by holding out hopes of self-government.

As soon as possible he escaped from Africa to India, where he engaged in another struggle with the civil power. As Kitchener got his way against Milner, so he got his way against Curzon, the Viceroy, and these were no mean opponents. In India Kitchener reorganized the Army into fighting formations which could provide an expeditionary force, thus preparing the model on which Haldane and Haig reorganized the Army in Britain, and on which he himself, ten years later, was to improvise his own New Army. In 1909 Kitchener was unemployed. The Liberal Government was afraid of him, and Morley, the Secretary of State, vetoed the appointment Kitchener coveted, as Viceroy. He was packed off to Australia and New Zealand, where in a few months he guided those countries in organizing their citizen armies on the British model, one of his best and simplest triumphs. Just then an appointment suited to his talents fell vacant, the post of British Agent and Consul-General in Egypt, where he was ruler of the land as much as Joseph ever was in the days of Pharaoh the Great. Ignoring the pashas and the Cairo politicians Kitchener devoted himself entirely to the welfare of the peasants, among whom his name is still remembered (or was when I was in Egypt in 1951).

He was on leave in England when war broke out and tried hard to sneak back to Egypt before he could be caught for home duty. The public call for Kitchener at the War Office was spontaneous and immediate. On 5th August the Press was demanding his appointment and on the 6th this autocratic, secretive, conservative old soldier became a Cabinet Minister in a Liberal administration with several colleagues whom he distrusted and several whose names he always forgot. He took them into his confidence as little as possible.

One other general might have been considered Sir John French's rival. Sir Ian Hamilton, also aged sixty two and commanding in the Mediterranean, had more varied fighting experience than any soldier in the Army. He had been with Roberts in Afghanistan; he had been knocked down and left for dead on the hill-top at Majuba when all the others ran away; he had done remarkably well in the Boer War, reaching the position of Chief of Staff to Kitchener; and when sent as an official observer with our Japanese allies in their war against Russia, his reports on Japanese tactics had strongly affected our war plans. Unlike the other generals, 'Johnny' Hamilton was an intellectual and a man of the world. He had written a book which you could read for pleasure; he knew the literary scene. In 1914 he was side-tracked in an unimportant post (which Kitchener had refused to take), and at first it did not seem that the war would bring him any high command, although he was known and trusted and liked.

An even better-known general was not mentioned at all. Of all the heroes of the South African War the favourite, after 'Bobs', was Baden-Powell, the Defender of Mafeking. In 1908 he produced what was the most beneficial consequence of the war by founding the Boy Scouts. Two years later, as a lieutenant-general, he retired from the Army to devote himself to his new activity and when war came Kitchener urged him to organize and use his scouts as messengers, coast-watchers, and for many other tasks.

The national revival after the defeats and disgraces of the Boer War was a widespread movement. Army reform, Haldane's territorials, the O.T.C.s, Roberts' rifle clubs, and Baden-Powell's Boy Scouts, all on a voluntary basis, pointed the way to Kitchener's Army.

2

The B.E.F. and the New Armies

SINCE March there had been a void in the War Office, brought about by the Curragh Incident, to which I must refer shortly. The Home Rule crisis had come so near to civil war in Ireland and so embittered was the tone of party politics in England that many of the Opposition leaders gave their open support to the Ulster volunteers. If civil war came the British Army in Ireland would be in a dilemma, since Ulster has always provided a high proportion of its officers. The Commander-in-Chief in Ireland forced the issue by asking his officers to declare what they would do in the hypothetical event of being ordered to march against Ulster. What they would do if employed to maintain impartial order in Ireland was one thing; how they would act in a civil war which good citizens were trying to avoid was another. Brigadier-General Gough, a Protestant Irishman, replied when directly challenged that he would rather resign his commission, and most of his officers followed him. Later Gough put himself in the wrong by demanding an assurance that he would not be ordered to march against Ulster. The Secretary of State, who imprudently gave Gough a written promise, was forced to resign and with him went his Chief of Staff, Sir John French, also a protestant Irishman. The Prime Minister courageously took charge of the War Office during the vacancy which was still unfilled at the outbreak of the European War a few weeks later.

When Sir John French withdrew, the most influential generals were Sir Douglas Haig, commanding at Aldershot, and Henry Wilson, the Director of Operations at the War Office, both of whom had been regarded as Sir John's young men. Wilson, again a protestant Irishman, was close with the Ulster leaders, if his own diaries can be believed, and closer still with the Opposition in the House of Commons. He fed them with military secrets, although he was the principal adviser to the Government on strategic policy. It was generally believed that Gough had acted on Wilson's advice.

The feud between soldiers and politicians, which was so lamentable a feature of the First World War in Britain, grew out of the Curragh Incident. Though French, Wilson, and Gough, the three Irish generals, were in disfavour with the Liberal Government their careers were not broken. So suddenly did the European crisis develop, and so light was Asquith's control of the War Office, that Wilson retained his key appointment, Gough resumed command of his brigade, and French insisted upon his right to command the Expeditionary Force in the event of war.

Unlike some other senior officers Haig had used all his authority and social influence to heal the breach between the army leaders and the Government, and he had successfully kept his own command clear of political wrangles. Yet this was the burden on the conscience of the soldiers and when news came on 28th June that an Austrian archduke had been shot by Servian terrorists at Serajevo it did not at first make much difference. There was always trouble in the Balkans and what could you expect of the Servians who had murdered their own king and queen, with peculiar brutality, only ten years ago? The Aldershot Command kept to its routine with the summer leave period in view. It was not until Thursday, 23rd July, that the Austrian Government sent so brusque an ultimatum to Servia as to make war probable in Eastern Europe, after which the Balkans began to crowd Ireland out of the newspaper headlines.

Fortunately Churchill was at the Admiralty and the Fleet, by way of a summer exercise, was practising mobilization at Portsmouth. On Monday, 27th July, Churchill decided to keep it mobilized, the only action by the British in the crisis which could conceivably have been regarded as bellicose. The Army, which had no Churchill—indeed no full-time Secretary of State—did not stir as the crisis gained impetus. On Tuesday Austria declared war on Servia; on Friday Russia began her sluggish mobilization; on Saturday Germany was at war with Russia; on Sunday, 2nd August, Germany invaded Belgium and British intervention became probable; on Monday the French, who had used extreme care earlier to avoid provocative action, were resisting the German invasion; and on Tuesday, 4th August, Sir Edward Grey sent the ultimatum to Germany which committed Britain to war within twenty-four hours if the Germans should not withdraw from Belgium. Only on that day were the War Books opened and the mobilization orders sent to the Army.

No one who lived through the year 1914 will ever forget the wind of change that blew through Europe that week. On 3rd August the German General Staff, not under parliamentary control, had released the mechanism of the Schlieffen Plan. Aggression on the French frontier set the military machine at work in France according to Plan XVII, which included a role for the British Expeditionary Force. If even then Britain had proposed to stay neutral the invasion of Belgium was an independent *casus belli*; it had been the sufficient cause of Pitt's war with the French Revolution in 1792. Gladstone in 1870 had warned both combatants that Britain would act against an invasion of Belgium by either side. An occupation of the Belgian coast would be a threat to Britain's vital sea-trade which could not be permitted, even if we were not already engaged by the gentleman's agreement with France to defend the Narrow Seas, while she defended the Mediterranean. Rightly or wrongly, the Belgian issue cleared the air so that within a few hours the national mind was made up, for war. The pacifists who a week earlier had included a large section of the nation, and perhaps a majority of the intellectuals, were reduced to a shrill handful of protesters. Strikes, unemployment, suffragettes, Ulster rebels evaporated and were forgotten.

Until the last day, 4th August, a great body of British opinion, including a section of the Cabinet, still stood for neutrality; and one of the curiosities of those days is the pacifist number of *Punch* written before the ultimatum but not published until the morning of the 5th when war had been already declared. While the political cartoon of the week was still concerned with Asquith's Irish policy, the world crisis received two mentions only: an article by A. A. Milne protesting that the 'war in Eastern Europe' was no concern of ours, and a set of facetious verses by Owen Seaman abusing the Servian Government as a gang of murderers:

> 'Well, if I must, I shall have to fight
> For the love of a bounding Balkanite;
> But O what a tactless choice of time,

>When the bathing season is at its prime!
>And how I should hate to miss my chance
>Of wallowing off the coast of France.'

The following number, issued on 12th August, was filled with abuse of Germany and praise for 'gallant little Belgium'.

(2)

So it was Sir John French who led the Expeditionary Force to France, taking with him so many senior officers as to make the War Office emptier still. Henry Wilson went abroad to conduct the operations under Sir John French in France which he had planned under Sir John French in London, a reasonable proceeding. More embarrassing was the departure to France of General Macdonogh, the Director of Military Intelligence, who left a void in London that could not be filled since no one knew what secrets he knew. Their places were taken by older officers called from retirement, who came to be known as 'dugouts', then a new word. Sir Charles Callwell, an entertaining writer of memoirs, who succeeded Wilson, is our main source for the inner history of the War Office in those days.

In every campaign a simple interplay of movement may be observed between the battle-front and the base. So great is the glamour of active service that in spite of all reason the earnest, the ambitious, and the generous-hearted fight their way to the front, while the easy going, the dull, and some who are merely prudent ensconce themselves in company with the shirkers, at the rear. Senior staff officers have opportunities of placing themselves and if they are worth their salt will place themselves well forward unless they are prevented and, since the best commanders, too, are struggling to the front, they are likely to take the best staff officers they can get. Best men forwards and less-good men backwards is so natural a process that it requires much resolution on the part of the High Command to reverse the flow and to keep an adequate number of good men for the essential work that must be done in the rear. There was no inclination to take this step in 1914 because the High Command expected the war to be short. If a decision was likely to be reached by a battle fought about the fortieth day after mobilization, why waste talent by withholding good men from the line?

At first there were no officers of sufficient seniority to question Kitchener's unorthodox notions in the War Office. Those who might have asserted themselves against him, and who were to assert themselves twelve months later, were packing their active-service kit to go overseas. On the second day after taking office, 8th August, Kitchener called for 100,000 volunteers for the first of his new armies, with the startling proviso that they were to enlist for three years or the duration of the war. Only one other person in authority suggested that the war could last more than six months. French and Wilson derided Kitchener's plan, but Haig agreed with Kitchener that there must be a long stern struggle for which a national army must be raised. He said so plainly at the Council of War on 5th August. However, Wilson's gibes and sneers, amusing though they might be, had no effect upon the course of events, since the mobilization plan worked smoothly, carrying him and French and Haig to France, where they were instantly engaged in the exacting Mons campaign, while Kitchener and the dugout staff officers at home had to create a new army out of nothing. He had no officers, no sergeant-instructors, no hutments, no uniforms, no weapons, no kitchens, no cooks, and here were 100,000 recruits, the vanguard of much greater armies, demanding only to be allowed to serve, and resting their entire faith on Kitchener who would manage everything. How it was done nobody can say, for the story has not been told except by individuals recounting their own experience. Two hundred and ninety-nine thousand men enlisted in August, 463,000 in September, and by then the channels were so choked that the flow of volunteers had to be stopped by raising the standards for admission. Long queues of men of all classes and ages in every town besieged the recruiting offices begging to be allowed to serve and furiously angry when they were told to wait. By the end of the year 1,186,000 volunteers had been accepted and in 1915 the figure was 1,280,000. After January 1916 National Service was introduced by stages, so that the flow was regulated.

The Expeditionary Force consisted of six infantry divisions and a cavalry division, soon reinforced by a seventh and eighth division composed of regular regiments withdrawn from scattered garrisons. The expansion of the New Armies took off from that point, so that Kitchener's first 100,000 were to be an army of six divisions, numbered 9th to 14th. Within a few weeks the men were available for twelve more divisions, numbered 15th to 26th, making two more armies. At this stage a number of British regular regiments arrived from the garrisons of distant colonies or from India and were organized as the 27th, 28th, and 29th divisions. Then came new Kitchener divisions, numbered successively 30th to 41st, completing the New Army of thirty divisions for which he alone was responsible. It was by Kitchener's management, too, that the original six regular divisions had been increased to eleven. It was his reorganization of the Indian Army that had released British troops from the Indian service, and he was responsible for advice on the organization of troops from the Dominions overseas, eventually four infantry divisions from Canada, five from Australia, and one from New Zealand, as well as formations of cavalry. The South Africans, in the first instance, were invited by the British Government to invade the German colonies.

The blind spot in Kitchener's eye was his mistrust of the Territorial Force. Designed for home defence in the absence of the Regular Army, it consisted in 1914 of fourteen infantry divisions which made up in enthusiasm for what they lacked in equipment. In July 1914 they were all under strength, by December they had received so many recruits that each division was ready to double itself and form a 'second line'. Kitchener consistently underrated the Territorials as soldiers, giving a low priority to their equipment and declining to make use of their organization for army expansion. They were not dismayed and since they were already half trained and half equipped they came into the fighting line sooner than the Kitchener divisions which had no training and no equipment to begin with. The fourteen Territorial divisions, numbered 42nd to 55th, went abroad between February and June 1915[1] and ten of their second-line divisions, numbered 56th to 67th, followed in 1916. The fourteen mounted brigades of yeomanry were mostly used in the Middle East.

When Kitchener met his death on 5th June 1916 the last of his divisions, 40th, was on its way to France, trained, armed, and equipped, and the fighting strength of the British Empire was seventy-five infantry divisions and nine cavalry divisions on active service, fifty-nine of

1. A few selected Territorial units had been sent abroad in 1914, as Line of Communication troops. The first in action were the Oxfordshire Yeomanry who fought a skirmish with German Uhlans at the Mont des Cats on 7th October. The action of the London Scottish at Messines on 1st November received vast publicity.

the infantry and four of the cavalry from the United Kingdom.

Kitchener's unwillingness to use the organization of the Territorial Force for expanding the Army was based upon a solider foundation of reason than is generally supposed. He had, indeed, formed a poor impression of the French Territorials during his boyish experience as a volunteer in the Franco-Prussian War; and had confirmed this impression both from the study and practice of warfare in his mature life. British generals, unlike their continental rivals, devoted much thought to the lessons of the American Civil War, in which the armies of the North suffered reverses because the volunteer regiments insisted on their constitutional right of going home, even in the middle of a campaign, as soon as their term of service was completed. In South Africa Kitchener himself had suffered from the same disadvantage. The volunteers of 1899 went home with Lord Roberts in 1900 when the main campaign was over, leaving Kitchener to raise a new army for the second, guerilla, campaign. The Territorial Force which Kitchener inherited from his predecessors in 1914 was partly under civilian control, through the nominated county Territorial associations, and it was raised specifically for home defence so that the Regular Army could be released for service overseas. Some Territorials in some regiments, even some whole battalions, had given a personal undertaking that they would go overseas if required, but they could not be so employed piecemeal. To convert the Territorials into an expeditionary force would destroy their immediate utility as home defenders and would require legislation which might be opposed in Parliament. It seemed better to make a fresh start by raising new regular regiments for a long period of service under direct control of the War Office.

Rightly or wrongly, this was the decision taken at a moment's notice in the national emergency. Afterwards the know-all critics pointed out that with his great prestige Kitchener might have got an Act of Parliament in 1914 to introduce conscription and to unite Regulars and Territorials in a single system. He had other problems to face and in the unfamiliar world of politics he could see at least that the conscription issue would split the Cabinet and might overthrow the Government. That Kitchener made the choice he did is not surprising. Let us reserve our astonished comment for his successor Hore Belisha, with all Kitchener's experience to profit by, who repeated the error in 1939 and heaped new errors of his own upon the confusion.

Kitchener would not have been able to create his armies without the foundation prepared for him by Haldane, and we may well stand amazed at the success with which he conducted his gigantic improvisations on that basis, not, of course, without some errors. 'No man has ever made war who has not made mistakes.'

(3)

If we may claim that Haldane was the best Secretary of State who has ever held the seals of the War Office—Kitchener being a portent, a comet straying into the system rather than a star of known magnitude —surely Hore-Belisha, five and twenty years after Kitchener, was the worst. Even the men of the Crimea did not produce more chaos, and it stands to their credit that even before their war broke out they had initiated some reforms. In 1914 Britain went to war with a plan, a fully equipped army which for its size was the best in the world—to say nothing of the greatest navy—and with a system capable of expansion. In 1938 there was no plan, no expeditionary force, and very little navy. What was available was a wealth of experience and a generation of middle-aged men, among them Hore-Belisha himself, who had fought in the First World War and could apply their knowledge. Hore-Belisha began by breaking the chain of promotion, superseding the generals whose careers qualified them for the highest places by two favourites, chosen, as it seems, for their romantic names. The Viscount Gort, v.c., proved himself a tough, competent, fighting soldier, but suffered the common fate of commanders in the opening phase of a war. Lord Ironside, who seems to have been made C.I.G.S. on the grounds that he was reputed the original of John Buchan's 'General Hannay', was a complete failure, though, no doubt, he did his best.

When we come to the expansion programme we observe that Hore-Belisha introduced conscription at such a moment, April 1939, that it upset the mobilization of the expeditionary force which was being hurriedly got together by robbing it of officers and N.C.O.s, and in such a way that the conscripts could play no active part in the coming crisis. They could neither be a new army, nor reserves for the Old Army, nor a home defence force; and since they were a complete age-group, all the boys of twenty, it was necessary when war came to sort out the essential technicians in order to return them to civil life. They had, however, publicity value—for Hore-Belisha—the only purpose they could serve. And while he managed not to provide the Regular Army with even the prototype for a tank or a support-aircraft, there was no lack of hutments with cots and curtains for his conscript boys.

It might at least be supposed that Hore-Belisha would profit by Kitchener's error over the use of the Territorial Army after so much discussion of this episode in the war histories. Not so! He took Kitchener as his teacher and bettered the instruction. At the same moment when he hamstrung the regular army with his conscription plan, he hamstrung the Territorial Force by expanding it upon its own organization. Every territorial unit, instead of bringing itself up to a state of efficiency, was ordered to double itself by throwing off a 'second line', so that on the day of war neither first nor second line was fit to fight. Nevertheless, the War Office had one valuable asset which had not been available to Kitchener or Haldane in the million or so of active middle-aged men then in their forties who had served in the First War. Here were the instructors, the staff officers, the administrators, and here the home-defence troops who might have released young Regulars and young Territorials for active service. It will hardly be believed that the upward limit for enlistment was fixed at thirty-eight years, while the civil-defence units, in September 1939, recruited only men over forty-five, so that the younger and more active survivors of the First War were excluded from both.

Until Hore-Belisha was dismissed in January 1940 chaos reigned. Only after Dunkirk was the Army allowed to begin to organize itself under the able command of Dill and Brooke, who had been passed over for promotion two years earlier. Before a real army could be formed almost everything done by Hore-Belisha had to be undone.

3

How to join the Army

ON 22nd June 1914 the Aldershot Command held a ceremonial parade in honour of the King's birthday. Four brigades of infantry, a brigade of cavalry, three batteries of field artillery, a battery of horse artillery, two companies of engineers, and a company of the Army Service Corps were out on Laffan's Plain, perhaps 15,000 men, all in the panoply of the old army and none of them aware that such a spectacle would never again be seen. There were perhaps 2,000 horses on parade and not one motor-car, except in the spectators' arena. We motored over from Fleet in the family car as sightseers and what most interested me, a schoolboy of seventeen, was that after the infantry had marched past, the artillery had trotted past, and the cavalry had galloped past the saluting base, no less than twelve aeroplanes of the Royal Flying Corps flew past. Rarely had I then seen even a single aeroplane and never before that day a whole squadron airborne.

The line regiments were in scarlet, the riflemen in green, the Eleventh Hussars in their cherry-coloured breeches, the horse-gunners in busbies and sling-jackets, the Highlanders in kilts and feathered bonnets. Each regiment marched with its band playing the quickstep, and among the old familiar tunes I particularly enjoyed that of the Army Service Corps, who trundled along at a round trot to the favourite 'nigger minstrel' air of *Wait for the Wagon*. But what we did not foresee was that within two months the Coldstream Guards would win new honours in the night alarm at Landrecies, that the Worcesters before the year was out would have tipped the scale of destiny by the decisive counter-attack at Gheluvelt, that the Oxfordshires, the old 52nd Light Infantry, would have broken the Prussian Guard, as their forerunners had broken Napoleon's Old Guard at Waterloo, and that within six months half of these hearty, healthy young men would be maimed or

dead. I asked what was the name of the handsome general in the cocked
hat who took the salute, and was told he was Sir Douglas Haig, a name
I had never heard before.

What did Haig and his senior officers suspect of the fate in store for
them? Continental Europe was quiescent; even the Balkans, where
wars had raged from 1911 to 1913, seemed to have settled down; and
the trouble-spot which gave anxiety to the senior officers at Aldershot
was Ulster, not the German frontier. If the soldiers on parade, that fine
Monday morning, had any misgivings about their future it was the
dilemma in which they would be placed if civil war should break out in
Ireland and if the British Army were called upon to intervene.

(2)

Let me focus my gaze upon a country vicarage at Fleet near Aldershot where these events impinged upon our quiet life. Discussions were
going on over my head between my parents in New Zealand and the
uncle with whom I was then staying. Was I to go back home or should
I be sent to school for another year in England to be coached for an
Oxford scholarship, two alternatives which, as July advanced, I found
equally unreal. Schoolboy-like, I thought I would break away and
fight as a volunteer in the war that seemed coming, and was heavily
snubbed by my uncle when I suggested it. Fight as a volunteer for the
Servians? What nonsense!

In those days, it must be remembered, there was no broadcasting.
The news came in the morning papers which from day to day grew
more alarming. In the afternoons I used to cycle down to the railway
station to pick up the evening papers from the London trains; there
were special editions now every afternoon, and with them came the
rumours running ahead of the news. Country after country was at war,
and by Friday or Saturday I was sure we should be in it and that I
should be in it too. It was going back to school that had become a
fantasy.

The vicarage was always lively with young people, my cousins'
friends, among them two gunner subalterns from Aldershot, Geoff and
Val, who often rode over to play tennis with the girls on Saturdays.
I asked Val what he would be doing if there was a war, to which he
replied promptly: 'We shall go to a rendezvous at Amiens on the left

of the French Army.' This struck me as odd. Why go to Amiens when there was a war in the Balkans? Only a day or two later we were ragging Geoff for taking his sword to be sharpened at the blacksmith's shop. 'You won't want a sword. You're only in the ammunition column'. On Tuesday, 4th August, a sultry afternoon, my uncle and I went for a long walk round by Crondall and Crookham to discuss my future in a mood of great unreality. Presently a sweating soldier on a bicycle stopped us to ask the way to Colonel So-and-So's house, and told us outright that he was carrying the mobilization order, an announcement that seemed fatal to our conversation. Late that night, after my usual bedtime, I rode down to the village street for news, to find three or four people staring blankly at a notice in the window of the post office: 'War declared.'

Apart from the universal call for Kitchener in Wednesday morning's papers the country was dumbfounded. There was no official information and no reliable news. No one could guess how the war would affect their lives and no one knew what should properly be done. Some people prudently bought up everything in the shops in case there should be a food shortage, others in shocked tones denounced them as public enemies for doing so. Rather vague committees sprang up to organize relief work—but for whom?—and offers of all sorts were made to patriotic funds. Should we turn in the family car, but first should we take a drive to Aldershot, to see what was doing?

Should we offer the spare bedroom for a billet? Or for a wounded soldier? Should we all go up to London where the streets were said to be full of processions and bands? Geoff and Val came over on horseback in service uniforms (with swords) to say good-bye, very reticent now about their movements, and we saw them no more. All the golfing colonels of that neighbourhood vanished. My cousin Evan, who had been rowing for his college at Henley, went back to Cambridge to join an officers' training unit called King Edward's Horse. The manservant, as he brought my cup of tea in the morning, discussed with me what we should do and soon joined the Hampshire Territorials. He too disappeared. Of course, there would be regiments of volunteers raised, as in the Boer War—but when and where? How to begin?

On the second day, Thursday, 6th August, it was announced that Kitchener was to be Secretary of State for War and that the Army was to be trebled in size. Five hundred thousand recruits were called for in a notice headed by the slogan 'Your King and Country need You'. On Friday the 7th, after only twenty-four hours in office, Kitchener produced the first draft plan for his New Army which was published in Saturday's papers. A hundred thousand young men between the ages of nineteen and thirty were invited to enlist 'for three years or the duration of the war'. So it was to be a long war.

The silent Navy had vanished into the North Sea; the Regular Army had moved to its war station—and I at least knew where that was—'Amiens on the left of the French Army'. I had the secret from a gunner subaltern and surely he must know. As soon as it was felt that the national interest was safe in Kitchener's capable hands the frenzy of the first few mad days subsided, and those who could not enlist began to utter a new slogan: 'Business as Usual.' For the civilians the best course, it was said, was to go on quietly with their work, trusting entirely to the father-figure of Kitchener, whose huge moustache and challenging eye now appeared on the poster designed by Alfred Leete. The First World War, like the Second, began with a 'phoney' period before the nation recognized what it was in for.

What was I to do? I certainly would not go back to school now, and in any case since school holidays had begun I had a crony to confer with in the village, Jack Sweet from Clifton. (Where are you, Jack Sweet? Are you still alive at sixty-seven years old?) An opening presented itself on Monday, 10th August, when *The Times* carried an advertisement for 2,000 young men 'of good general education' between the ages of seventeen and thirty, 'cadets or ex-cadets of O.T.C.s', to whom temporary commissions in the Army might be given. We jumped on our bicycles and rode over to Aldershot to enquire, and, knowing no better, we asked advice of a redcap (military policeman) at the corner of Queen's Road. He looked at our newspaper and gave the professional opinion that this would be a matter for the Adjutant-General's branch. Believe it or not, we battered our way into the office of the Adjutant-General on the sixth day of mobilization, the day on which the Expeditionary Force began to cross to France.

The room was full of bustling staff officers in khaki, wrestling with mountains of lists and schedules and files. Though we were not inside for five minutes, some young staff officers took an interest in us. Two or three left their work for a moment to look with a kindly eye at these lanky schoolboys with their absurd enquiry. Warning us off Aldershot, they advised us to try the depot of the Rifle Brigade at Winchester. Next day we took train to Winchester with a letter of introduction and actually persuaded an elderly colonel 'dug out' from retirement (though I rather think the word 'dugout' had not yet come into use) to put our names on a list. Since I had little confidence in this, I went to London to call on the New Zealand High Commissioner, who then possessed a shabby little office in Victoria Street, most unlike the glass tower over which his successor presides today. He too took my name, promising to slide me into any New Zealand contingent that should appear. Since there seemed nothing more to do, I returned to Fleet to wait with what little patience I could muster, and was soon consumed with chagrin on realizing that the authorities were not tumbling over one another to find a military appointment for Charles Carrington, aged seventeen and quite unqualified. Evidently I had better be nineteen for official purposes.

It was a cloudless August, pleasant enough for riding around Hampshire on a bicycle, reading eight or ten newspapers a day, and sticking pins in maps of Europe to illustrate military situations of which we knew almost nothing definite. On 18th August the Press Bureau announced that the B.E.F. had been successfully transported to France, and the one journalist who got a view of them described a regiment coming ashore singing 'It's a Long Way to Tipperary'. This tinkling little tune had had no vogue and was never a natural favourite with the troops, but since the singing of 'Tipperary' was the first, almost the only, human touch recorded of our fighting army, the public snatched at it. 'Tipperary' was plugged by the civilians who made it into a national anthem. French civilians, warming to their new allies, took a fancy for it, and in time the tune worked its way back into the army. Recruits in England felt obliged to march to 'Tipperary', and the legend became rooted.

This was about all we knew of the B.E.F. until on a hot Tuesday evening, 25th August, the papers came out with the news that Namur had fallen, that the British were hard-pressed at Mons, and that there had been many killed and wounded, the first indication of the tendency of the Press Bureau to gloat over bad news. Three days later it was revealed that the Allied armies were in full retreat. On the 26th Lord Kitchener, as Secretary of State, made his first report to the House of Lords. This and his later speeches were candid and factual, restoring

D

public confidence. The armies were fighting well, in spite of suffering 2,000 casualties—the heaviest loss in any battle since the Crimean War —and he was assured of the First 100,000 recruits for his New Army. On the 31st he spoke again of the battle of Le Cateau and of the cavalry fighting, which, as those who stuck pins in maps could see for themselves, meant a considerable withdrawal. The news grew worse in the first week in September, but was lightened on the 5th by accounts of Russian victories in East Prussia which, unfortunately, proved fallacious. It was at this crisis of the war, when the fall of France seemed to be threatening, as in 1870, that London began to seethe with rumours, true and false.

On 29th August it was officially announced that the German Army had burned and looted the town and university of Louvain as a reprisal because Belgian partisans had sniped at German troops. No such measure had been taken in European warfare since the seventeenth century. Reports began to filter through from many parts of France and Belgium that the Germans, especially in Von Kluck's First Army, had made a practice of seizing the leading citizens of each occupied town as hostages for the good conduct of the populace. In town after town—at Visé, Andenne, Aershot, Malines, Senlis, and many others—batches of innocent hostages had been massacred in order to terrorize the recalcitrant. This was the policy of 'frightfulness' (*Schrecklichkeit*) which was announced in published German orders as their professed intention. It had no precedent in the history of civilized warfare. The easy-going British, with their Victorian respect for German culture, treated these reports at first with scepticism—or at any rate I did—but the confirmation came from German sources. They did it and they were proud of doing it, and in the long run it had a disastrous effect upon their cause. The inevitable consequence was a call for reprisals in the same mode, but when Lloyd George went to Kitchener to urge him to retaliate, Kitchener swept him aside. 'Don't talk to me of atrocities,' he said. 'All war is an atrocity.' The accounts of hostages massacred were unfortunately true, and such episodes were repeated by the *Wehrmacht* in the Second World War on numerous occasions. While the British heard with a growing sense of horror what the invasion of Belgium and France meant to the civil population, they consoled themselves with a romantic belief that reinforcement for their retreating armies was on the way. Many years ago I worked through a dossier prepared by the late Sir Henry Hadow on the myth of the Russian armies passing through England. The evidence there assembled was so rich and well attested that many a man has been hanged on flimsier proof of guilt. Yet no Russian soldiers passed through England in reality.

In the first few days of the war two Russian armies had invaded East Prussia with confident ease. Their early success reassured the Western nations at a moment when the Germans were advancing into Belgium. The great majority who knew little of the military factors put a simple faith in the onset of the 'Russian steamroller', and quoted the text from Amos, V.19—'as if a man did flee from a lion and a bear met him'. Not knowing that the Russians were already defeated at the Masurian Lakes before the end of August in the campaign that made the names of Hindenburg and Ludendorff, they continued to believe in the Russian steamroller.

Who initiated the rumour that a Russian army, brought by sea, was passing through Britain on its way to the Western Front is unknown. It spread by the 'grapevine', with new variations every day; it was believed in France; it was believed in Germany where the General Staff during the Antwerp campaign kept an uneasy eye on the Flanders seaports in case a Russian army should leap ashore. It was current before the end of August and grew in force during September; it died away only as the situation of the Allies improved and the need for a miracle was less apparent. By mid-month the sceptical view prevailed and the celebrated joke that 'he knew they were Russians because they had snow on their boots' appeared in *Punch* on 23rd September. I have my own Russian story. About 1st September, when I was visiting an aunt in Birmingham, we were so convinced of the truth of the story that we went down to Snow Hill Station to watch the trains. The ticket-collector at the barrier confirmed our beliefs. Of course, he said, Russian troop-trains had been passing through all night. Not having been on night duty he had not seen them, but the next train, he understood, was due at four o'clock. Unfortunately we could not wait till four o'clock.

My early attempts to join the Army had proved abortive and my visit to relatives in Birmingham was paid in a mood of frustration. The town was in an elevated state with a recruiting campaign at its height. Birmingham was raising a 'city battalion' at its own cost and from its own resources. I persuaded my parents, by cabling round the world, to let me enlist and, pretending I was nineteen, put down my name at the Town Hall on 6th September, the day—though I did not know it—that the tide turned on the Marne. Three days later, as one of a long queue, I was 'attested', medically examined, sworn in, handed the King's symbolical shilling, and was dismissed to await the calling-up order. Again nothing happened for four weeks and while the Battle of the Marne was fought and won I was riding round Warwickshire on my bicycle. But I was a soldier, drawing pay at the rate of one shilling, with subsistence allowance at the rate of two and ninepence per day. Twenty-seven and sixpence a week was a good wage for a working man in those days.

When the calling-up notice came it was characteristic of 1914 that proceedings began with voluntary church parade. On Sunday, 4th October, the members of the City Battalion would meet in St. Martin's Church and on Monday would assemble at New Street Station, wearing buttonhole badges and bringing hand-baggage. There were as yet no uniforms to be had and a bonus of ten shillings was given to every man who arrived with a good overcoat and a pair of stout boots. At Sutton Coldfield, our destination, we were met by guides and sent off in twos and threes, haphazard, to be billeted in private houses. Most had enlisted as parties of friends, but I, a stranger, was lumped in with three others: a clerk, a commercial traveller in a small way, and a gas-fitter with whom I 'mucked in'; that is, shared everything we possessed. The gas-fitter (Fred Kernick. Are you alive, Fred?) was a serious leftish trade unionist who read Marx and said very little, and we lived together happily for six months in the back bedroom of a working-class cottage. The landlady now took our two and ninepences, on which she fed us lavishly, and I lived on my shilling a day. Cocoa in the canteen was a penny a cup; Woodbine cigarettes a penny for a packet of five; a pint of beer in the public bar cost fourpence; seats at the movies once a week were sixpence; and the pit at the old Empire in Birmingham, where we went occasionally, cost a shilling. My pin-up girl was the adorable Vesta Tilley, who impersonated a Kitchener recruit that season, singing:

'I joined the Army yesterday,
So the Army of today's all right.'

But we were hard-worked and tired in the evenings, which were mostly dull. I walked out with a girl who served in a baker's shop, with great propriety, as we were both desperately shy. All this by the way. The serious business of life was learning to be a soldier.

A thousand young men in their holiday clothes (with overcoats and stout boots) appeared in a mob on the parade ground, and were confronted by the colonel, Sir John Barnsley, in a blue uniform. Though I had a letter of introduction to him in my pocket, it didn't seem appropriate to deliver it just then. With him were about twenty lively looking young men, some of them in the uniform of the university O.T.C. and some in overcoats and stout boots. Another group of twenty or thirty, apparently from a different stable, were middle-aged, tough, and weatherbeaten; with a broomstick up each backbone and old-soldier written on their features. They pushed us into a long line which they divided by four, whereupon a loud-voiced sergeant-major (in overcoat and stout boots) started to bark like a dog at each of the four companies. We were subdivided again into sixteen platoons, to each of which was allotted a young officer from the O.T.C. party and a sergeant from the group of old soldiers. Now we were away and at once began to drill. It did not take long to learn that the officers knew little more than we did about soldiering; and not much longer to learn that what the sergeants knew was largely out of date. In my company all depended on the sergeant-major, a forceful character with all the latest military information, or so we supposed. My captain for the first few days was one of the Birmingham Members of Parliament, by name L. S. Amery, but when he was swept away to higher spheres we got an elderly major with a South African War medal and no vices that I remember. The sergeant was a benevolent old gentleman, quite forty, who admitted that he didn't know the modern drill-book; and it was he who entertained me with tales of his favourite General Buller. As for my platoon commander, I thought poorly of him. I couldn't think why he was where he was and I where I was though I liked being a private soldier.

Since I had no friends as yet, I had sidled in among a group of boys of my own age when the line was formed, and presently discovered that two or three, like me, had falsified their attestation papers. After a week or two, when they had sized us up, the sergeant-major picked out section commanders who were made acting, unpaid, lance-corporals. I could think of no reason why this barren honour should not fall on me and was hurt when the sergeant-major's eye fell on my neighbour in the ranks, Jack Sangster. Since, I observe, he is now a great financial tycoon I am obliged to admit that the sergeant-major's eye may have been penetrating.

Weeks went by when we had no uniforms, no arms, no apparatus for teaching the military techniques. Marching, squad drill, physical training, was all that we could do from dawn to dark, and we were avid to become soldierly. When it rained someone lectured us on map-reading (without maps) or on musketry (without rifles), so that the rate of progress was limited. Since everything was lacking, all our interest was centred on the next item of equipment and when it would come. The country had run out of khaki cloth and in November we were put into blue uniforms with a handsome red piping, because a large stock of material for postmen's uniforms had come to light. Before Christmas we mostly had rifles—not real rifles but an out-of-date pattern 'for drill purposes'. By January we got our 'equipment', the harness of belts and braces and pouches that enable soldiers to become beasts of burden. Surely we must go to the front soon. On the other hand pessimists began to say that we were destined for home service or for garrison duty in some colony, with the consequence that two or three daring spirits deserted, to enlist in some other corps which, as they thought, was higher on the list for embarkation. On the whole, the best way to jump the queue for France was to get yourself selected for an officer's commission, since young officers had the heaviest casualties and the highest replacement rate.

We were so concentrated upon our own progress towards the war that we had little time for speculating on strategy. I knew less of the autumn fighting than I had known of the summer fighting, being no longer free to read the papers and stick pins in maps. What we now cared about was how to get to the Front and how to behave when we got there. Returned soldiers were still such rarities that only in late November did I acquire first-hand information about life in Flanders. A corporal of the Welch Fusiliers turned up in our street and proceeded to tell us the tale. 'I've been at Eeper,' he said, 'the place that you call Wipers.' I did not find his reminiscences edifying, as they were mostly concerned with loot and mademoiselles, but I thought he was genuine and I learned about warfare from him. A few days later I met a wounded sergeant of the London Scottish at a rather stiff dinner-party. It was a sign of the times that he and I were in common soldiers' uniforms while everyone else was in full evening dress, but I managed to get some talk with him when the ladies went upstairs and the men sat on over their wine. Yes, he had been in the famous action of the London Scottish on 1st November and what he remembered best of it was running for his life with the Prussian Guard after him. Could this be true? Did British soldiers really run away? Perhaps I wasn't quite so silly as the letters I then wrote to my mother seem to imply.

Kitchener's Army was rapidly taking shape. In the new year we understood that the half-million recruits were now organized in five armies (K.1 to K.5) of six divisions each with a systematic progression in equipment and training. K.1, the first 100,000, would be ready to make the jump in the early spring, but we in the Birmingham Battalion, now established in the county regiment as the 14th Royal Warwickshires, were only in K.5. The caution with which our colonel had postponed the day of call-up until he could collect officers and N.C.O.s had lost us some precedence, though it had ensured efficiency. Since military stores were to be issued in strict priority off the production line, advanced training was dependent on the rate of delivery. Khaki uniforms, webbing belts, service rifles, horses and transport, signalling gear, machine-guns at the rate of two for a battalion, would arrive in sequence and each issue would warrant a further stage of our education. We should move to a concentration area, fire a course with live ammunition, dig entrenchments, go on divisional manœuvres, expose ourselves to inspection by Kitchener himself, and embark—like lemmings drowning in the Arctic Sea.

At the New Year of 1915 I went on leave, to London, where I heard George Graves sing 'Sister Susie's sewing shirts for Soldiers' in the Drury Lane pantomime, and to the vicarage at Fleet which was still beset at week-ends by subalterns from Aldershot, and livelier than ever with fun and games. The house was full of young men in Kitchener's Army, all of whom had begun, like me, in the ranks and all of whom had got commissions. Why should I not try again? Colonel Addison, of the 9th York and Lancaster, who had recently been billeted on my uncle, seemed fair game. Some letters passed and I found myself, in my blue uniform with my buttons notably polished, in the officers' mess at Barossa Barracks trying to make a good impression at an interview.

There was no further test and in one day, 23rd February 1915, toughened and six months older, and knowing my drill, I jumped from private soldier to second lieutenant. I was a better bargain for the York and Lancasters than I would have been for the Rifle Brigade the previous August, but still an innocent child.

4

The First Year

THE rivalries and disputes between the generals in the first campaign of the 1914 War were largely unknown to the public. Even the sequence of events at the front and the outcome of particular battles had not been made clear in the meagre statements issued by the Press Bureau. That French's Army had given the Germans a hard knock at Mons, that it had made a fighting retreat to the Marne in order to conform with the strategy of Joffre, that the Germans had been stopped and driven back to the Aisne, and that all had then turned on securing Antwerp and the Channel ports, was about as much as the man in the street had grasped. Except for the guarded statements made by Kitchener in the House of Lords, little was accurately known of particular actions or of the regiments engaged, or of the commanders' names, other than General French. The official communiqué, no more than a paragraph, was issued to the press agencies in the afternoon and was rushed into print in special editions of the evening papers, then sold at a halfpenny. Out of reach of the news-stand and the running, shouting newsboy there was no news. The morning papers, mostly sold for a penny—even *The Times* came down to a penny for a short time—repeated the same communiqué with such embellishments as they could produce. 'Our military correspondent', from an armchair in London, contributed an article based on general knowledge of the science of war, not on superior information. A team of official reporters with the Army, who wrote under the collective name of 'Eyewitness', supplied elegant essays on army life which were so heavily censored as to convey no news, and were commonly described as 'eye-wash'. Otherwise the Press relied on extracts from Allied and enemy journals which seemed not to be so severely restricted, and on such gossip as it could obtain from refugees, wounded soldiers, and political journalists who had found out something for themselves, especially in Belgium before it was overrun. The Navy was so silent a service that neither Frenchmen nor Germans appreciated its contribution to the battle; the Army had no notion of publicity or of propaganda as a weapon; and Kitchener's addiction to secrecy was part of his legendary reputation.

What the country lacked in information it made up in rumour. The dramatic episodes were wildly exaggerated, so that the cavalry action at Nery became a feat like Balaclava, the night alarm at Landrecies a regular Battle of Hohenlinden, and General Gallieni's use of Paris taxis to move a brigade from the garrison a portent in modern war. Though there was more said—and much more to be said—about the French armies of 1914 than about the Expeditionary Force, the British public could hardly be expected to realize how small a part, even though a decisive part, it had played in a great campaign, as one army and that a small one, out of nine. It is doubtful whether the Kaiser ever, in fact, uttered the oft-quoted sneer about the 'contemptible little British Army', which at once adopted the adjective as a nickname to be proud of. Mons, Le Cateau, the Marne, the Aisne, Ypres soon passed into history as the heroic, legendary, age of the war, from which there were few survivors.

Not many of the British appreciated that these were regarded by the French as minor incidents in the Battle of the Frontier. The continued retreat was alarming, since everyone over sixty could remember the French collapse in 1870. In every family Grandfather feared the worst, and it was this consideration that made the sudden halt and counter-offensive on the Marne so unexpected as to be miraculous. When the Allied armies advanced to the Aisne in September spirits rapidly rose and not only the aggressive French generals supposed that the decisive battle had already taken place. The optimistic Henry Wilson ventured an opinion that we should reach the German frontier in four weeks. It was the German stand on the Aisne that revealed the strength of the defensive, since the earlier battles had been affairs of mobility and manœuvre. When the Germans dug themselves in on the north bank of the river it proved impossible to shift them, as the trench warfare, which was to last three years, began. The so-called 'race for the sea' was a continuous attempt by each army to outflank the other, a race which the Germans won because they had the most men and the best railway communications. The troops they first threw in to the fight in

Flanders were new formations of very young soldiers, who made up in keenness what they lacked in military knowledge. It was these young soldiers who were laid low by the rapid rifle-fire of the British infantry in the first stage of the Battle of Ypres, which the Germans remember as the '*kindermord*' ('massacre of the Innocents'). In the later stages they were reinforced by the best regulars the German Army possessed, including the Prussian Guard. They too were shot to pieces by the 'old contemptibles', who saved the Western Front and the alliance in its second great crisis—the first having been the Marne—and lost half their numbers in the process.

The true nature of the First Battle of Ypres, and its two crises, on 1st and 11th November, when the shock was taken by Sir Douglas Haig's 1st Corps, was appreciated by the public rather slowly. It was not so dramatic as the 'miracle of the Marne', with no sudden or violent change of fortune. The newspapers at the time had more to say of the operations on the Belgian coast when Churchill scraped up marines to hold Ostend for a few days, and when his half-trained, half-equipped Royal Naval Division was sent to reinforce Antwerp. Kitchener, always able to work with Churchill, produced a division of Regulars withdrawn from colonial garrisons, the 7th, which fought its way through from Ostend in time to close the gap at Ypres. This was spectacular, but the hardest fighting was done by Haig, who rode forward through the Menin Gate and took personal command at the decisive point on the critical day. The Battle of Ypres was a skilful operation in which Belgians, British, and French were better led than the Germans, and we should not forget that it was an Allied battle in which General Foch co-ordinated the action of the three national armies.

In the black days of the retreat there had been a moment when Sir John French despaired of his allies and made ready to retire on the Channel (as his successor Gort was obliged to do twenty-five years later). Though he was overruled by Kitchener, who ordered him to conform to Joffre's plan, his pessimism was not forgotten and when the British Army was moved from the Aisne to Flanders it was sandwiched between two French armies under Foch. Though the battle was won, by the efforts of all the combatants, the fighting qualities of Haig and his men would not have had their effect had not he and Sir John French and General Foch supported one another.

(2)

We entered the year 1915 in a mood of easy optimism and ended it in gloom. In the spring, it was supposed, the Allies would attack and break the deadlock in France, restoring the war of movement. The first step was Neuve Chapelle, 10th March 1915, an experimental battle not unlike the Dieppe landing in the Second World War, and like it a failure from which many lessons were learned. Rather against his own inclination, Haig was ordered to mount an offensive at a point selected by the French command. Neuve Chapelle is interesting because the technique of launching a trench-to-trench attack was there elaborated and the difficulty of moving forward from a break-in to a break-through was demonstrated. Every later battle until Cambrai was a variant of the Neuve Chapelle method.

Strategic surprise was impossible, because the enemy could not fail to be aware of the intense activity and the accumulation of stores behind the British line, which must mean trouble coming. Tactical surprise was, however, complete, as the Germans got no inkling of when or where in particular the British blow would fall, or whether there was to be a sustained offensive. The troops were assembled and ammunition was piled up for a three days' battle, as much as could be spared. For the first time the whole of the front to be attacked was reconnoitred from the air, so that the assaulting troops could be briefed on photographic prints. The German barbed wire was bombarded by field-guns with low-bursting shrapnel which successfully blew away the obstacle on at least part of the front. For this new type of battle the tactics of open fighting were abandoned and the assault was delivered as in siege warfare. Instead of advancing by 'fire and movement', with infantrymen covering one another by rifle-fire as they moved in alternate groups, the whole front line advanced together, keeping as close as possible to the protective curtain of fire—the barrage, as it came to be called—laid down by the artillery. The guns did not concentrate on specific targets but spread their fire along the whole enemy front line, so as to force the defenders to keep their heads down. When the barrage lifted on to the second-line trench the wave of attacking troops rushed forward.

The first assault at Neuve Chapelle was successful on the greater part of the front attacked. Within an hour or two the British held the

German front line and the village and had made some lodgments in the second line. They had taken many prisoners and had not suffered heavy losses. Now was the time when supporting troops should have exploited the success by 'leap-frogging' through, which on this occasion and on almost every other such occasion proved too difficult a task. Even after a successful attack the confusion was so great that hours passed before the second phase could begin. Signal sections were dispersed, signallers killed, and wires broken, so that at headquarters in the rear messages did not arrive, or came late, or brought contradictory reports from different sectors. After the barrage had lifted machine-guns opened from the flanks, making it impossible for reinforcements to move up. The leading troops had outrun their artillery, which dared not fire, not knowing how far forward our men were. Stubborn enemy groups fought on in the battle-zone.

In the first phase, the assault, the advantage lay for a short time with the attackers, if the guns had done their work. In the second phase the advantage passed again to the defenders. While the attackers were weakened, exhausted, confused, and now deprived of their artillery support, the defenders could prepare a new line on familiar ground, under cover of their artillery; and their reserves could come up fresh to counter-attack when they were ready.

On the second day a German counter-attack was beaten off and on the third day the British ran out of ammunition. The battle fizzled out, the British having taken a village and 2,000 prisoners at a cost of 11,000 killed and wounded. The pattern was repeated a dozen times by all the armies, enemy and Allied, during the next three years. Heavier bombardment, a complex fire-plan to neutralize every danger-point, 'mopping-up' parties to deal with pockets of resistance, five or six methods of sending messages, 'contact' aeroplanes to fly low and locate the leading troops, a 'creeping barrage' that was made to move slowly forward as the gunners raised their sights after every round, new devices for each new battle, did not solve the problem. Though in 1917 and 1918 the armies became much more mobile, they never in that war succeeded in maintaining the momentum of the attack.

Western Front battles after Neuve Chapelle may be classified as: attacks with limited objective, battles of attrition, and breakthrough battles—the third being a hypothetical class since in France the breakthrough was never quite achieved by either side. The French Army perfected the method of seizing a feature of ground by a sudden rapid assault delivered with great violence after careful preparation, and then of breaking off the action as soon as the objective was gained. The battles of attrition, which have given posterity so deep an impression of horror, were sustained methodical offensives—one Neuve Chapelle after another—with a pause for reorganization between phase and phase. The breakthrough, which all the commanders hoped to achieve in 1915, for which Nivelle produced a blueprint in 1917, and Luden-dorff another in 1918, remained beyond the reach of both com-batants; with the consequence that very few people foresaw, in 1939, that it had been made possible with a higher degree of mechanization. Perhaps the 'walkie-talkie' radio set was the most significant of the new devices that came up. In the First War, in a less mechanical age, the defensive remained dominant; in the Second the advantage had moved to the attacking side.

(3)

If we may describe the experimental battle Neuve Chapelle as a partial success which at least revealed the obstacles that must be over-come before victory was reached, no such comfort could be claimed by the Germans for their next burst of activity. In April 1915 they added a new horror to war by making an attack behind a cloud of chlorine gas, at the junction—inevitably a weak spot—between the British and French armies near St. Julien north of Ypres. The British left was held by the Canadians, new to the line, and the French right by Algerian troops. Although there had been a rumour that the enemy intended to use poison gas, it was not much credited and no counter-measures could be taken until it was known what poison would be discharged by what method. Terrifying as it was on its first appearance, a cloud of volatile, soluble, chlorine, issuing from cylinders dug into the German front trench, was a clumsy, uncertain weapon of war. The German command threw it away with a great deal less forethought than Haig was to use, a year later, in releasing his secret weapon, the tank.

The Algerians bolted and the first the Canadian commanders knew of the disaster was that the French artillery on their flank suddenly ceased fire when the gas-cloud reached them. Though there was now a mile-wide gap in the line, the Germans—just as scared of their own gas as were its victims—showed little initiative. No preparations had been made for a general advance and all that happened was that the front-line troops gingerly moved forward a little. The heroes of the day were the Canadians, who stood fast and let the gas flow over them, though they had no warning, no protective measures, and no knowledge of the extent of the danger. Bending back their flank they prepared to defend their position with no thought of retreat, very wisely as it turned out, since the gas-cloud soon blew past while those who ran away ran with it. Some forgotten genius, who recognized the smell of chlorine, passed the word that a pad of rag, soaked in urine—a chemical easily procured —would give protection if held against the mouth and nose. Within four days every man in the British Army was provided with a medicated pad to breathe through.

The half-hearted German penetration into the gap was the beginning of the long and bloody Second Battle of Ypres. The local commander was Sir Horace Smith-Dorrien of the Second Army, who was already in bad odour with Sir John French because he had fought the Battle of Le Cateau against French's orders (and, what was more provoking, had won it). He withdrew from the exposed tip of the Ypres salient, which the new German advance had made untenable, and wanted to draw back his whole line to a well-sited position. This French would not allow, and decided to change this army commander, who had a knack of being right when the Commander-in-Chief was wrong. The anecdote told of 'Wully' Robertson, the ranker general, that he alone was bold enough to convey the Chief's decision to the fiery Smith-Dorrien with the plain words: "Orace, yer fer 'ome', is authenticated. Horace went, and the British Army was obliged, on a point of honour, to hold the exposed Ypres salient for the duration of the war.

Before proceeding with the 1915 campaign I shall say a few words about that unsatisfactory weapon, poison gas. It produced a reaction in the emission of clouds of moral indignation, which in their turn, were neutralized when it was understood that we might gas the Germans, with the aid of the westerly winds, more efficiently than they could gas us. At the Battle of Loos, to which I shall be coming shortly, we secreted cylinders of chlorine in our front line and found them as uncertain an aid as they had been to the Germans at Ypres. In the Battle of the Somme we concealed our movements with screens of smoke in which a modicum of poison gas was diluted to oblige the enemy to take it seriously, but the campaign of unpleasantness went in their favour when in July 1916 they began to mix with their chlorine the far more deadly phosgene which could not be detected by its smell and could penetrate the gas-masks then in use. Before the end of the year we were driven to carrying box respirators, which some will remember as issued to the whole nation in 1939. The 1917 campaigns produced gas-shell fired by the artillery of both armies, and mustard gas as a missile. During the last two years of the war we were all accustomed to sniffing the air and saying: 'Best take care. A touch of mustard about this morning', with the mental reservation that more than a touch was deadly. I do not think that poison gas won any decisive advantage for either side in a battle of the First World War. What gas could do, if a small area was drenched with gas-shells, was to deny it to the use of either army. With proper discipline and effective gas-masks good soldiers could defy a gas attack, which merely added another un-pleasantness to their comfortless way of life.

To strike a personal note, I add that gas was one of the few weapons of war which did not frighten me, and during the Somme I once slept a night in a gas-mask, too tired to take it off. It gave me a secret satis-faction, when going round the trenches with my colonel, to notice that he was made miserably apprehensive by a smell of gas, which meant little to me. This made me feel better when he seemed to ignore high explosives, which reduced me to gibbering terror.

(4)

In May 1915 the French launched their general offensive on the Western Front and failed to break the German line. The British con-tribution to this was the two subsidiary actions at Aubers Ridge and Festubert, of which we need say no more than that these battles were like Neuve Chapelle over again but rather worse. They were the last fights of the old Regular Army and perhaps revealed it as battle-weary. Meanwhile the centre of public interest had moved away from the Western Front and supplies were being diverted for other campaigns. In Germany the general staff had decided to hold its ground in France until a decisive victory had been gained over Russia, and to that they gave their main attention in the summer of 1915. In Britain a large section of political opinion, led by Churchill, was for transferring our main effort for the year to the Mediterranean. In Feburary the first attempt was made to force the Dardanelles by the Fleet alone, and on 25th April the first landing was made on the Gallipoli Peninsula by the 29th Division of regulars, the Australian and New Zealand Division, and The Royal Naval Division of marine volunteers.

I do not propose to relate the story of Gallipoli, because I wasn't there and because readers may be referred to Alan Moorehead's book for a perceptive account in a modern idiom. Gallipoli caught the imagination of the public in a way that the Western Front battles of that year did not, and the eventual failure of the campaign had a sobering effect. No one could doubt that our troops had fought with great courage and efficiency and that the cause of failure lay in the higher direction of the war. Politics being what they are, it was inevitable that there should be a demand for a scapegoat to take the blame. But in war someone must lose a battle if someone wins it, and one explanation of our failure at Gallipoli is that the Turks have been known for centuries as the most stubborn defensive fighters in the world, and in Mustafa Kemal they produced the outstanding battle-winner of the war, not a great strategist but a fighting commander like Rommel in 1941. He had just that *coup d'œil* that Sir Ian Hamilton lacked.

The British supposed, too, that they had some reputation for stubborn defensive fighting and after the first landings at Cape Helles and Anzac Cove (so named from the Australian and New Zealand Army Corps), the troops ensconced upon these narrow rocky slopes were defending themselves with little likelihood of pressing on. As in France, so in Gallipoli, every attack lost momentum, every operation degenerated into trench warfare, with some differences. While the soldiers 'on the peninsula' were always under enemy observation, hardly out of range of machine-gun fire, they were not exposed to artillery bombardment on the scale of the Western Front. As such campaigns do, Gallipoli absorbed soldiers. Most unwillingly the War Office released for the Mediterranean Territorial and New Army divisions which they had intended to send to France, without gaining the victory that always seemed just over the crest of the hill. When it was decided to make a further landing no troops were available except raw untried divisions, and the choice of a commander proved unfortunate. The Suvla landing of 6th August, not so bloody as the earlier landings, stands as one of the lost opportunities of military history. It is odd that the pattern was repeated with curious fidelity at the Anzio landing in the Italian campaign of 1943, with troops and commanders who should have known better. Gallipoli was the one chance granted to the Allies for forcing a decision by opening a new front, and when it failed the opportunity vanished for ever. Soldiers who had fought on the peninsula, like the survivors of Mons and Ypres, were respected as veterans of a memorable event. National myths are often based upon legends of heroism in disaster; and it was Anzac Cove that placed the soldiers of Australia and New Zealand under the searchlight of the world's observation. The three 'colonies', Canada, Australia, New Zealand, built their national reputations upon the valour of their armies, the Canadians at Ypres, the two southern countries at Gallipoli.

Later in the war the wishful thinking of imaginative statesmen was directed again and again to diversions of effort into the Mediterranean, which became steadily more unprofitable. All the logistic advantage, after 1915, was on the side of the enemy, and the later campaigns in Greece, Mesopotamia, and Palestine were no more than side-shows, recognized as such by the soldiers of all ranks. Troops consigned to these operations got little public notice and endured the fate of forgotten men.

As 1915 advanced, a growing sense of failure in our war effort, both on the Western Front and in the Mediterranean, produced friction between the fighting troops and Whitehall, between the War Office and the Admiralty, between the service chiefs and the politicians. Public opinion was divided and diffused until attempts were made to concentrate it by the tycoons of Fleet Street and the Conservative opposition. In mid-May crises were reached over the Army and Navy commands.

Sir John French, not a subtle politician, unwisely placed his reputation in the hands of a gossip-writer named Repington, a socialite who had been obliged to resign his commission in the Army under a cloud, and who was then working for the megalomaniac Lord Northcliffe. Sir John, who had been complaining of the shell shortage for months, briefed the Northcliffe Press, which, with characteristic impudence, inflated his case into a 'munitions scandal', making it the occasion for violent personal abuse of Kitchener. The consequence was an equally hysterical reaction in Kitchener's favour on the part of the public, who made it clear that the old man was still the nation's hero. Whoever was to be blamed for shortcomings it was not to be K. of K., who then received the public recognition of his sovereign's confidence in the form of an earldom and the Garter. Lord Northcliffe had overreached himself, and Sir John French, about whom the generals in France were growing uneasy, was left in isolation, having also antagonized the War Office by his intrigue with Repington.

At the same moment the Navy was convulsed by the sudden resignation of Fisher, the First Sea Lord, as a protest against the conduct of the Gallipoli campaign. No one could induce him to return to duty and a political crisis then blew up, of which Churchill was the victim. The Conservative leaders were bidding for power in a new coalition government in which the hated Churchill would be excluded from high office. They would have liked to be rid of Kitchener also and for a moment there was a chance that he might have been made Generalissimo in France, until the demonstrations of his popularity scared the politicians who dared not remove him from the War Office.

(5)

Mr. Asquith's coalition of 1915–16 was a bad government in which there were continual conflicts between the Liberal and Conservative elements. It has to its credit two successes which are relevant to my story: the reorganization of the War Office under Sir William Robertson and the formation of the Ministry of Munitions, both at the expense of Kitchener. To appreciate the 'munitions scandal' one must think oneself back into a world of laissez-faire in which there was no Ministry of Defence, no Ministry of Munitions, no Ministry of Labour, no conscription, even for the Army, and no hint or suggestion of the compulsory direction of munition workers. As the senior field marshal, Kitchener had assumed powers of command immensely greater than those exercised by any previous Secretary of State for War. Churchill has put it on record that the Cabinet never once overruled him when he had given his opinion on a military matter during his first great year of office. For the soundness of his views I shall quote Lord Hankey, who knew all the secrets and all the national leaders of his day: 'Kitchener', he writes, 'showed himself the most far-sighted soldier and statesman of his time. It was he who at the beginning of the war foresaw and declared that we were in for a long war. He it was who conceived as in a flash the great armies which bore the brunt of our cause in the later stages of the war. He it was who raised, and before his untimely death had brought to completion this great engine of military power. . . . Granted that he made mistakes—and who did not in those bewildering days . . . the great outstanding fact is that within eighteen months of the outbreak of war, when he had found a people reliant on seapower, and essentially non-military in their outlook, he had conceived and brought into being, equipped in every way, a national army capable of holding its own against the armies of the greatest military power the world had ever seen. That is the achievement beside which all else pales. That is the standard by which Kitchener's place in history must be measured.'[1]

The conversion of a nation of civilians into a nation of soldiers was a task within his mighty powers, but the parallel mobilization of industry, another unprecedented revolution, was entirely beyond his constitutional authority. Hardly less remarkable than the formation of Kitchener's armies is that he housed and fed and clothed and armed them and despatched them overseas before the Ministry of Munitions had got into its stride. Much more than that, the plans were made, the contracts signed, and the production lines were at work for most of the armament expansion before Lloyd George took over. We must never forget Churchill's considered verdict on industrial mobilization for war: the first year you get nothing; the second year a little; the third year as much as you want. Northcliffe's 'munitions scandal' was his observation for the first time that you can teach soldiers to drill and to shoot in six months but that to build factories and train workers to produce precision instruments like shell-fuses requires at least two years, a consideration that was no news to Kitchener, whose target date for the release of his Armies, fully munitioned, was the summer of 1916. Like his other forecasts, it was right.

When the six divisions of the B.E.F. went to France in 1914 as the best-equipped army in the world they were provided with enough ammunition to fight three or four battles which might last three or four days each, and the replacement rate from the recognized armament firms was appropriate to such a campaign. The French and German armies had comparable scales of supply but for armies of sixty to eighty divisions. While all were short of shells by the spring of 1915, the

1. Lord Hankey, *The Supreme Command, 1914–1918* (George Allen & Unwin, 1961), p. 508.

French and Germans merely had to double their output under the stress of war, whereas the British had to double their output for the six divisions and, at the same time, create a new munitions industry for an army ten times as great. Tenders must be put out to private firms who had to tool up new machines operated by trade unionists who were bitterly hostile to the dilution of skilled labour. The placing of contracts, the negotiating, and the inspecting of firms working voluntarily, for profit, was an appalling burden to place on the shoulders of Kitchener and his staff of military 'dugouts'. There was no means of ensuring dates of delivery or of checking the quality of production, and he had no statutory authority to enforce compliance.

Rifles are precision instruments which cannot be efficiently made by mass-production. Kitchener's armies were partly equipped with Canadian and Japanese rifles, and the small-arms ammunition was mostly made, after December 1914, in the United States. The production of artillery was always behind schedule; in July 1915, when Sir John French had 100 heavies and 1,200 field-guns in France, only one-third of the contracts for new guns had been completed. Shells, of which there were never enough, were coming off the line at a rate that had increased from 3,000 a month in July 1914 to 174,000 a month in the spring of 1915. Vastly greater numbers of shells could have been released if it had not been for the shortage of fuses—again precision instruments. The greatest shortage was of high explosive shells for the heavies, and as the quantity increased the quality declined. We had 2,000 machine-guns in 1914 with an output of fifty a week. There was not much point in stepping up the contract beyond 200 a week since the deliveries did not reach this figure. Experiments were ordered with the new Lewis gun in August 1914 but only 600 could be delivered in the first year. Mills bombs were put in hand in March 1915 but were not plentiful until the autumn.

The problem was not in the planning and ordering but in the contracting, inspecting, and labour-management, matters which the War Office could not control. When Kitchener had created a national army Lloyd George performed an equal miracle by mobilizing the whole nation for war production, the essential problem, as always, being priorities. Were skilled men to be withdrawn from the armies for munition-working, and were the factories to be combed out for cannon-fodder? How were the trade unions to be engaged in the national effort? Should ships, or guns, or tanks, or shells, or aircraft, or motor-lorries come first in order off the production line?, since you can't do everything at once? This was Lloyd George's proper work as Minister of Munitions, though Kitchener was loath to relinquish responsibility even in this unfamiliar field.

(6)

In the summer of 1915 Kitchener seemed to have regained his authority in the councils of the new government and, so far as his armies knew, his was still the master hand. I saw him in July for the last time, with the King, inspecting our division on Hindhead Common, and thought him the greatest man in the world. Very different was the opinion of his colleagues, as the reminiscences of many contemporaries prove. The work at which he excelled, the great improvisation, was completed and in the War Office it was time to resume the routine of acting by rule and method.

The Gallipoli campaign had a bleak outlook after the failure in August at Suvla, and politicians both in Britain and France wrangled over conflicting views. The adherence of Italy to the Allies and of Bulgaria to the enemy, the conquest of Servia, the struggle to draw Greece in on one side or the other, presented many possible courses of military and diplomatic action, all dominated by the Gallipoli campaign. Should we and could we push on? Should we and could we withdraw? And, if either, what should be our next pressure-point? All the experts were at odds, and Kitchener, for the first time in his life, vacillated. At last he had found a problem too complex to grasp, or was he growing old and tired? Perhaps if he had been relieved of the War Office and had been sent as High Commissioner and Commander-in-Chief to the Mediterranean he might have achieved one more miracle of improvisation; and when in November he went to look at the Peninsula for himself it seems that his colleagues hoped he would not come back. He decided, then changed his mind, then finally gave an order for the withdrawal from Gallipoli, an admission of defeat in the theatre of which he, personally, had been the master. A few months later he had to concede another defeat when a British force surrendered in Mesopotamia.

But, like almost every other high-ranking professional soldier, Kitchener was a Westerner and believed that the decision must be reached in France. The autumn offensive by the French armies produced another deadlock, and again the British were persuaded to co-operate by an attack not of their own choosing. For the third time that year Haig's First Army was ordered to make a prepared assault on a designated section of the front. The Battle of Loos, 25th–27th September 1915, differed from Neuve Chapelle and Festubert only because it was on a larger scale with seven divisions in the front line, and because four divisions of Kitchener's Army took part. Again the attack lost momentum and again the reserves failed to make progress when thrust into the gap made by the assaulting troops. Controversy has raged over two divisions, which should not have been entrusted with this supremely complex task on their first day in action. In Haig's view they were wrongly placed and released to him too late.

Sir John French was in poor health that autumn, which gave the War Office an excuse to withdraw him politely from his command, and in December Haig became Commander-in-Chief as of right, with complete self-confidence, with the support of Kitchener and the War Office, with the entire approval of the Army, and with the friendship of the King as a powerful buttress to his position. French had no legitimate complaint, as he retired loaded with honours to make way for a man ten years younger. While Haig's appointment seemed to be inevitable, some of the consequent promotions were more unexpected. Mr. Asquith now decided to restore the old system at the War Office by putting in Sir William Robertson as Chief of Staff (C.I.G.S.) with full powers to advise the Government on strategy and to issue orders to field commanders by authority of the Army Council. Thus Kitchener, who had already lost control of munitions, lost control of strategic planning and for the last six months of his life gave up the military dictatorship which he had exercised for fifteen months, without constitutional authority but at the wish of the nation; and now our military planning began to take a conventional shape. Kitchener was left merely as Secretary of State, a political appointment which he did not relish and for which his talents were not suited, though he accepted it with good grace, giving his support to Robertson and Haig. Six months later he was drowned at sea on a visit to Russia, a dramatic end to a unique career. The whole nation and the Army went into deep mourning. The last of his New Army divisions was on its way to France at the time of his death.

While Kitchener, though he hated publicity and ignored the arts of propaganda, was never out of the public eye, 'Wully' Robertson, his successor as military adviser to the Government, was an obscure figure. The stories that are still current about 'Wully' were whispered in the world of the clubs and messes, not published in the Press. He was never a popular hero with the rank and file, which is surprising since he was the first example in the history of the British Army of a private soldier who carried a field marshal's baton in his knapsack. Self-taught and self-made, with no money and no influence, he fought his way up the ladder, actually by way of a crack cavalry regiment, and died a poor man, though a field marshal and a baronet. Simple, pious, and honest, he was devoted to his working-class family and in moments of stress reverted to the homely accents of his provincial youth. Such a man might have been a popular hero like Ernie Bevin in the Second World War. Again, unexpectedly, he was not a swashbuckler but an office soldier, all of whose experience was on the staff. A master of logistics, he could prick the bubbles of more imaginative war-makers with a few unquestionable facts and figures. To the torrents of Lloyd George's eloquence he replied, raising his bushy eyebrows, which were enough to terrorize lesser men, with the grunted remark: 'I've 'eard different,' and there the matter ended. He was firm as the Rock of Gibraltar. Unfortunately, like Haig, whom he supported through thick and thin, he had no gift of speech and though he expressed himself on paper with formidable lucidity he had no political talent for talking an opponent over.

Leaving him in charge we can return to the worm's-eye view of the war.

5

Kitchener's Army

THE 9th York and Lancasters were colliers from the West Riding, a rough, tough lot, and if there are better or braver men in the world I have yet to find them. Being in K.3, they were further forward than the Birmingham Battalion with their training, were armed with service rifles, and had khaki uniforms, which seemed to bring much nearer the glorious day when we should get to the front. Soon after I joined them the whole division, the 23rd, marched by road from Aldershot to Shorncliffe Camp in six days, spending the nights billeted in Surrey villages that were not yet suburban. Can it be true, or have I dreamed it, that I saw yokels wearing smock-frocks? This march was so near to active service as to gratify me enormously, and when settled for the spring in East Kent, far away now from protecting relatives, I threw myself into the postures and revelled in the fantasies which the earlier stories of Rudyard Kipling had taught me to regard as appropriate to a subaltern in a line regiment. Never again have I been so immersed in the life of a group, so convinced that everyone was as ready to conform as I was—and indeed most of them were. It did not distress me when some of the officers proved unequal to their task, or when old soldiers who had been given sergeant's stripes on sight revealed themselves as what the Army called 'King's hard bargains', since all that was in the tradition.

The colonel was a pleasant, quiet, Regular officer recalled from half-pay, not a dynamic man but a responsible soldier with right principles about training troops. At his elbow was Major Lewis, the second-in-command, a striking character with some resemblance to 'Wully' Robertson. A 'ranker', he had been a Guards sergeant-major and from him we all learned our discipline and drill. I happen to know that he was forty two years old, which I thought a great age. Perhaps the best schoolmaster I ever had, Major Lewis impressed upon me and my friends one lesson at least, that young officers have no privileges and no rights but only duties. Woe betide any subaltern who ever so much as enquired after his dinner until he had seen his men fed and made comfortable, or who kept them standing at attention when they might have been standing at ease.

The other officers were amateur soldiers, two or three of the seniors having Boer War medal ribbons on their chests. As the year drew on, new faces began to appear in the officers mess and it was not difficult to distinguish them into two classes. Rarely and significantly, there would be a captain or major, home wounded from France, to be quickly snapped up as a staff officer by brigade or division. More often it was some pleasant easy-going incompetent who had been sifted out and pushed into the back areas. Best men forwards into danger, and less good men backwards into safety, the eliminating rule of war was at work. Very wisely, the cadres of officers were overfilled so that a lurking fear began to creep into my consciousness: that some would be left behind when we went overseas. Who would be sent back to a reserve battalion as incompetent? I asked myself.

During March and April we had company training down in Kent. In May we moved to Maidstone to dig a defensive system of trenches, against invasion, along the whole ridge of the North Downs. (It vanished and was not to be found when wanted again in 1940.) June, July, and August we spent again in the Aldershot Command at Bordon Camp, happily because we knew that this meant the final preparation. I took over Quebec Barracks from a Highland regiment of the 9th Division, one of the first of Kitchener's Army to go overseas, and was professionally shocked at the disorder in which they left their quarters. Bordon Camp, set among woods and heaths, was an ideal training ground through which we romped all that hot summer, at battalion and brigade training across country, with marches and bivouacs, always preparing for a war of movement. We spent long days on the ranges at field firing and liked to think that we had almost achieved the standards of the Old Contemptibles at accurate rapid-fire with our rifles. The technique of trench warfare, which we still supposed to be a passing phase, was talked about but not practised since no one had any experience of it, and we were not provided with any of the trench weapons. Towards the end of our time we began to specialize and every subaltern, as well as commanding a platoon, made a study of machine-guns, signalling, or whatever it might be. I understudied the transport officer, and when he could spare me, I rode all the pack-ponies in turn. We possessed thirty horses, thirty mules, water-carts, field-kitchens, and a dozen limbered wagons—articulated pairs of two-wheeled carts which could be driven across country.

In the evenings we dined in mess, paying rather more than the usual attention to the traditional rules about which we had read in little books of etiquette. No Regular regiment, I am sure, was as meticulous as we were on such momentous questions as never mentioning a lady's name at the mess-table or never bringing a sword into the ante-room (or whatever it was). We 'sirred' and 'saluted' a great deal more than the Brigade of Guards. It was also a revered custom that once a month there was a guest-night, which every officer must attend, when the King's health was drunk with honours (paid for by the Prince Regent, who had allowed every officer an additional sixpence a day for the purpose) after which the proceedings ended, when the senior officers had tactfully withdrawn, with a rough-house. Never again, I surmise, shall I climb round the room from mantelshelf to cornice to window-ledge, without touching the floor, or drink a pint of beer while standing on my head.

When I first applied for a commission I had some doubts whether I could live on my earnings and it may be interesting now to give the answer. Subalterns' pay had recently been raised from five-and-three-pence to seven-and-sixpence a day, which we thought a handsome gesture of Kitchener's. There were, in addition, extra allowances—as well as the 'Regency allowance' which I have mentioned—for special duty or for living rough. It was annoying that one's allowances were lowest in regular barracks like Bordon Camp where one's mess expenses were highest—over five pounds a month. (But if they were too high Major Lewis would have something to say, since young officers were discouraged from living beyond their means.) One of the minor advantages of going overseas was that mess bills shrank while earnings were increased by a special field allowance of half a crown a day. In my first year as a subaltern my total income from pay and allowances was just over £200, on which I paid six pounds income tax. I had also received an outfit allowance of fifty pounds which provided easily for sword and revolver as well as for two service-dress uniforms, a greatcoat, and all the accessories. At the end of my first year I had a few pounds in hand.

Two years later, when I was an acting captain in France, with increased allowances, my basic rate was eleven and sixpence a day and my actual earnings over £300 in a year. This was wealth, although I now paid nine pounds in income-tax, and I saved seventy pounds.

It was not the comfort of being a man on a salary, nor the fun in the officers' mess, nor the rare week-end leaves to London, nor the pony-riding, nor the healthy open-air life, but another factor which I did not then appreciate, that made this year so satisfying; I was in love with my platoon. The whole of my affection and concern was for the forty Yorkshire miners, collectively and severally, with whom my life was so unexpectedly linked. For me the national effort, Kitchener's Army, the battalion, were vague concepts while here, concentrated, was an entity in which I could take a sensuous enjoyment. To see their healthy faces, to hear their North Country accents, to feel myself one of them, to cosset them, and even to bully them, gave me the deepest contentment I had yet known; and my love-affair was to be disrupted.

Two days before the battalion left for France the colonel sent for me to say that in accordance with a regulation beyond his control I was to be left behind, even though he had given me a good 'confidential report'. Well, I was still only eighteen years old, and didn't look a year older as I pretended to be. Anyone would have been disappointed but I was more than that; I was heartbroken. When the battalion marched away to the station (27th August 1915) they sang a silly chorus which still rings in my ears:

'Kitty, Kitty, isn't it a pity,
In the City you work so hard . . .'

As my platoon waved their good-byes I felt finished, disgraced, and my war over, though it had not yet begun. But teen-age troubles are tiresome to read about, and I have another type of military unit to describe. First let me write off the 9th York and Lancasters, whom I still recollect as a well found, well trained battalion. Ten months later, in the great holocaust of the 1st July 1916, they were in the leading wave of the assault made by the 8th Division against the German line at Ovillers. The bombardment had not been effective in destroying the

German machine-gun posts to right and left, and when the barrage lifted the machine-gunners wiped out two brigades of the 8th Division as they marched straight to their front in unfaltering lines. So much for the prolonged cross-country training in open warfare. The 8th Division lost 5,500 men out of 8,500 who had gone into action: the German defenders lost 280 men. Colonel Addison and Major Lewis and almost all my friends died on the German wire.

Now let us move to the Reserve Battalion. When the 23rd Division went to France each of its units discarded a number of convalescents after illness or accident (and there are always a great many accidents among men whose life is spent handling dangerous weapons); super-numeraries like myself who felt slighted; shirkers and slackers of various kinds; and a residue of inadequate young men who had no remarkable vices nor virtues. After a few days of uncertainty the whole mixed bag of us were sent off to dreary half-finished hutments on Cannock Chase where I spent the next ten weeks in great dejection. It does not now seem surprising that the staff provided to run this establishment, which was given the loathsome name of a 'Young Officers' Company', were themselves second-class soldiers, the dregs of the senior ranks as we were the dregs of the junior. Perhaps we might have had worse luck than to get an amiable, idle, boozy colonel, who was a decent fellow when sober, and an adjutant who had been, I think, an auctioneer's clerk. He ran his office well, under conditions that must have been exasperating, but was not our idea of an adjutant. Most of us were smarting under the slur of dismissal by the regiments to which we were devoted, and were indignant at our reduction to the status of officer cadets. The authorities made efforts to organize classes of in-struction which we derided, as we believed ourselves to be more up-to-date than our teachers; and since we claimed to know the King's Regulations better than the adjutant did, we made the poor man's life a misery with complaints and objections. The mess, inevitably, was abominable. All this I thought scandalous, until I grew chary about using the word. When a whole nation is mobilized the natural leaders find their way to the front rank where enthusiasm is general and where willingness makes allowance for deficiencies. By the law of averages there must be a place for those who are not up to the mark, a sink or residue, and I'm inclined to applaud my boozy colonel and un-military adjutant for doing their best with intractable material.

My friends and I had one object only in view—to find a means of escape. Not long after the 'Young Officers' Company' was formed came the Battle of Loos, with a long casualty list for the 10th York and Lancaster, which enabled a number of my fellow-victims to escape to France, the haven where they would be. The 9th were not in that battle and in the whole autumn lost only one officer, a friend whose place I coveted but did not get. We all pulled what strings we could get a grip on, with a fair measure of success, since the War Office, in the last days of Kitchener's dictatorship, was in considerable chaos. One of my friends overcalled his hand by appealing to a great-uncle whom he had never met, a very elderly field marshal, and received this reply or words to this effect: 'Field Marshal Sir Evelyn Wood acknowledges receipt of a letter from 2nd Lieutenant So-and-So, and begs to inform him that he (the Field Marshal) spent many years at the War Office combating the baleful effects of private influence'.

I remembered my friends in Birmingham. My uncle, who was serving with a Territorial battalion, the 5th Royal Warwickshires, in France, persuaded his colonel to apply for me. A transfer from Kitchener's Army to the Territorials was unusual—I think irregular—but it happened; and I was ordered away from hateful Cannock Chase to a reserve unit of the Royal Warwickshire in Birmingham. This led to a change of occupation, as we were called in to run a campaign under Lord Derby's scheme for getting potential recruits into an order of priority. Night after night I attested and swore in recruits at a little office beside New Street Station with another subaltern, R.M.S. Saundby, both of us stretching our wings to fly: metaphorically in my case, to the service battalion in France; actually in his to the R.F.C., his first step to the rank of air marshal.

Late in December I was ordered abroad and sent on embarkation leave which I spent at Fleet, with my aunt and my three elder brothers who had all come to England. The eldest, Philip, was a theological student at Cambridge and not liable for military service. Christopher, on sick leave from Gallipoli, was a regular soldier on the staff of the New Zealand Division, with an appointment that had given him the rare experience of being present at all three landings—Helles, Anzac, and Suvla. Gallipoli staff officers did not luxuriate in châteaux far behind the line. The third brother, Hugh, also a career soldier, was an interesting wounded hero swathed in bandages, having been cut about by a Turkish bomb in Quinn's Post. This was a happy reunion—our last—but so besotted was I that I did not grudge it when I got my orders for France on Christmas Day.

After a few days at the Harfleur Base Camp, where all the talk was of hand grenades, trench mortars and barbed wire, I joined the 1/5th Royal Warwickshire in the trenches facing Gommecourt Wood, secretly gratified that I had reached my goal irregularly, before my nineteenth birthday.

6

The Old Front Line

THE front on which the British had fought the Battle of Ypres ran from the canal bank two or three miles north of Ypres, round the town in a pronounced salient and then through low-lying farmland and scattered copses which rose slightly above the fens. A mound on the sixty-metre contour, Hill 60, was no great mountain, but south-west from Ypres there was a range of low hills overlooking the plain, much as the Gogmagog Hills overlook Cambridge, growing a little higher to the west as the Cambridgeshire hills rise towards Royston Heath. Thus the Messines Ridge was a swelling and Kemmel behind it was a notable eminence. North and east from Ypres there was nothing but wet plain, just off sea-level, land once reclaimed from the coastal marshes and artificially maintained, like the English fenland, by drainage channels and dykes. South of the Messines Ridge which Allenby's Corps had lost after a sharp fight in October, the line went down again into the flats through Ploegsteert Wood—which everyone called 'Plug Street' —and close round the little market town of Armentières ('Armenteers'). This was a quiet sector and mademoiselles were still to be found living in the town in 1915, within a mile or two of the Germans.

Beyond Armentières the line ran out into a colliery district, a bleak harsh plain with slag-heaps (called 'fosses' on the French maps) and dingy rows of miners' dwellings where battles often ended in street fighting from house to house. Near La Bassée, which the Germans held, the British line ended and the French took over. The redoubtable General Foch commanded the northern group of armies along the fringe of a mining, manufacturing area, the French 'Black Country'. In the distance could be seen the smoking chimneys of Lens, now working for the enemy, and beyond that lay Lille, the French Man-chester. Here was territory worth regaining and Foch pursued his policy of the offensive, in attack after attack, with little success. Until the end of the war the Artois industrial area remained in German hands.

Ypres to La Bassée was no more than thirty miles. At the reorganization after Ypres the British Front was for a time reduced to a sector of no more than twenty miles, which the French thought a wretchedly small contribution for Britain to make to the defence of the Western Front; it was hardly more than the Belgian sector and Belgium was a small country in enemy hands. The German front-line troops now knew the fighting quality of the British and it was perhaps not they but the French who underrated the 'contemptible' little British Army.

Whenever the British Commander-in-Chief found himself a little stronger his intention was to thin out his line and draw back some divisions into reserve so as to form an attacking force, which could never be done while the French were insistent that the British should take over more frontage. During the next year the British sector was extended north and south. A pocket of French troops to the north of Ypres between our men and the Belgians were replaced by the British in April 1915. In the summer a new British Army, the Third, under Allenby, was formed to take over a sector farther south, and when a Fourth Army was formed under Rawlinson it held the right wing while Allenby relieved Foch's men in Artois. By the spring of 1916 the British held a continuous line from Ypres to the Somme Valley near Bray, a length of seventy miles. For many months this front stood firm, with no loss or gain of more than a few hundred yards of ground at any point, and with no change at all at most points. It is remembered as the Old Front Line—about which the Poet Laureate has written an eloquent book—and for the rest of the war battles swayed backwards and forwards from this line. Some sectors of it were held continuously for three years, and one sector, which Smith Dorrien had sited as a reserve position for the 2nd Corps during the early days of the Battle of Ypres, stood unchanged from November 1914 to April 1918. The Old Front Line passed through three well-marked regions: in the north, about Ypres, the fenland of Flanders, like Cambridgeshire, where it was impossible to dig deep without striking water and where the defences were breastworks of sandbags; the Artois industrial area about La Bassée, like South Staffordshire, where underground workings suggested tunnelling and mining warfare; and the open chalky downland

F

of Picardy, the Somme country which resembles Wiltshire with its long bare slopes and occasional deep fertile river valleys. 'Going north' to Ypres, or 'going south' to the Somme meant a different kind of warfare and new discomforts.

Even at its full extent the British Old Front Line was less than a quarter of the Western Front, threequarters being held by the French Army, but the British front, except for a few small sectors, was always active while much of the French front was dormant for half the war. Not that the French High Command wanted to make it so. '*Tout le monde à la bataille*' remained their slogan, but the French soldiers who fought so well when committed to battle were remarkably resistant to pressure from behind and did not budge if there was no good reason for budging. The whole Western Front may also be considered in its three sectors: from the Channel coast to Noyon on the Oise it ran north and south, and the active part of this sector was held by the British; from Noyon to Verdun it ran east and west and this active front was held by the French; from Verdun to the Swiss frontier it turned south-east, and after 1914 saw no large-scale battles. There was rarely any suggestion that the British should take over a quiet sector; they were brought in to extend the front of attack.

The effect of the 1914 campaign which left the armies lined up facing one another, engaged in perpetual conflict, was to make any withdrawal a dishonour. On both sides, in the crisis of the battle, the word had been given to stand to the last man and the last round of ammunition, and both armies had indeed so stood. On the German side, to withdraw would be to admit a second defeat which they were far from ready to do; on the Allied side, to withdraw would be to subject more French or Belgian villages to the German terror. Mere stubbornness prevailed so that the cold-blooded principles of strategy hardly came into play. The armies stayed where they found themselves at the end of the 1914 campaign and dared not leave their front lines to enemy occupation, even if a stronger position could more cheaply be held a mile or two back. In this rigidity the Germans were more irrational than the Allies, and it was a German general, Von Below, the opponent of the British on the Somme, who threatened with court martial any officer who lost a trench.

While the Allies' war aims were simply to drive the Germans out of France and Belgium it was natural for them to say 'Take any step forward but take no step back'. On the other hand, the Germans had no intention of annexing the plains of northern France and therefore no reason for occupying them a day longer than was profitable. They had got the iron-mines of French Lorraine, the collieries of Artois, the manufactures of Lille, and so long as these could be retained the swamps of Flanders and the downs of Picardy were of no consequence. It was not until February 1917 that they made up their minds to do what they should have done in November 1914, to retire out of the Noyon salient to a shorter, more defensible, position. We had no such lucky course to take. The British Army, cramped in the narrow strip, no more than thirty miles wide at its narrowest point between Gomme-court Wood and Abbeville, had no room to manœuvre. For us the alternatives were to go forward or to stand fast. All our plans were geared to going forward and all our instruction was designed to keep us thinking of it. We were not to resign ourselves to the prospect of a sedentary campaign in the trenches but to look forward to the day when open warfare would be resumed as in the heroic days of 1914, when 'the cavalry should go through'.

On their side the Germans were being taught to stand on the defensive and consolidate their gains. The Schlieffen plan, or rather the version of it that Moltke had bungled, was abandoned and the new High Command under Falkenhayn set out to get command of the situation in the east before making a second onslaught on France. The roles of the belligerents on the Western Front were thus reversed in 1915; Germany stood on the defensive while France and Britain were committed to the offensive, as the French General Staff desired. No wonder the Germans designed more permanent trench-lines than ours, since our intention was to leave our trenches behind and capture theirs. It proved to be a long job.

Trench warfare and open warfare called for different weapons. The Germans had begun the war with careful plans for besieging the great fortresses of Flanders and had therefore provided themselves with heavy howitzers, trench mortars, and grenades. We had no intention of attacking any fortresses and even if the pre-war army had asked for these weapons, the Treasury which refused money even for the machine-guns which the soldiers said were essential, would have rejected any such hypothetical proposal with contempt. The Army was obliged to do its best with rifles and bayonets which were cheap, and fortunately they proved the best weapons for the 1914 campaign. The opinion of good commanders at the front was that no decision could ever be reached with the weapons of trench warfare. The hand-grenade might be necessary in that phase but the rifle would assert itself again. Soldiers should not be seduced from their true war-winning weapons by an addiction to the devices of the trench-warfare season. Meanwhile, some special weapons must be improvised for this phase and the British must begin at the beginning. There was not even a prototype for a trench mortar, and only a few experimental grenades. The museums were ransacked for bombs and mortars that had been used at Sebastopol. In addition to their numbers the Germans enjoyed one other advantage over French and British by their deployment of heavy artillery in the field. The German 150-millimetre howitzer, which we called a 'five-nine' (150 mm. = 5.9 inches), was their stand-by throughout the war and one of the most effective weapons used by any army. It outranged our 4.5-inch howitzers and fired a much heavier missile, usually a high explosive shell charged with T.N.T. which burst with a cloud of black smoke and was therefore called a 'Jack Johnson', after the negro boxer who had recently won the world's heavyweight championship. Our howitzers fired lyddite, which burst with a yellowish white smoke, and not very much of it. In addition, the Germans had a few heavier batteries of 305 mm. (eleven-inch), and even one battery of Austrian 420 mm. (seventeen-inch) howitzers with which they had reduced the fortifications of Liege.

7

Cushy Trenches

IN AUGUST 1915 when the British front was extended southwards into Picardy, the 48th Division took over from the French a quiescent sector facing the wooded village of Gommecourt, the most westerly point of the old front line and reputed one of the strongest positions on the German front. It was never captured in battle and none of our raiding parties succeeded in penetrating the German trenches in our sector. Our positions too were strong, and German raids failed to enter our trenches. Gommecourt, a hamlet, and ruined château standing in a wooded park, was one of three small villages set in a triangle about a mile apart from one another, on the watershed of northern France. East of Gommecourt the streams flow towards the Scheldt and the North Sea; west of Hebuterne and Fonquevillers, the two villages which we held, they flow westwards towards the Somme estuary and the English Channel. The open meadow between the three villages, so smooth and clear that we called it 'the racecourse', was our No Man's Land, lying along the 500-foot contour. But the country was flattish, chalk covered with a cap of clay, and these low undulations were not hills that a civilian would notice. To us soldiers every fold in the ground where you could come out of your hole to bask in the sun, just free of direct observation, every bank or hedge behind which you could jump to shelter, was a feature of the landscape, to be studied and remembered. The country was arable and thinly populated, with long open spaces between the few large woods and villages, so that the least rise of ground might give you a distant view over enemy territory and no less might expose you to enemy observation, and to a round of shrapnel, if they thought you a worth-while target. I have looked across the country in quiet times and seen French peasants ploughing in the distance behind the German lines; then looked back and seen others ploughing far behind our own.

Gommecourt was an ideal tactical position, like Agincourt, like Waterloo, like Le Cateau, situated behind a reverse slope with observation posts forward on the crest, so that the defenders could not be directly observed. The top of the rise was in No Man's Land, and Fonquevillers also lay behind a reverse slope which covered our shelters from their sight. The strength of Gommecourt, heavily entrenched and wired against direct attack from the front, was its command of the country to either flank. The hundred guns ensconced in the 'dead ground' behind the wood could enfilade the whole British front to southwards and proved a decisive factor in the defeat of our 7th and 8th Corps on 1st July 1916.

From the day we took over Hebuterne and Fonquevillers we knew that sooner or later we should be called upon to climb out of our trenches, pick our way through the gaps in our own wire, line up in No Man's Land, standing, at the high port, with bayonets pointing straight upwards, and race across to the assault of Gommecourt Wood. If not us, then someone else here and we somewhere else. The problem was wire. There it was, three thick belts of it, in full view 400 yards away, and I may say that in the Second World War I never saw a wire entanglement as formidable as even one of the three belts at Gommecourt Wood. If it were sufficiently minced up by our preliminary bombardment, if we could snip our way through the remaining strands with wire-cutters, why then we could jump down into the German trench, perhaps eight or nine feet deep, to engage in combat with such armed men as we might find there. All that could be observed, by men on watch through loopholed steel plates concealed at vantage-points, by patrols prowling along the German wire every night, by air photographs which revealed the tracks used by the Boches to their observation posts and gun positions, was noted and collated daily by our intelligence officer. We knew the German routine almost as well as our own; the habits of their patrols, the routes of their working parties when they came out at night to strengthen the wire, the emplacements in their front line from which machine-guns uttered a morning 'strafe', the location of battery positions behind the wood—though we never saw them—which carefully registered each new construction in our trenches with a few ranging shots. Not often did we see a Boche, sometimes a head and shoulders leaping past a gap in his parapet, a working party on the wire caught for an instant in the glow of a Very-light at which they would 'freeze' and stand still, hoping not to be noticed, perhaps a shadowy figure by night in No Man's Land. We heard wagon-wheels in the distance as their transport brought up the rations, the thumping and scuffling of their night-workers, distant coughs and sneezes, and once I caught the unmistakable sound of a sergeant-major bawling-out a soldier for some misdemeanour which I could well imagine.

At night their line would suddenly come alive with Very-lights which they fired far more profusely than we did: from time to time a machine-gunner, fortunately committed to a German punctuality of routine, would traverse our front to discourage night-walkers. At dawn you could see lines of blue smoke rise from their front line when you too were cooking bacon over a charcoal brazier. All day long the front was quiet, or if not everyone grew anxious to know the reason why. In fifty years I have never been able to rid myself of the obsession with No Man's Land and the unknown world beyond it. This side of our wire everything is familiar and every man a friend; over there, beyond their wire, is the unknown, the uncanny; there are the people about whom you can accumulate scraps of irrelevant information but whose real life you can never penetrate, the people who will shoot you dead if they catch a glimpse of you, even miles away behind the line. Only the other day I found this dread and defiance of the unknown rising into my consciousness as I looked over the Wall at Berlin.

Our division, the 48th (South Midland), consisted of pre-war territorials from Warwickshire, Worcestershire, Gloucestershire, Buckinghamshire, Oxfordshire, and Berkshire. Our brigade, the 143rd, consisted of four battalions, the 5th, 6th, 7th, and 8th Royal Warwickshire. The division held a front of about four miles as the bullet flies, much longer following the trace of the trenches. All three brigades were in the line, side by side, each with two battalions 'up', one in close support, and one back in reserve doing what was ironically called 'resting'; which meant that six battalions out of the thirteen[1] in the division held the line. Each of these front-line battalions would

---

1. Three brigades of four battalions each. The thirteenth was a Pioneer battalion of fighting infantry, specially trained in field engineering. In 1918 brigades were reduced in strength from four to three battalions.

normally have two of its companies 'up' and two held back in supporting positions which I shall describe presently. In my battalion, the
5th Royal Warwickshires, at Fonquevillers, each company had three
platoons actually posted in the front trenches and one standing to arms
as an 'inlying picket' under cover, ready to act in any emergency at two
or three minutes' notice. If this may be taken as typical, though the
dispositions of each battalion varied with the lie of the land, the six
front-line battalions at quiet times held the whole divisional front with
about thirty-six platoon posts, and since a platoon could rarely put
more than thirty men on duty, we may conclude that the divisional
front was held by about 1,000 out of its, say, 10,000 infantrymen.

In quiet trenches, in good weather, the men on duty in the front line
might have a rather easy time. In the mild autumn of 1915 tales were
told of men crawling out into the long grass of No Man's land, when
off duty, to smoke and read their home letters undisturbed. By day the
number of sentries was reduced and if your trench was in good order
and your rifle clean there was nothing much to do and a strict limitation
on what you could do, since the least show of life would bring a quick
reaction from the enemy. Men on duty—and in my regiment we did
not place a man more in the line than was necessary—never took off
their boots, or equipment, or unshipped their gas-masks, and kept their
rifles at hand, loaded, and with bayonets fixed. It was unlikely that
there was a deep dugout in the front trench—certainly not at Fonquevillers—and if there were such a shelter it was unlikely that the men on
duty would be allowed to use it, since everyone must be ready to jump
up on to the firing-step ready to shoot over the parapet in a few
seconds. By night this was a serious matter, since not many nights
passed in even the quietest trenches when some alarm was not given to
stand to. At the first streak of dawn everyone stood to and remained
with rifles loaded on the parapet, with fingers on the trigger, until the
light was strong enough to show that no attack threatened that morning, whereupon all who were not on sentry duty 'stood down',
snuggled up with a greatcoat in a corner of the trench, and got what
sleep they could.

When it was wet it was a different story, as the trench, in spite of all
your efforts at drainage, filled with slime, and the rain infiltrated the
back of your neck. No shelter and no chance of shelter until tomorrow
night. When the line became active no one doubted that you were

posted there to take whatever unpleasantness was coming over. The worst would not happen more than once in your military career.

(2)

The Fonquevillers sector was as near as we ever came to a model set of defences for fixed trench warfare. Back in the heroic age of 1914, during the race to the sea, French and German infantry had confronted one another here and had dug themselves in where they happened to be at the end of a skirmish. The first front line followed the string of rifle-pits (fox-holes they were called in the Second World War) which men had scrabbled for themselves with their entrenching tools, under fire. Step by step, as labour and expert assistance from the corps of engineers was available, this line of pits was joined into a continuous trench and was covered by an apron fence of barbed wire. Sometimes the casual sinuosities of the firing line were retained; sometimes a new trench of firing bays set out in straight lengths with traverses, or kinks, at regular intervals was traced and dug by working parties of soldiers brought forward at night. Week by week the position was improved, when it became clear that the line was fixed there for the winter. The Germans were most assiduous at defence works and had no difficulty over supplies, since they ruthlessly looted houses and cut down trees to provide themselves with building material and furniture, and impressed the French civilians to work for them.

The French Army was more ingenious than ours at supplying home comforts. Their trench shelters were hollowed out under banks and lined with hurdles cut from the hedges, which they also used to revet the sides of their trenches so that the earth would not cave in. These shelters were cosy rather than secure, which did not so much matter since the French intended to go forward in the spring, while on the other side the Germans had gone to ground for a longer period. All through 1915 they stood on the defensive in France, to which end they made almost permanent fortifications, equipped with deep dugouts, tunnelled out by mining engineers in the solid chalk. I never saw a 'mine dugout' until I captured a German trench. The standard pattern was a length of plank-lined tunnel under the parapet, ten feet or more below ground level, to which you descended by a steep flight of fifteen or twenty cellar steps. Every mine dugout had at least two such entrances and in the Leipzig Redoubt near Thiepval I have seen dugouts connected underground, with eight or nine narrow stairways up to different fire-bays. No such shelter was ever provided for the British, chiefly because it was our policy to attack not to defend, but also because neither the slave labour nor the looted building materials were at our disposal.

British defence works depended on sandbags such as our grandfathers had used at the siege of Sebastopol, and on barbed wire, a legacy of the Boer War. The art of filling and laying sandbags—bonded like brickwork, sloped at the most effective angle, and hammered flat with a spade—was a British trench accomplishment. They resisted weather, stopped bullets, and had a resilience that was valuable even against high explosive; and, in addition, you could use an empty sandbag to carry the rations, to hide away some loot, to wrap round your legs as a protection against mud, or to camouflage the top of a shiny helmet. A French dugout shelter strengthened by a few pit-props across the roof with two courses of sandbags and a bursting charge of road-metal was thought pretty good protection in the simple days before the Battle of the Somme. 'It will keep out,' we said, 'anything but a direct hit from a five-point-nine.'

During the wet weather that autumn the Fonquevillers trenches collapsed into mud, not so overwhelmingly as in the swamps of Flanders but unpleasantly enough to bring about a change in our tactical plan. Back in 1914, to which our military thinking so often recurred, the urgency of the situation was such that every man had been crammed into the front line. The infantry all in a row won the decisive battle with rifle-fire, in the old romantic tradition of the 'thin red line' of Balaclava and Waterloo. It was magnificent, but not war. Every trained officer knew that the essential next move was to thin out the line so as to defend the position 'in depth', by well-sited posts supporting one another with cross-fire, and to withdraw as many men as possible into reserve. So long as the battle was maintained it was dangerous to do so and in some sectors it was never done.

Our battalion, and subsequently our division, were among the first to revert to the established principles of warfare, and after the summer of 1915, that is to say as soon as we were battle-trained, we never again held a continuous trench-line manned shoulder to shoulder. Almost everyone came round, sooner or later, to this rational view as it had been laid down in the Field Service Regulations, but a characteristic of the 1914 War was that it created its own orthodoxies and its own conservatism. Some of the officers and N.C.O.s who had served through the first winter in the trenches felt unsafe unless they manned a continuous front where they could stand up, now and then, to fire five rounds rapid over the parapet, while the enemy snipers picked them off from concealed positions. Many a lugubrious war story begins with taking over a new sector of front and finding, to the storyteller's dismay, that there was 'no proper front line', as though soldiers had a sort of right to dugouts, continuous trenches, and a protective fence of wire.

Operations for us facing Gommecourt Wood began at dusk when the transport columns arrived in Fonquevillers. Four or five limbers from Bayencourt three miles back, each drawn by a pair of mules, drew up under the shelter of a brick wall which would at least stop bullets in case the enemy machine-guns, only a thousand yards away, should open fire. Shelling was not likely in those simple times when gunners were not much disposed to fire blind at a mere noise. A year later both sides had become more prodigal with ammunition and made a practice of putting down barrage fire at random intervals on likely crossroads where transport might assemble by night. There were two battalions in Fonquevillers, a dressing-station, an artillery brigade, and I forget what else, so that the village street was lively with horse traffic, but no motor-vehicle except a light ambulance van to take away the day's casualties and two or three despatch-riders on motor-cycles. Single men, even single horsemen or cyclists, could usually cross the plain from Bayencourt by day without drawing fire, but vehicles or groups of men marching would quickly attract a 'whizz-bang', so that reliefs and stores came only in the evening convoy.

Parties of men in a sequence that needed careful preparation and traffic control came down from the trenches to the dump in the village to collect the night's requirements: dry rations made up in bundles according to the strength of the front-line posts; trench stores—planks, pit-props, duckboards, coils of barbed wire, sand-bags in bales; boxes of rifle ammunition (S.A.A.) and Mills bombs; gallon jars of rum (never let out of sight of a responsible officer); the mail (if there was any) with 'comforts' from charitable societies at home and food parcels from their families for the lucky. There was water medicated with chloride of lime and tasting of the petrol cans in which it was carried; there was

hot stew in two-gallon 'dixies' from the field kitchens. All this was to
be sorted in silence and manhandled in the dark to six muddy ditches
half a mile away across the fields and to various dugout shelters along
the lanes. Show a light or make too much noise and the enemy would
open fire. Was there a little give and take? An unspoken agreement that
'they' might get their rations up while 'we' got up ours? Perhaps so in
1915–16, but not twelve months later; and any concession that might
be made for transport in the village stopped far short of the front line,
where no allowance was made or expected by either side and any good
target was instantly fired at.

Carrying parties loom up in the memory as the most persistent,
fatiguing, hateful chore of the war in France and Flanders—everything
by hand. The trench stores would have been a heavy burden for fresh
men walking on good roads by daylight. In the dark, in the mud, it
was so much worse with the added nightmare quality that came from
the conformation of the trenches. A roll of barbed wire spitted on a
stake and carried by two tired men is at any time an awkward burden.
Now manœuvre it along a deep muddy ditch in the dark. You cannot
see more than five steps ahead because trenches always zig-zag so that
the enemy cannot enfilade them by finding some point from which to
shoot straight along the line. It would be trouble enough to work your
two-man load round corner after corner if you could see your way,
but you slip in a shell-hole under foot; your helmet is whipped off your
head by a trailing wire; you catch your slung rifle on a projecting root;
you tear your hand or your sleeve on the damnable wire-coil; you
stumble and your mate swears at you; and round the traverse you find
yourself face to face with a stretcher-party carrying out a casualty.
Someone has to lay down his burden, clamber up and slither over the
muddy bank, and stand in the open while the stretcher takes the right
of way. Just then the Boches put up a Very-light which illuminates the
scene with a pallid hue like the sodium lighting on some of our main
roads. The casualty looks ghastly, and you, standing in the spotlight,
feel as if the whole German Army was looking at you. If they have
seen you and do realize that this trench is full of men they will think it
well worth two rounds gun-fire on a registered target. The spent Very-
light falls unpleasantly near, like a rocket-stick from the neighbours'
garden on Guy Fawkes Night, and leaves you blacked out, with your
night-vision spoiled, to slip down into the ditch, scrabble for your load

in the mud, and soldier on. You've lost touch with the men in front and don't know where you're going until the sergeant's hoarse whisper makes it plain that the delay is all your fault.

(3)

Now look back to company headquarters in the sunken road which we call 'Thorp Street' after the address of our barracks in Birmingham.[1] It is an old French dugout, scooped out under a bank with hurdles against the earth walls and a roof reinforced with stout timber and sandbags, giving just room for a very small table made of old boxes, and two bunks made of wire netting stretched on frames. Opening out of it is a still smaller den, in which an officer's servant is cooking over a charcoal brazier that gives the cave its characteristic smell, and a signaller is testing a field telephone that works intermittently. The signallers, privileged people, have a secret life of their own and maintain endless conversations full of technicalities and private jokes, with an occupational hazard of no small seriousness. Very often their conversation stops dead. 'Dis—' says the signaller, and goes out alone into the night, presumably under fire, to follow his line across the fields until he finds, and mends, the break, perhaps disconnected by a shell-burst, perhaps by the carrying party of the last paragraph stumbling against it.

The quartermaster-sergeant, who has come up from Bayencourt with the ration wagon, reports to the captain. He brings the officers' mail; parcels from home; yesterday's London papers (and remember there was no broadcasting in those days, so that this is our latest news); the local paper; the *Bystander*, perhaps, with the week's Bairnsfather cartoon, or *La Vie Parisienne* with a colour-print of a pin-up girl by Raphael Kirchner; the rum ration carefully allotted at the rate of a gallon-jar for every sixty-four men; and the day's gossip. 'Sit down, Quartermaster, and I'll see if I can find you a drop of whisky. No, there's none left. Have you brought another bottle?' 'Yes, sir, and a hell of a job I had to find it'. In accounts I've since read of the 1914 War officers' messes are described as floating in liquor, but I find no such liquidity in my memory. Whisky—at seven and sixpence a bottle, a subaltern's daily pay—was a rarity which we husbanded. A spoonful

1. The Thorp Street notice-board is now displayed in the Imperial War Museum.

in a tin mug of chlorinated water was what the captain took and what he gave, I hope, to the quartermaster-sergeant, who regaled him with the rumours from the back areas, perhaps with talk of the whole brigade going out 'into rest'.

There is much to be arranged—platoon reliefs, hot food, ration parties, carrying parties, the lucky handful to go on leave to England, billets when we move into support next week; and now the captain can organize the night's work, knowing who and what has 'come up with the rations'. And now he turns to me, the subaltern on duty. There are three of us, for we are as usual under strength, one commanding the 'inlying picket'—a cushy job indeed, since there's nothing whatever to do except to be available at two minutes' notice, night or day; one on duty 'in the posts' with his platoon; and one—that's me—for night duty.

'Finish your dinner' (bully-beef stew, tinned apricots, weak whisky and water), 'Carrington,' says the captain, addressing me like that because this was long before the age of easy Christian naming, 'and get along up to the posts. Send Wilson down here for his dinner. I'll come round myself with the rum ration about nine o'clock. The Sixth' (our sister battalion) 'have delivered a load of wire and pit-props at the top of Fifth Avenue, and 'D' Company have fifty men out in front of the right sector. They're sending a patrol along the whole front at midnight, coming in at "Long Sap" about two a.m. Password "Vancouver". The brigadier thinks it might make the Boche think that the Canadians have relieved us, if they heard it. Just like him. Does he expect us to shout it out? The bloody fool! Never mind. That's what it is—"Vancouver". Hurry up.'

I pull on rubber waders up to the thigh, slip into my goatskin jerkin, like Robinson Crusoe's with the hair outside; buckle on a webbing belt and a loaded revolver, sling my gas-mask—this is before the days of respirators and my protection is a stinking hood of medicated flannel with an eyepiece of talc to look through; clip an electric torch—a clumsy ineffective article in those days—to my belt; and pick up my trench stick, a longish cudgel with which I can feel my way in the dark but which I've decorated at the business end with a binding of barbed wire to make a more formidable weapon of it. My helmet? Yes, I have one They're new devices in the spring of 1916, still rather scarce and issued only to troops in the front line.

It's disconcerting that as I step out into Thorp Street a sheaf of Very-lights shoots up from Gommecourt Wood and a German machine-gun chatters over on our right. The captain comes out of the dugout asking angrily: 'What's the Boche got the wind-up about, now? They must have spotted our carrying-party, blast them!' Then whizz-bangs begin to come over, one-two-three-four, three times repeated, a harsh, screaming roar ending in a metallic clang and a burst of sparks, three or four hundred yards away where we suppose 'D' Company's wiring-party to be.

'You'd better go to the right post to check up,' he says, and turns into the dugout.

So it's there that I go first, putting a bold face on it before my orderly, a young soldier with a slung rifle and fixed bayonet. I don't much like going in this direction and the twenty men in 'Leicester Square' post don't much like being there. The shells have been all about them and one so near as to throw up stones in the face of the sentry, who's scratched and bleeding. 'Shall I send him down to the aid post?' asks the sergeant. 'No, fix him up with your field-dressing and let him report at sick parade in the morning,' I reply. The sergeant thinks that 'D' Company has copped it, as he heard them calling for stretcher-bearers, but the night is quiet now, frosty and star-lit with a light ground-mist rising and I decide to walk along the front while the visibility is good. 'Be careful at Short Sap, sir,' says the sergeant. 'There was someone moving out in front and they're quick on the trigger tonight. Our patrol's not due in till two o'clock'.

And now I am to make a confession. That our wiring-party had lost a man killed, a few minutes ago, did not seem intolerable. Only last week I had taken a Lewis gun out into a shell-hole and had dispersed a German working-party with the best intentions of killing one or two of them; murderous exchanges that had a sporting quality, like hunting big game. Neither then did I, nor now can I, find in my conscience any sense of guilt at this barbarity. Never, indeed, have I been more light-hearted than when I climbed over the parapet and strolled along the front, outside the wire where the going was easier, with my revolver loaded and cocked in my hand. I was a green young soldier then, utterly happy to find that I could do this thing and was not afraid. I had passed my initiation. Blame me if you like, but understand me. I was accepted.

'When will the stern fine "Who goes there?"
Meet me again in midnight air?
And the gruff sentry's kindness, when
Will kindness have such power again?'

The most sensitive of our wartime poets found the generous warmth
of our own men to be the strongest element in our bemused mentality.
The failure was that it did not embrace the enemy, in a like predicament
over there, or even our neighbours in the adjacent sector.

8

'We and They'

In the first winter of the war a Regular officer named Bruce Bairnsfather was serving with his regiment, the First Royal Warwickshire, in
cushy trenches near Messines. Having a knack for drawing caricatures
he decorated his rest billet at the deserted farm of *le petit Douve* with
sketches of soldiers' heads. The *Bystander*, a shiny weekly, reproduced
some of these sketches which caught on with the Army at the front.
The spirit of the trenches, so fatally misinterpreted by romantic
patriots at home, was more nearly expressed in the Bairnsfather car-
toons than in any literary formulation. The soldier recognized himself
and read more meaning into these bold unsubtle drawings than the
civilian could identify. Throughout 1915 their vogue increased and
reached its climax—I should guess—in the second winter of the war
when the New Armies were coming into the line as young soldiers to
learn their trade from the veterans of the first year. The Bairnsfather
style was modish; he had but one comment to make and having made
it he had no more to say. No one is likely to allot to him any element
of that timeless quality that distinguishes great art. He served his day,
and even those who were addicts in 1916, waiting anxiously for Friday's
mail and the next Bairnsfather cartoon, may now wonder what they
found in his work that induced them to pin it up on the dugout wall.
He established a myth, perhaps a lasting myth, of 'Old Bill' and 'Young
Bert', and the predicament to which they reacted. It was not the same
after the Somme, and the soldiers lost interest in him.

The old soldier, 'Bill', a short stocky plumpish man of thirty-five or
even forty, with a heavy moustache, is a type to be found in all professional armies; he is pictured as a *'grognard'* in the prints of Napoleon's
grande armée in similar style. Completely cynical about national or
political issues, he is nevertheless a dedicated man, immersed in his

G   97

military tradition, exemplified by the use of Hindustani words picked up from the Indian Army. On duty he is irreproachable, punctual in his duties; his buttons are always polished, his rifle clean, a state of affairs which he attains with the minimum of effort. Having thus adjusted himself to the routine his whole endeavour is directed towards the ease and comfort of 'number one'. Though recognized as a good soldier, he avoids promotion since responsibility calls for extra duty. He never shirks and he never volunteers. Since he has the trade of soldiering at his fingertips, he knows exactly how to make himself comfortable under the worst conditions, and never misses any good thing that is going. Old Bill's attitude to his officers is kindly and condescending, since it is understood on both sides that, like Nanny, he knows best. Even the formidable sergeant-major uses some caution in disciplining Bill, who has the Manual of Military Law by heart and appreciates exactly how far the sergeant-major can lawfully go. He is not a very honest man, retaining old-fashioned notions about a soldier's right to plunder (which in the British Army had, somehow or other, come to be disfavoured), and it's more than likely that he keeps an illegal Crown-and-Anchor board in his kit, with which to conjure Young Bert's pay into his own pockets. But we must do justice to Old Bill by saying that in the line he never fails. He can and will fight, and the young officer will be wise to use his experience. When the sergeant is killed it is Old Bill who takes command and carries the platoon through, without waiting for promotion. Even at his age he has more physical stamina than Young Bert, a wide-eyed boy, very much the volunteer. What more need I say about Bert than that he strongly resembles the author of this book?

Between the young and the old soldier of the caricaturist's vision there was room for all the varieties of human nature. As individuals each had his burden to bear but the soldier's life is essentially a social experience. A corporal and six men in a trench were like shipwrecked sailors on a raft, completely committed to their social grouping, so that no one could have any doubts about the moral and physical failings of his pals, since everyone's life depended on the reliability of each. If Bert was 'windy' and Bill an invalid who ought to be in hospital it was no use complaining, and if the lance-corporal was a nice nitwit and the corporal a capable bully there was no escape from their impact. Bill and Bert, the corporal, the lance-jack, and the others must sink or swim together. At that level so small a group stood solidly against the world with a remarkable unanimity. Without doubt an infantry section thought of itself as 'we', but who were 'they'? In a manner of speaking, all the rest of the human race could be so classified: the mysterious unknown enemy across the wire; the bloody munition-makers at home who were earning high wages and seducing your girl-friend; number four platoon in the next trench who made such a noise that they woke up the enemy gunners; the trench-mortar section that came up from its 'cushy' billets, fired a few rounds, and went away leaving us to take the retaliation; the Fifth Loamshires that we relieved last week and hadn't done their share of strengthening the wire; and, of course, the staff who could conveniently be blamed for anything. That tale was older than Harry Hotspur:

> 'But I remember when the fight was done,
> When I was dry with rage and extreme toil,
> Breathless and faint, leaning upon my sword,
> Came there a certain lord, neat, trimly dressed
> . . . and still he smiled and talked;
> And, as the soldiers bore dead bodies by,
> He called them untaught knaves. . . .'

Between Hotspur, dry with rage in the front line, and that aide-de-camp from G.H.Q., 'perfumed like a milliner', there were many layers of authority.

When at last relieved from the front line, the section rejoined the rest of the platoon in some barn or dugout where all, perhaps thirty or even forty, were crowded together, the small group melted into the larger as the platoon resumed its corporate life. Next day when 'we' march out into rest the four platoons move in a single column, lulled into unity by the rhythms of drill and keeping step. Certainly the infantry company, with 150 men at duty, is 'we'. At the head rides the captain, who hands out our pay-packet and signs our pay-books once a week; behind him marches the sergeant-major with his two aides, the orderly sergeant and the orderly corporal, who actually detail men for jobs, parade the ration-parties, and distribute the post. In the rear comes the quarter-master sergeant from whom we hope to wheedle a new pair of boots tomorrow, and the company cooks with the field kitchen brewing our tea as it trundles along. We are all insiders in this group and petulantly jealous for its rights and privileges. This evening our company will be with the permanent unit in which the whole of a man's period of service may be spent. To be 'struck off the strength' and posted away to some other battalion is an uprooting which we dread, since all our personal records, our reputations as soldiers, our wartime acting rank, our little perquisites and cushy jobs, our places on the leave-roster, derive from the battalion. If posted away the acting major will revert to the rank of captain; the lance-sergeant will be a corporal again, the lance-corporal a private, Thomas Atkins will lose that coveted post as storeman or company clerk, and we shall start at the bottom of the list for leave.

The battalion has an office, with clerks and typewriters and records. It has its showpiece in the quarter-guard with a posh sentry strutting up and down, and, in addition to the colonel, a grandee who holds himself a little aloof from the other officers, there is his deputy, the senior major, his staff officers, the adjutant and the quarter-master; there is the transport with its twenty wagons and sixty horses or mules, the quarter-master's stores and a row of technical departments each under a senior N.C.O.: the provost sergeant, the sergeant signaller, the pioneer sergeant, the armourer sergeant, the sergeant master-tailor, and the sergeant master-cook. These dignitaries, and their assistants, are believed by the rank and file to lead a luxurious life since, mostly, they stay behind with the transport when the companies go up the line. All, however, are trained soldiers who may at any time be returned to duty with their platoons, and all will be called upon to fight in an emergency. Every regiment has its tradition of the day when the cooks and the batmen were pushed in to plug a gap in the line.[1]

The colonel of an infantry battalion was traditionally the Commanding Officer, 'the C.O.'. All below him were subordinates who could lay the blame on his shoulders for what went wrong, and might even give him the credit for what went right. While the colonel was one of 'us', above and beyond the colonel lay a region of authority about which the soldier in the line had the haziest conception. At that point in the hierarchy we all became conscious of 'they'. Above the

1. Sergeant C. Haynes, our sergeant master-cook, volunteered for a turn of trench duty. He was killed commanding a platoon in my company at Passchendaele.

colonel's head was 'brigade' which neither rationed nor fed us and which impinged upon our lives mainly with peremptory orders to pack our kit and go somewhere else, delivered by a despatch-rider who was likely to herald discomfort or danger, like the messenger in a Greek tragedy.

Our brigade was unusual in consisting of four territorial battalions from one regiment, the 5th, 6th, 7th and 8th Royal Warwickshire, the 7th being raised in the county and the others in Birmingham, which was well known as a recruiting area for the fighting regiments of the old army. Our original men were 'townies' who knew one another at home and, in the patriarchal world of fifty years ago, not only was the squire captain of the company in which his villagers served, but in a town battalion the manager of a firm might raise a company from his own workmen. We had a B.S.A. Company and a Mitchell & Butler's Company with the chief salesman as its colour-sergeant.[1] There were few Regular officers or N.C.O.s in a Territorial battalion. When I joined our only Regulars were the sergeant-major and the Command-ing Officer, Colonel G. C. Sladen, who was seconded to us from the Rifle Brigade. The C.O. was a handsome well-dressed man of thirty-five with an incisive manner and, as I discovered when I twice found myself in very hot spots with him, a clear head for an emergency. He had the soldier's gift, 'an eye for country'. If I were to meet such a man today when I am old and grumpy I fancy I should write him down as aggressive and a little self-indulgent with not enough intellectual ability to justify his arrogant manner; but I might be wrong. At nine-teen years old I gave him my unstinted admiration and perhaps he deserved it. What I liked about him was the uncompromising way in which he confronted brigade, from whom he stood no nonsense. The brigadier of those days was just like the popular image of a brigadier, inclined to find fault as if that were his aim in life. He was what I thought very old indeed, possibly fifty-five. To me he was a figure of fun—poor man—and I may as well relate here as anywhere how I scored off him.

I was holding one of the front-line posts at Gommecourt in fine spring weather when a spy brought word that the brigadier was on his way to inspect the line. My post was the only one thereabouts with a clean continuous communication trench and so was a favourite with

1. Sergeant-Major F. Townley, M.C., D.C.M. He was recommended for the V.C.

visitors from higher up. We had spent the morning on a new drainage scheme, penning up a mass of slime behind a temporary barrier while some new outflow was being dug, quite an amusing game of mud pies. Picking a moment when he was half-way up the deep and winding trench, we broke down the dam, releasing a tidal wave of stinking sewage which washed the brigadier away like Pharaoh's host in the Red Sea, after which we resumed our undisturbed course of life in the front line. This is all that I can remember of an eminent officer and I fear it does him scant justice. There came a day when our Colonel Sladen was promoted brigadier and, as brigadiers go, he proved a good one. From that day on I felt that brigade was on our side and certainly I was on their side.

Beyond brigade lay something called 'division': a body of 20,000 men commanded by Major-General Sir Robert Fanshawe. At first, to a young soldier, this did not mean much, until one got a grasp of the system of reliefs, which arranged our lives in a recurrent pattern like some old-fashioned square dance. As we moved through the sets, like pieces on a chess-board, we relieved or were relieved by the support company, the support battalion, the support brigade. Our sister battalion, the 6th, with which we changed places in and out of the trenches every eight days for months on end, was on familiar terms with us, and the other infantry battalions not much less so. In your trench, as well as your own officers and men, there was a forward observation officer (F.O.O.) from the Divisional Artillery, a machine-gun section from brigade, and you got to know the sapper officer who came up to plan the more elaborate defensive works, and the party from the Royal Sussex (Pioneers) who came into the line to perfect them. In rest billets you shared amenities, the baths, the cinema, the concert-party, the Expeditionary Force Canteen (E.F.C.—which in the Second World War was called a N.A.A.F.I.). After six months in the line you knew every unit in the division by sight and had friends in most. Rarely did you move outside the divisional area or meet men of other divisions. Embracing the *esprit de corps* of the battalion, that link which was so deep-seated that men were shy about it, so shy that they didn't give it an English name, the divisional spirit was the strongest influence. It grew steadily and was fostered by the tradition of old battles. One of the favourite legends of the war was the German Black List, of which one was always hearing new versions. They were supposed to have circulated a secret list—I doubt whether there was any truth in it—of the British divisions in an order of priority for their formidable quality as fighters. Some divisions had so great a reputation as to appear in everyone's list and the typical order as I often heard it given was: the Guards, the 51st Highland Division, the New Zealanders, and then the division in which you happened to be serving.

Our General Fanshawe ('Fanny'), a quiet sandy little man in his fifties, bore no resemblance to the figure of fun which the satirists offer as the type of a British high commander; he was more like Chaucer's Knight. Every soldier in the division got to know that 'Fanny' spent more days in the front line than any of them. He was easy and pleasant-spoken and he liked to drift into a trench wearing an old raincoat over his rank badges so that the men were not intimidated. It would never have occurred to me to sweep him away with a torrent of sewage. Fanny's foible was his conviction that we were there for one purpose only, to drive the Germans out of France. One of his favourite gambits was to encourage sentries in the front line to complain about their discomfort. Then he would quietly chip in: 'The Germans over there have got very good dugouts. You can go and take them as soon as you like.' But he never let us down, never took an unnecessary risk, and never committed the classic error of generals in the First World War, which was to go on battering away at a position long after the opportunity to capture it had vanished. I shall have more to say of 'Fanny'.

If I am more favourably disposed than some old soldiers to the officers I served under it is because my battalion, brigade, and division had an unusually strong sense of unity, and because my colonel, brigadier, and divisional commander were men whom I could respect. Now look higher. In the battle of Verdun the French command invented the principle of *roulement* which became the common practice of all armies in those murderous battles of attrition. The Corps Commander stood firm and fought the battle, while divisions were rolled through his hands in succession, brought into action, bled white, and then taken away for a blood transfusion in some other more healthy corps area. Unlike the division, which maintained a permanent establishment wherever it might be, the corps, and above that the army, were merely headquarters and staffs which administered whatever divisions were rolled through. All my service in France was in the same battalion, brigade, and division, but we were under command of five or six different corps and of three different armies from time to time, hardly knowing one from another. The war histories now make play with myths about the generals, of which the soldier in the trenches was unaware. While every man in my company knew Brigadier Sladen and General Fanshawe by sight I doubt if one in ten of them knew the Corps Commander's name. I have long supposed that I was an expert on the Battle of the Somme and have gone into print more than once on the character and conduct of the generals. For some time we served in General Jacob's 2nd Corps and I can give you my word that for once we felt a difference, after a spell with Hunter-Weston's deplorable 8th Corps. When I was checking my references to write this book I found to my surprise that our most spirited action, the flank attack at Ovillers on 16th July 1916, was fought under the direction of Morland's 10th Corps, not under Jacob's 2nd.

The remoteness and anonymity of corps headquarters were such that the Corps Commander, inevitably, was blamed. Heaven knows, we grumbled and joked about brigade and division, but within reason. Knowing them, we made allowance. Corps we did not know and, since battles in France were mostly disastrous, the Corps Commander was rarely popular. We formed some vague impressions: rations were unusually good in the A.N.Z.A.C. Corps to which we were once attached, but you had to be spry to protect your horse-lines from rustlers; Maxse's 18th Corps was efficient if only the general would leave you alone a little; Haldane's 6th Corps was the very devil as he allowed no rum ration, and so on. Discrimination went not much further. After the war I asked 'Fanny' which was the best Corps Commander he served under. 'Oh, "Putty", (Sir W. Pulteney, 3rd Corps) he said. ' "Putty" let me do exactly what I liked.'

The Army Commander was so far away as to count for nothing in our lives. I served in the Third and Fourth Armies for many months without catching a glimpse of either Allenby or Rawlinson or anyone from army headquarters. My only contact at this level was with Gough of the Fifth Army whom I once met out riding within sight of the Hindenburg Line. He reined in his horse and talked very civilly, which I appreciated. There was nothing in the First World War remotely like the proud tradition of the Eighth Army in 1942-3, which Montgomery deliberately fostered. The fashion then had swung right round and the best generals again believed in showing themselves to the troops.

The B.E.F. in France was so huge and ponderous a machine that no one except Haig could impose his personality upon it, or at least no one did. The generals were just as deeply involved in the machine as were the rank and file, with a range of action that was severely limited by material factors. The feeding and clothing and housing of two million men, who were continually on the move, grouping and re-grouping themselves in ever-changing patterns of concentration, and who every few months were faced with a catastrophe on the cosmic scale like an earthquake or flood, presented problems of storage and transportation that precluded sudden changes of plan. The build-up for a battle required such masses of supplies and munitions, such elaboration of movements by road and rail, that it could not be concealed and, once set on foot, could change direction only at the cost of chaos. As a feat of organization the staff work of the B.E.F. was supremely efficient, far more so than in the armies of any of our allies. Regarded as a machine for putting soldiers into battle it could hardly have been bettered; it was what the armies did when they got there that is open to criticism.

The commands, and the higher staff appointments, were kept in the hands of Regular officers, with rare exceptions, and these mostly in the 'A' and 'Q' branches of the staff which dealt with manpower and materials respectively. The 'G' branch, which dealt with operations, intelligence, and training, was reserved for professional soldiers with a staff college education. The comical assertion that the generals were 'donkeys' does not stand up to a moment's criticism. To begin with, they achieved the first object of a military commander, which is to gain and retain the loyalty of their men. When generals behave like 'donkeys' their men refuse to follow them, as did the Russians, and, at the end of the war, the Germans. There was not a sign or hint in the British armies of political unrest until the war was won, from which it might be deduced that the men were 'donkeys', but in respect of the officers only that they knew how to lead. The corps of professional soldiers, on the whole, lined up behind the school of Haig and Robertson who said from the beginning that the war would be long and hard and could be won only by fighting it out on the Western Front. Their appreciation proved to be correct and they won after fighting it out in the way they had foretold. Again, they carried the agreement of the soldiers with them in this unattractive programme. No one can make soldiers fight if they have no heart to fight. The French armies in 1917 decided that they had done enough and refused to follow their leaders into further mass-attacks. Not so the British, who still had confidence in their generals. Who were the 'donkeys'? The men who ordered the attacks at Passchendaele or the men who obeyed the orders although they knew that the Russians had stopped fighting and suspected that the French were resting on their arms?

Attempts to make scapegoats of Haig or Gough break down on the fact that no one else could do any better, certainly not the German generals. The sideshows in the Mediterranean by which Lloyd George hoped to find an easier way to win the war produced similar massacres and deadlocks without bringing about a decision. The generals promoted by politicians as rival war-winners made no better progress than the conventional leaders whom they superseded or, if they made progress, did so by orthodox manœuvres more efficiently conducted. There was no easy way out, no escape from the simple dilemma—fight your way through or stop fighting.

The deadlock in which the army commands of every country were held is well shown by a local action fought near Vimy in March 1916. At that date Sir Henry Wilson asked for a command at the front and was piqued because Haig gave him only the 4th Corps when he thought he deserved an army. By a strange coincidence, the officer who might have been described as Wilson's opposite number in the German Army also applied for a command and was given the corps front facing him. This was General Freytag von Loringhoven, a lifelong staff officer, and the expert in Germany on collaboration with their Austrian allies. He wrote a book on strategy which I had read in translation. Both generals were spoiling for a fight and were determined to show what brains could do when applied to the problem of the Western Front.

Freytag got authority to mount a local attack with three divisions against 'the Kink', a salient projecting from the British line. If you applied enough force, and accepted the cost in casualties, it was not difficult to bite off a salient, though more difficult to hold it when captured. In this neat little operation, a moderate amount of blood was shed. Freytag captured the salient; Wilson put up a stout defence and recaptured part of what he had lost; and a tidy sector of quiet trench was reduced to horrid confusion. Wilson begged for permission to mount a general counter-attack but Haig, busy with preparations for the Somme, refused to divert men and munitions merely to save Wilson's face. Result: a win on points for Freytag, and not one penny-worth of progress on either side towards winning the war. Both Freytag and Wilson soon found their way back to staff appointments and might console themselves with the reflection that all their cere-bration had failed to produce a single tactical idea. They were just as much 'donkeys' as the other generals—or just as little.

The simple rule, 'blame the Corps Commander', would pass when one was young and ignorant, but won't do as an historical verdict. In their station of life, I now suppose, the Corps Commanders did their best, or I shall try to credit them with doing so. Above the Corps Commanders whom we condemned on insufficient evidence, and above the Army Commanders of whom we knew nothing, was the C.-in-C. I wish to place it on record that never once during the war did I hear such criticisms of Sir Douglas Haig as now are current when his name is mentioned. There are channels of communication between human beings which the psychologists have not yet identified, and this silent man made himself known to his two million soldiers by tele-pathy. He was trusted, and that put an end to discussion. Looking back, I convince myself that I can see faults in his character and errors in his judgment—which is only to say that I have now enough knowledge to consider him as a human being.

In those days we used to envy the generals for the splendours of the châteaux in which they lived while we grovelled in the mud, but, having been a staff officer in the Second World War, I've shifted my point of view. Sir Douglas Haig lived in a modest country house near Montreuil with a staff, I believe, of 200 officers. He rode every day for exercise and a fine sight he was, as I saw him once near his advanced headquarters at Beauquesne, with a trooper riding in front bearing his Union flag, a group of red-tabbed staff officers at a decent interval, and an escort of lancers with fluttering pennons. I do not think he enjoyed pomp—a simple, thoughtful man. It is when I compare Haig's G.H.Q. with Eisenhower's S.H.A.E.F. that front-line jealousy begins to rise in me. While Eisenhower was still in Algiers the current jibe was that he had more officers on his staff than Washington had soldiers at Valley Forge, and the Byzantine luxury of the successive resting-places of S.H.A.E.F. as it traversed Western Europe was disquieting. My memory is of rooms filled with one-star generals of the Army and the

Air Force, and their British equivalents, all desperately trying to convince one another that they were busy while they applied the principles of Parkinson's Law. It had not come up in the First World War.

9

The Battle of the Somme

IN THE trenches in the early months of 1916 we were impressed by the stubborn defence of Verdun, so that the French Army never stood higher in our estimation. While we had always appreciated their élan in the attack, it was a revelation to learn that they could also fight a defensive battle against odds, like our stand at Ypres and on a much greater scale. At the same time, none of us doubted that our role would be 'a spring offensive' of equal magnitude. With our eyes on the ponderous strokes that were delivered and parried, week after week at Verdun, we could hardly suppose that our 'great push' would be a push-over. We hoped, and we intended, to break the German front wide open, not with a single effort but by a succession of hammer-blows, and we understood what an incomplete victory meant. After 1st July, which I must presently describe, I wrote to my mother: 'We shall break through, and the War will be over by Christmas,' then added dubiously, 'or perhaps it will be another Verdun'.

The first indication I got of the coming battle was some gossip from an A.S.C. officer who told me in April that the Fourth Army would 'go over the top' in June after feints and diversions along the whole British front. Something of the sort became obvious in May when our quiet sector began to liven up. More troops were brought south, narrowing our front, and allowing us to withdraw a whole brigade at a time for rest and training ten or fifteen miles back. Let me here recall the beauty of the Authie Valley that pleasant spring: the 'Dell' at Sailly where we cut down green branches to make ourselves rustic booths in a copse ringing with bird-song, the camp at Couin Château with spacious views up and down the little river, the Bois de Warnimont, and the deep secluded vale in which that charming village, Gezaincourt, was hidden. The devastating tide of war was to sweep away every pleasant thing to the eastward of this neighbourhood but did not quite reach the Authie Valley, which is almost unchanged today. since traffic roads and urban development have also passed it by.

When we returned to the line,[1] not in Fonquevillers which had been taken over by the 56th (London) Division but in Hebuterne, opposite the southern face of the Gommecourt salient, preparations for the battle were on such a scale that they could not be concealed from us, nor from the enemy. Technical superiority in the air, which moved from side to side as new types of aircraft came into use, was in our favour that season. We now rarely saw German aircraft as we had seen Immelmann's famous squadron aggressively over our lines in the early spring; and we watched the skies full of our men, photographing, spotting for artillery and, on one glorious day, shooting down the whole row of German observation balloons. (During the Somme Battle I once counted thirty balloons and forty aircraft in the sky together.) On the ground the array of new batteries of heavy guns, concealed in every copse, was equally impressive and it would have surprised us to learn—so starved had the British been of artillery support—that this great concentration was still only half as dense as that which the French and Germans thought necessary for battle. We did not now think of strengthening our own defences but of digging assembly trenches, lines of approach, deep cable trenches for telegraph wires, and new 'jumping-off' positions nearer to the enemy, where No Man's Land was too wide. The official historian criticizes our corps, the 8th, for not having dug forward trenches but I can assure him he is wrong. On the night of 5th June 1916 our whole battalion moved into No Man's Land and dug a new front line, as I remember well, because our covering party had a fight with a German patrol, identifying them as men of the 66th Regiment, and, no doubt, they identified us too. The German guns then opened fire as we dug, and wounded, among others, my friend Edward Carter, the adjutant. To my great surprise I was made his temporary substitute. I think I was a good platoon commander, and later a fair company commander, and I'm sure that at just nineteen years old I was a bad adjutant. Yet when I think meanly of myself it sustains me to recall that I was adjutant of an infantry battalion on 1st July 1916.

1. During this trench tour we received news of the Battle of Jutland and the death of Kitchener.

It was my business to run an office—a line of activity in which I had no experience—to cope with confidential and secret correspondence, to issue the daily routine orders and the occasional operation orders, to receive the instructions and enquiries from brigade behind our backs, to anticipate the needs of the companies in front, to stall off minor troubles from the colonel if I could deal with them myself, to be on duty for twenty-four hours a day, and to answer a hundred questions from high and low. We lived in a farmhouse concealed among orchards in the village of Hebuterne, above ground until, about the third day of the bombardment, we were driven into the cellar by enemy shell-fire. Our headquarters was within machine-gun range of the Germans who, now and then, fired a few bursts blindly in our direction, traversing round from left to right so that one usually had time to jump for cover before the bullets came whipping through the leaves. I stayed here thirteen days from 22nd June to 5th July and took my clothes off only once, for a quick wash all over.

The colonel and I had a command post, obligingly constructed for us and 'camouflaged' (a new word in those days) by the divisional engineers. No sooner was it ready than the Germans scored a direct hit on it with a rather large shell at a time when, fortunately, we were not at home. Whereupon we decided to fix our battle position in an open trench behind a hedgerow from which there was a long view across country towards Serre and Bucquoy. I was much concerned with the state of the Serre Road which ran through the lines, since I should have to organize the movement of our transport along it when the general advance should begin—not, we thought, on the first or second day of the battle. The senior major teased me for my anxiety, assuring me that all we needed would be the officers' mess-cart, since he had a case of champagne in store for celebrating the coming victory. Six months were to pass and a million men to be killed or wounded before British wagons could trundle along the Serre Road.

We had now been told what was to be our role in the battle, though not much about the Commander-in-Chief's plan. We and the 7th Battalion were to hold the line in front of Hebuterne and were to discharge a cloud of smoke and poison gas, so as to mask the fire of the concentrated artillery behind Gommecourt Wood. On our right the main attack would be delivered by the Fourth Army, while on our left a subsidiary attack would be made by the Third Army. The remainder of our division, which we were to rejoin when our special task was done, was held in reserve to exploit the gains of the attacking troops. Ours was thus the left-hand battalion of Hunter-Weston's 8th Corps and Rawlinson's Fourth Army. We were on friendly terms with our neighbours a few hundred yards away, the 13th Londons (the Kensingtons), the right-hand battalion of Snow's 7th Corps and Allenby's Third Army. As adjutant I was now in daily contact with the brigade staff and often with the divisional staff which controlled our artillery and engineers. It only occurred to me later that at this difficult key-point in the battle I never received a visit from any staff officer from either army or from either corps headquarters. They stood off at a distance and discharged peremptory orders at us.

My notebook is full of detailed instructions, largely relating to intricate traffic plans. Every day ten or twenty distinct carrying-parties had to be brought forward from the two reserve companies to bring stores of many different kinds—gas-cylinders, smoke-bombs, trench-mortar ammunition, anti-gas equipment, sandbags, materials for trench repair for the first phase, and a wholly different assemblage of articles for the second phase when we would advance, as well as food and water. Everything must be checked, receipted in writing, and then must be manhandled from the dumps in the village to various points in the labyrinth of trenches, often under fire. The officers or N.C.O.'s must be briefed, guided, and routed, going up by one communication trench and down by another, must not block one another's way, and must not interfere with the normal routine of trench reliefs, still less with the movement of fighting patrols which visited the German wire every night. Four times in succession did we attempt to raid the German line so as to secure the necessary identification, and four times we failed, with loss. We understood that our Intelligence was searching for the 2nd Guard Reserve Division, which was thought to have relieved the 66th Regiment at Gommecourt—as indeed they had. They proved to be the most active opponents we ever met in No Man's Land and I'm obliged to admit they had the best of it. Patrol fights were very much unlike any notion you might get of them by reading the desiccated official reports. After long creeping about in the dark and the cold there would be sudden bomb-explosions and bursts of fire, with no means of knowing who was firing at what: scurrying; eddies of panic; and drawing off with your wounded if you could find them; the whole thing often rather unheroic.

In this battle, for the first time, we used the code-word 'Zero' for the day of the assault, which was, of course, kept secret, and the five days of preliminary bombardment were designated 'U', 'V', 'W', 'X', and 'Y' in the artillery programme. All the preparations were complete and we approached 'Z' Day with confidence. except that we felt neglected by corps headquarters, which had callously ordered us to attempt raids every night without preparation, and had taken no other notice of us.

The main attack was launched by the Fourth Army with eleven divisions in line, and was supported by two sudsidiary attacks. On the right, French divisions under separate command advanced on both banks of the Somme; on the left the Third Army attacked the flanking bastion of Gommecourt Wood. The French, behind an artillery concentration twice as dense as that of the British, gained a complete tactical success, five divisions against two. This was the first of those brisk little battles, with limited objective, in which the French Army was to excel. Having secured the British flank and carried their front forward to the right-angled bend in the Somme opposite Peronne, they dug in, considering that they had done their share and contributed little more to the battle which took its name from the river. There was some justice in this, for one of Haig's stated objectives was to take the pressure off the French Army, and on the next day, 2nd July, the German command closed down the Battle of Verdun.

The Fourth Army assault was successful on the right, made some slight progress in the centre, and was a total failure on the left. Even where the British succeeded in advancing, their losses were so shattering that the leading troops were capable of little further effort. On the whole northern half of the front, an extent of ten miles, the young soldiers, mostly Kitchener's men or Territorials, marched to their deaths in marshalled lines. At ten or twelve points the German front was penetrated, but north of the Ancre River, a tributary of the Somme, these incursions were eliminated by German counter-attacks or, in a few instances, ended with the recall of survivors from untenable isolated posts. The subsidiary attack on Gommecourt ended in total defeat. The British losses that day were 57,000 of whom 19,000 died, the most concentrated massacre in modern military history.

Let us narrow our gaze to Hunter-Weston's 8th Corps (31st, 29th,

H

and 4th Divisions with 48th in reserve) which attacked on a front of about four miles, against the German lines from Beaumont Hamel to Serre. Twenty-nine infantry battalions, 'went over the top' on this narrow frontage, which is to say that the action of this corps alone was comparable with the British share of the Battle of Waterloo, always remembered as a hard-fought, bloody action. At Waterloo Wellington deployed thirty-four British battalions and won a decisive victory for a loss of 7,000 British killed and wounded; Hunter-Weston, with his twenty-nine battalions, lost 15,000 men in a day, without securing a foothold in the German front at any point; and his was one of six British corps—six battles of Waterloo in a row, and four of them massive defeats. On the left, the two attacking divisions of the Third Army (56th and 46th) failed in their attempt to pinch out Gommecourt Wood, since only the right-hand claw of the pincer got a hold. It was this episode that I witnessed.

The morning of Saturday, 1st July, broke clear and fine; later the sky clouded and the day grew sultry. We stood to at 6.30 and as I left the village for our forward trench—wildly excited at actually being in the centre of a great battle—the air quivered with bombardment of a new intensity, to which the Germans gave the name of drum-fire. Gusts of shrapnel were stripping the trees of their leaves, which lay in a carpet on the ground as if it were autumn, so that our lurking-place would soon be uncovered. All well at our headquarter trench and messages from the smoke-throwing party to say they were ready! Ten minutes before zero I sent the code-message by landline to brigade and, half an hour after zero, reported again that the poisonous smoke-cloud was blowing steadily away. No need for us to put on gas-masks. At 7.30 someone said: 'There they go!' and on our left we had glimpses of a few men of the London Scottish in their hodden-grey kilts, running forward into the smoke. That was all. That and a growing hullaballoo of noise. On the right towards Serre, no visibility. You could hear the battle but you couldn't see it.

Sharper detonations punctuated the drum-fire as German shrapnel burst with bright flashes over our front line, three or four hundred yards in front of us, until the smoke-candles burned out and the enemy could see that there was no movement on our front. Within an hour the landscape had cleared and though it must have contained 10,000 men, not one could be seen. To right and left the noise continued;

our heavies were still firing over our heads, and machine-gun bullets—
'overs' from someone else's fight not aimed at us, I think—came
cracking past our ears. We could see nothing, and we knew nothing.
When the bombardment slackened the colonel and I made a tour of the
line, walking about rather freely in the open with a facility that was
new to me, and made me glow with satisfaction. Strange but true that
it was safer to wander behind the lines in a battle when the leading
troops were busy firing on one another than on a quiet day when
keen-eyed snipers were searching for a target. At 11.25 the London
Scottish sent us word that they were in the German trenches and held
some prisoners. About the same time we reported to brigade that we
could see Germans collecting in the trenches opposite us. There was
nothing we could do about it.

Soon after 12.00 we saw larger groups of Germans in the distance
moving across country towards Gommecourt and disappearing into
the communication trenches. We engaged them with rifle-fire and
with the one machine-gun in our trench at over 1,500 yards range,
which was worthless. I twice rang the corps artillery on a telephone that
faded and finally broke, but got no reply except that it was not a target
for them, but in the area of the 7th Corps, to whom we had no line.
We sent a message to the Kensingtons on our left and after long delay
were told that their artillery considered it was in our area. Meanwhile,
the German counter-attack was delivered and was accompanied by a
crashing bombardment on the whole of our front. For the second time
they scored a direct hit on our headquarters, with a heavy shell that
burst on the parapet, throwing the colonel, the sergeant-major, the
two leading company commanders—who had been summoned for a
conference—and me, in a heap on the trench floor. But shell-fire is
chancy in effect and only one of us was wounded. Then calm descended
on the battlefield. No news at all. A hot bright afternoon with grumb-
lings of noise in the distance. At 7.30 the Londoners sent word that they
were all back in their own trenches, all—that is—that could run. A
wounded Scotsman crawled across our front and lay there writhing.
One of our officers was just about to bring him in when I heard of it
and gave him a positive order not to risk his own life until dusk, which
made him very angry. There were plenty more lying out, a few
hundred yards away. That evening a German medical officer with a
white flag arranged a truce for half an hour to collect the wounded on

the front of the Londoners, a rare civility in the 1914 War, much frowned on by both higher commands.[1]

How meagre had been our experience, yet our small contribution had been successful. We had formed the curtain of smoke just where it was required, we had drawn fire which might have been aimed at the attacking battalions, and had isolated the Gommecourt operation from the main battle. Before the war ended, a German report on the Battle of the Somme came into my hands with a full account of the defence of Gommecourt by the 55th Regiment of the 2nd Guards Reserve Division. I was able to correlate it, phase by phase, with what I had seen and with the records of the attacking units, and I award the 55th Regiment my certificate for the best demonstration of minor tactics I ever encountered in either world war.

They held the Gommecourt salient with two battalions and twelve machine-guns, covered by an immense mass of artillery; the third battalion, with fourteen machine-guns, was in reserve at Bucquoy, three miles back. On the north face of the salient, the Fonquevillers side which we knew so well, four battalions of the 46th Division attacked one. The wire was uncut and though they broke in at one point they were quickly driven out. When they were stopped the German front company advanced from its trenches into No Man's Land and drove off those of the attackers who had not been killed by the machine-guns. In half an hour all was over, and the four attacking battalions were destroyed. Of this action we at Hebuterne knew nothing and afterwards heard very little, though we were only a mile away.

On the southern face, the Hebuterne side, four battalions of the Londoners attacked, with three in support, seven against two. Here the wire was cut so that they overran the first and second trenches and reached the village in which was an entrenched work known as the Kern Redoubt. Within half an hour of zero the commander of this kernel of the defence had received a written account of the British

1. Our Fourth Army issued an order forbidding such fraternisation. The enemy could not be trusted and would take the opportunity to reconnoitre our positions. Stretcher-bearers who came too close must be driven off by fire. A few weeks later, when a strange colonel visiting my trench near Thiepval ordered me to open fire on German stretcher-bearers, I flatly refused, and I'm obliged to say that a few minutes later we came under accurate shell-fire.

penetration with an accurate sketch. Already a pioneer company had regained one trench, and a counter-attack by the defenders of the redoubt was ordered. No German unit ever moved back. Those who were not overrun advanced against the Londoners and when a platoon or company went forward, its reserve group spontaneously closed up behind it. It was 9.30 when news reached the regimental commander who at once ordered the battalion from Bucquoy forward. By 11 o'clock the commanding officer (Major Tauscher) had made his reconnaissance, had assembled his men, and hard marched two miles. At 12.30 he began to deliver the attack which I observed. All the German units co-operated in containing the Londoners, pressing them back and closing in from both flanks. The most exposed were seventy men of the London Rifle Brigade, under Lieutenant Petley, who did not retire until ordered to do so at 4.30, and who then fought their way out. It was 9.45 at night before Major Tauscher reported all clear in the German lines. The assault across No Man's Land had been broken by machine-gun fire. The later fighting was all with bomb and bayonet in deep trenches, so that observers half a mile away could see nothing.

It is usually a problem of some statistical difficulty to compare casualties since armies make returns in bulk, for frontages and over periods that are not likely to correspond. In this instance we have no such anomalies. The 55th Regiment which held the whole of the salient reported losses of 6 officers and 449 men between 24th June and 2nd July, their strength before the battle being about 1,900. The seven assaulting battalions of the 56th Division lost 114 officers and 3,181 other ranks out of a strength of about 5,000. The four assaulting battalions of the 46th Division lost sixty-nine officers and 1,283 men.

By way of general comment on 1st July, let me quote the words of the official historian, Sir James Edmonds, a stout defender of Sir Douglas Haig's policy as a rule. 'This terrible toll . . . was partly due to the optimism of G.H.Q., to the use of out-of-date tactical formations, and to place, date, and time being forced on Haig by the French; but it was mainly due to the insufficient number of heavy howitzers and to the large amount of defective ammunition, so that the damage done to the strong enemy defences was much less than expected . . . and the German units, instead of being found dead or demoralised, put up a most stout-hearted defence.'

(2)

How do you know when you have lost a battle? No one in front can
tell what is happening a mile to right or left. In the rear the general
waits for messages that fail to come, since wires are cut and runners
killed. Those who have advanced send back optimistic reports and
those who have retreated don't advertise the fact. At every level—
brigade, division, corps, army, G.H.Q.—there is confusion and uncertainty, chiefly on account of the sectors from which no report, good
or bad, has filtered through. Commanders are killed, and their subordinates—scattered and fighting for their lives—are unaware that
control has collapsed. The best troops have vanished into enemy
country, so that no one can tell whether they are still holding out in
forward positions where reinforcements might reach them. As for
losses, when dead and wounded are scattered over the landscape and
thousands of stragglers are away from their units, who can begin to
count the cost?

In my central position I did not learn that the counter-attack had
been successful until 7.30 in the evening. My opposite number in the
German Army was not assured of it until two hours later. What time
was it when news of the defeat at Gommecourt was received at
G.H.Q., and was the report accepted as final? I do not know but from
published sources it is clear that neither Rawlinson nor Haig appreciated on 2nd July how gravely they had been defeated on the previous
day. They agreed that the Gommecourt attack had been useful as a
diversion and that the 8th Corps had done badly, even though relieved
of pressure by it. South of the Ancre, they thought, the fighting was
still going in our favour although the troops had captured only part of
their objective. Haig's staff estimated the casualties at over 40,000 'which
cannot be considered severe,' he said, 'in view of the numbers engaged'.
Even without the comment that this estimate was too low by 50 per
cent the modern reader will shudder at this dreadful familiarity with
blood and destruction.

Haig was for exploiting success on the right, but Rawlinson, who
was fighting the battle, thought we should first widen the gap by
capturing the high ground from Longueval to Pozières, and Haig
accepted the opinion of the man in charge, as he had already accepted it
over the infantry formation to be used in attack. His suggestion had

been to probe the enemy front with strong fighting patrols before the assault, and it was Rawlinson who had preferred to advance in 'waves', that is in parallel lines of men almost shoulder to shoulder behind the barrage Having consulted Rawlinson and having deferred to his views, Haig was obliged to spend the next day resisting the importunate demands of the French who had at last got the British moving and proposed to keep them at it. When Haig suggested that they should join in exploiting success on the right, Joffre—strongly backed by Foch—repudiated any such proposal, insisting that Haig should renew his unsuccessful attacks along the whole front, and here Haig, in spite of his wish to conform with the grand strategy of his allies, firmly drew the line. Minor operations, which in any other war would have been thought great battles, to reduce pockets of German resistance at Mametz, Fricourt, La Boisselle, kept the Fourth Army engaged for the next ten days until Rawlinson's second attack was ready, the Battle of 14th July, which differed sharply from the Battle of 1st July. North of the Ancre the front was allowed to lapse into quiet. South of it Haig reorganized the command, inserting a new Fifth Army under Hubert Gough whose task was to widen the gap by pushing northwards into the German flank against the villages of Ovillers and Thiepval, where frontal attacks on 1st July had been as bloodily repulsed as those at Serre and Gommecourt.

It has often been hinted that Haig was bad at choosing his lieutenants. He had a preference for young men, and Gough, aged forty-five, was by far the youngest Army Commander on the Western Front (excepting the German Crown Prince). At the same time Haig's strong sense of loyalty to his own subordinates made him unwilling to dismiss well-tried old veterans. 'Hunter-Bunter', who to us had become a figure of fun, the very image of a brass-hat as represented by the caricaturists, with features, voice, and manner, all in character, was, nevertheless, the hero of Gallipoli and could not be just sacked like an office-boy. He was moved to a quiet part of the line and allowed to go on commanding a corps on a front where nothing ever happened. The only time I met him, after the battle, I thought him not quite sane, but I dare say I was not a very good judge. At any rate we were glad to be done with the 8th Corps and found Sir Claud Jacob's 2nd Corps in Gough's Fifth Army many times more efficient.

Rawlinson's second assault was a surprise attack by night, very carefully prepared. The neighbouring French general, contemptuous of British tactics, as well he might be, said that if Rawlinson succeeded he would 'eat his hat', and the next day Rawlinson sent him a new hat, for the Fourth Army took its objectives and hit the Germans very hard. He was now well established on the high ground and there followed two months of severe struggle for a series of key-points to which the Germans clung with grim determination, Delville Wood, High Wood, Pozières, Mouquet Farm, Thiepval, Ovillers. 1st July had been a disaster, a colossal miscalculation; the fighting from then until the end of August was of quite another character and the British had the best of it. All German plans for the summer were dropped and the High Command resigned itself to a hand-to-mouth defence, throwing division after division into the battle without winning another tactical success. At every point the British made progress and at every point the Germans counter-attacked in vain. Perhaps there have been no more obstinate battles in history, and German historians admit that in the Somme fighting their great regular army bled itself to death, as the small British army had done in the 1915 battles. Never again did they fight as well. Casualties? The most careful analysis implies that the cost to Germany was rather greater than the cost to Britain, but there was a debit balance of 50,000 on our side for the losses on 1st July. The British Army learned its lesson the hard way, during the middle part of the Somme Battle and, for the rest of the war, was the best army in the field.

Enthusiastic amateurs when the fighting began, the British were soldiers at the end, with the cynical notions and the prudent habits that professionals exhibit. Lieutenant Petley (I don't know whether he is still alive) and his seventy heroes versus Major Tauscher and the 55th Regiment, was a contest of 'Gentlemen versus Players', a formula that only the English understand. There was an inclination on 1st July to go over the top dribbling a football or blowing a hunting-horn, which would have been laughed at six months later. Two battalions of our brigade, the 6th and 8th Royal Warwickshires, had been lent to the 4th Division on 'the day' and, I like to remember, had got deeper into the German lines than any other unit in the 8th Corps, retiring only when ordered to. (Their losses: the 6th, twenty officers and 436 other ranks; the 8th, twenty-one officers and 569 other ranks—say 75 per cent.) Major Townshend, a sporting type in the 8th, went over the top with a shot-gun—no bad weapon for trench-fighting—and a terrier to flush the game. He survived, and told me afterwards that he had bagged two or three brace, which doesn't seem as good a joke now as it did at the time.

During Rawlinson's second phase the 48th Division carried out a series of co-ordinated attacks, by brigades and battalions, into the German flank at Ovillers. Here on 1st July the 9th York and Lancaster, with many others, had marched against uncut wire and had been shot down in rows by flanking machine-guns which, theoretically, should have been silenced by our bombardment. From our starting-point at La Boisselle a fortnight later I could see the grassy slope strewn with bodies, like St. James's Park on a fine afternoon, and did not know that these carrion men that smelt upon the earth were my friends. On the night of 15th/16th July our battalion put in a flank attack, which has been thought worthy of one line in the official history.[1] Without pre-liminary bombardment we crossed a thousand yards of open ground and occupied a knot of trenches in rear of the defenders of Ovillers. It fell to me to lead the assault, and to hold the farthest point we reached against a German bombing attack, which might have been pressed more resolutely if they had known our strength—or rather our weak-ness—and how we had got there. By such tactics the Division con-tained the garrison of Ovillers and compelled its surrender on the afternoon of the 16th, for what we thought a moderate cost in casual-ties. They were the Prussian Guard again, a crack regiment known as the 'Cockchafers'. This was a battle fought in summer heat, conditioned by chalk dust, not mud, and, like Hotspur, we were 'dry with rage and extreme toil'.

A week later, the Australians, recently come from the Mediterranean, carried the village of Pozières on our right, after some of the bitterest fighting of the war. We organized a heavy attack by bombing along the trenches in their direction but failed to force our way through. Here we learned to distrust the fashionable tactics of the year—'work-ing up a trench' with bomb and bayonet—and quickly reverted to the rifle, which my Colonel Sladen had always recommended. One of our other battalions, brought up from reserve, solved the problem of the Pozières 'bomb-stop' by capturing it 'over the top', not without loss

1. I have described it at some length in *A Subaltern's War* which I wrote under the pen-name of 'Charles Edmonds' (Peter Davies, 1929 and Icon Books, 1964).

They allowed us three weeks' holiday and even a convoy of buses to take us out of the line, and recruited our strength before the next operation with a draft of disbanded cyclist troops from Huntingdonshire—one of the best drafts we ever received.

North of Ovillers, the top of the ridge overlooked Thiepval and the Ancre Valley like a Wiltshire Down. On our side it was defended by system beyond system of trenches cut deep from the hard chalk and linked with dugouts that might better be described as underground corridors; to the left, the Schwaben Redoubt; on our front, the Leipzig Redoubt; facing either way and stoutly defended. On 18th August the Warwickshire Brigade carried the Leipzig Redoubt by a sudden attack with limited objective that the French could not have bettered; and since it was watched from across the river by the Army Commander, the Corps Commander, and several journalists it received wide publicity. The 5th and 6th battalions, with their flank covered by the 7th, went over the top, in waves that followed close behind the barrage, the first 'creeping barrage' we had ever seen, an unexampled concentration of fire by eighteen batteries on this small front. In the first assault the casualties were few and were mostly caused by our own shells when our eager men risked themselves too near. Better that than massacre by the German machine-guns. The Germans were overrun before they had time to man their defences, so that many were killed and 400 were forced to surrender with nine officers, a high proportion. Better still, their reserves put in an immediate counter attack, over the top, which we shot to pieces with rifle-fire. This, we knew, was the right way to set about our business and we had no doubts about who was winning the Somme Battle. 'Mopping up' the battlefield, as always, was an untidy affair which required a whole day of patrolling, dugout clearing, and very nasty bomb-fighting which I remember only too well; and before we left the line we had a further tour holding Skyline Trench which, as its name implied, seemed to be the favourite target of the whole German artillery. We had got there and we stayed there; the skyline just then was what our division was fighting for. Since we spent September out in rest in the Authie Valley and further away in remote untouched villages where our men helped the peasants to get the harvest in, I can pause to look back at the general panorama.

Rawlinson had now beaten the Germans off the high ground, and they conceded a win on points by dismissing their Chief of Staff,

Falkenhayn, all of whose plans for the Western Front had failed, was packed off to Rumania where he could snatch a cheap victory, and was replaced by the duumvirate of Hindenburg and Ludendorff, with dictatorial powers over the German war effort. On their first day in office, 23rd August, they admitted the failure of Falkenhayn's strategy by ordering the construction of the so-called Hindenburg Line, to which they could retreat when they were ready, or when they were obliged to.

I speak of the Somme Battle as I saw it, and as it affected the soldiers I knew. The 48th, a well-commanded division but of no outstanding fame, had captured strong positions from first-class troops, inflicting at least as many casualties as it suffered, had taken several hundred prisoners, and was conscious of its superiority. We were not intimidated by the war of attrition and after our September holiday were ready for anything; never, I think, in better heart. On 31st August I wrote home: 'They are beaten. The only question is whether they can hang on till winter'; on 26th September: 'The Push is going on and is more successful every day.' In a month's fighting, for which we could show some prizes, the division had lost eighty-eight officers and 2,418 other ranks—say, a quarter of our fighting strength, much less than the average of the unfortunate divisions that had been sacrificed for no visible advantage in a few hours on 1st July.

In September Haig decided to make a third attempt to force the decision. As on 1st and 14th July, so again the troops were given definite objectives, and provision was made for exploitation by cavalry, if a breakthrough should be achieved. This was the battle in which experiments were made with tanks. The first I heard of them was from another subaltern, J. C. Siddeley (now Lord Kenilworth), who told me we possessed armoured cars that could cross trenches and wire. I flatly refused to believe him; and was surprised two or three days later when the famous report was issued after the attack on 15th September, of a 'tank'—whatever that might be—marching into the village of Flers with the Hampshire Regiment cheering behind it. We were only twenty miles away, and neither then nor weeks later did we know what a tank looked like, how big it was, or what was its performance. The secret was wonderfully well kept, and could not have been kept if Haig had waited to conduct an experiment on a much larger scale. As another much-criticized commander, 'Bomber' Harris, has said, it is as great a mistake to try to fight with the weapons of the next war as with the weapons of the last. And the lesson to be learned from the battle of 15th September was that the Mark I tank had almost no value except for the lift given to our morale and the shock to the German morale by the rumours about our secret weapon. Haig had to use the material that was ready; to suggest that he should have closed down his operations and given the enemy a free hand for nine or twelve months while the inventors cured the teething troubles of their new baby is to talk neither politics nor strategy. He believed, and for what it is worth I and my friends believed, that there was still a chance of fighting the decisive battle before the autumn and for such a prize everything must be staked. You never know whether you are going to win a battle; you can only try your hardest.

So Haig tried out his forty tanks. Thirty-six started; some were ditched; some broke down; some were shot up; eleven crossed the front line; and four or five made a useful contribution to the battle. Whatever the front-line soldiers thought, the German command was not impressed and took no steps either to make tanks or to prepare anti-tank devices as a result of this experiment. How fortunate it was that their inadequacy was revealed before a large order was placed for them. Nevertheless, four days later Haig asked the War Office for a thousand tanks of better design, and when, a year later, the Mark IV tanks arrived, with many modifications, we at last had a war-winning weapon.

Every new invention has to meet the criticism of sceptics and the mere force of inertia so powerfully operated by second-rate men who don't like change. The strongest opposition to the tanks was, as might have been expected, in Whitehall. In France many of Haig's best commanders, who had seen the poor performance of the early tanks, disliked them. Even a year later the Australians were distrustful, taking the view that they gave more trouble than they were worth, and even at Cambrai there was one commander who preferred to have no tanks with his infantry. Gough was an early convert and used one of the few survivors of the first battle for the capture of Thiepval on 26th September.

The September battles went pretty well for us and badly for the Germans, without producing the desired breakthrough. Though I was not there myself, I had a long letter from my brother Hugh, at least as enthusiastic as I was about our prospects, and describing his adventures between High Wood and Flers. He had not seen a tank. But the besetting fault of Haig now showed itself in the stubbornness with which he refused to hold fast when the autumn rains set in. It is fair to add that Joffre never ceased urging him to attack on the whole front. In October we went back in the line at Fonquevillers where we sedulously practised for a new assault on Gommecourt Wood, in which my part was to have been to charge the very beak or snout of the salient with my platoon and one tank (which we never saw). Fortunately for me, Haig came forward and reconnoitred the front personally, one of the only two occasions on which I saw him in France, and cancelled the operation. If it had gone forward I should not now be writing these lines.

Soon afterwards we moved south again into the main battle zone and saw something of the final operations in November, when Gough, very skilfully by the standards of 1916, captured Beaumont Hamel. It was announced as a victory that, after four months' fighting, we had at least secured the objectives of 1st July, though it was too late now for the breakthrough. Well, we had given the German Army some good hard knocks. Next year, we did not doubt, we should finish them off.

10

Not so cushy trenches

THERE was no end to one's military education. Schools of instruction in all technicalities and at all grades sprang up behind the front with a deal of rivalry between corps and armies as to the fare provided for students. Sergeants and 'young officers' (how I disliked that patronizing phrase!) were much exposed to educational treatment and if they had the greatest share of danger in the line they enjoyed the perquisite—now and then—of being 'sent on a course'. At least it would be safe and comfortable, at best it might be a mere holiday—a 'binge'. Ten days at the machine-gun school at Camiers, though it was on the seashore near Le Touquet, gave me little pleasure in November 1916. It was too late in the year for the seaside and too cold for camping out in tents under the pine-trees. In a way I was glad to rejoin my battalion, by one of those long-drawn-out journeys in a troop-train at five miles an hour, even though I knew that the division had gone back to the Somme.

It proved to be a new raw camp of the rounded iron shacks that we called 'Elephant Huts' at Scott's Redoubt near Contalmaison in the middle of the devastated area, a commanding height from which you could get a view for four or five miles in any direction over a landscape entirely composed of mud. After four months' fighting the Boches had been pushed back seven miles and were now so far away that we were safe at Contalmaison from all except very long-range shell-fire. Here was my battalion and here were my friends, very jealous of my seaside holiday, because—they said—the daily working-parties clearing a road through the shattered stumps of Mametz Wood were the hardest and worst chores that anyone could remember. There was something particularly cloying about Somme mud. Perhaps the chalk in the subsoil gave it a gummy quality like half-dried cement which made the going even worse than in the porridgy mud of Flanders. Oh, we were

experts in mud! A light railway had been engineered across the battlefield from Albert to the highest contour, above the wood which lay in
a slight hollow, and if you took this toy train up to the height of land
the Somme country lay around you like a map. Behind, was the pretty
valley of the Ancre still showing some winter verdure, and there
stood the Albert Basilica against the sky with its huge gilt madonna
knocked sideways by a shell. Right and left ran the ridge from Delville
Wood to High Wood (where my brother, Christopher, had been
killed in October), from High Wood to Pozières, from Pozières to the
hill above Thiepval, the watershed which had been the original
objective for 1st July, the starting-point from which we were to have
exploited the victory that was never won. Carrying the eye round
from Pozières I could see Ovillers, where we had fought two battles in
July and August, now deserted by a host that had moved on. The
countryside looked as if a tidal wave had flowed over it. You could see
ten or a dozen villages, all with names still remembered by old soldiers,
and not one with a house or barn standing. There might be a spike of
brickwork where the church had been, or not even that, merely
mounds of rubble and discoloured soil, hedgerows looking deader than
they need in November, and woods that were clusters of bare poles.
The tall poplars in which the French delight were stripped of their side
branches, their foliage scorched, trunks snapped off short with splin-
tered ends like monstrous shaving-brushes. Every yard of ground had
been ploughed up by shell-fire and was tainted with high explosive, so
that a chemical reek pervaded the air. The smell of burnt and poisoned
mud—acrid is, I think, the right epithet—was with us for months on
end, and through it one could distinguish a more biotic flavour—the
stink of corrupting human flesh. In the thirty square miles around us
the best part of 200,000 men had been killed in the last few months and
had lain unburied, or been buried hastily in shallow graves, or buried
and blown out of their graves again. I think 7,000 corpses to the square
mile is not much of an exaggeration, ten to the acre shall we say, and
your nose told you where they lay thickest.

After a battle you buried your comrades and saw to it that their
graves were marked with a wooden cross and a name. If you had time,
and if it was not too dangerous, you did as much for other British dead.
The enemy came last in priority, and more than once I have cleared a
trench of its defunct tenants by throwing them over the parapet where

someone might or might not find and bury them when the battle was over. There were so many live inhabitants in the landscape as I saw it at Contalmaison in November 1916 that corpses had been cleared off everyone's premises, unless you went up to the new front where it was too dangerous for burial-parties to work. But in rolling forward the armies left desert areas behind, where no one had either need or inclination to go, in winter dreary beyond description, inhabited only by giant rats, fattened on corpse-flesh, in summer strangely beautiful with carpets of wild flowers and loud with skylarks. Clumps of scarlet poppies sprang up wherever the chalky subsoil had been disturbed by digging or by shell-fire. Long afterwards you could find corpses in nooks and corners of this wilderness as I found one at La Boisselle in 1921. When I was a boy I was very superstitious, suffered from 'creepy' feelings when I was alone, and was afraid of the dark. This nonsense was completely obliterated by the genuine horrors of the battlefield and I remember surprise at my own unconcern. I never heard a ghost-story at the front.

If you looked eastward from the ridge you could see a broad vale— of mud—with the land rising in the distance to a skyline, still in enemy hands. Straight through the centre of the landscape ran the Roman road from Albert to Bapaume, the main axis of the Battle of the Somme. Westward, behind us, it was thick with traffic, and all the valleys were crowded with tented camps and hutted camps, with horse-lines and battery positions and dumps; eastwards, the road and the countryside lay empty to the eye, though occupied, as we knew, by the fighting troops who lay low until it was dark. The ridge had not been finally captured until the first attacks made with tanks in September, when it was late in the year to press on with the battle. This, I should say, was the fault of Haig's tactics, that he was too stubborn to remain content with a partial success. Up to this point, the Somme Battle, which the French generalissimo conceived as a battle of attrition, could be justified. It was the attempt to push on in the vain hope of forcing a breakthrough, so late in the season, that may be condemned. Not till 26th September did the three villages, which I could now see before me—Martinpuich, Courcelette, Thiepval—come into our possession, and then the rain and the mud began to prevail. The last stage of the battle took us down the hill into a new valley of humiliation where the enemy again had the command. Why did we go on?

However, go on we did and the line had been pushed down the forward slope, in full view of the enemy guns to the village of Le Sars, a little salient astride the Bapaume Road. Not only was it commanded from the Bapaume ridge; it was dominated by a monstrosity. Beside the road, which rose up the slope beyond Le Sars, and only 500 yards away, was a round barrow, a prehistoric tumulus, standing up like Silbury Hill beside the Bath Road. What Gallic chieftain slain by Caesar in the land of the Ambiani lay buried here we neither knew nor cared, but this outgrowth, which we called the Butte of Warlencourt (pronounced just as in English) terrified us. A dome of gleaming white chalk from which all the vegetation had been blown away by shell-fire, it was the most conspicuous object in the landscape by daylight or moonlight. The Butte seemed to tower over you and threaten you with its hidden machine-gun posts, which—I now believe—were quite imaginary. Motoring past it the other day I was astonished to see what an ordinary inconspicuous little mound it is. At Contalmaison, when I rejoined, we had orders to take over the Le Sars front, facing the Butte of Warlencourt. We did three tours in this sector in November and December, the worst in my experience, coming back for periods of 'rest' between them to Scott's Redoubt camp.

(2)

On 13th November 1916 there took place the last active operation of the Somme Battle, when the Durham Light Infantry of the 50th Division attacked the Butte of Warlencourt. We had moved to Prue Trench, a reserve position far down the forward slope, and enjoyed a view from the stalls, just as on 1st July we had watched the assault on Gommecourt from Hebuterne trenches. In those nineteen weeks we had become connoisseurs of the seasonal mode, having captured Ovillers and the Leipzig Redoubt, and having held them against counter-attacks; and we could appreciate just what the 'Geordies' were going through. Battles of the First War were rarely spectacular, since the shrapnel barrage obscured visibility. A great noise and a smoke-cloud filled the valley in which now and then one saw distant figures moving, aimlessly it seemed, like ants in a disturbed anthill. I am sure I saw them swarming over the lower slopes of the Butte, which I'm sorry to say they did not capture.

I

We were strung out in a shallow, winding trench with no better cover than a cavity in the parapet roughly boarded over. There was not much shelling near us, but in the afternoon a German aeroplane flew low along our trench, shooting it up, a new development in the art of war. It was a 'pusher' monoplane with its engine and airscrew behind, and a gunner in a nacelle that protruded in front of the pilot. Round he went, and round again, while I ran for my Lewis gun. Was I not fresh back from the machine-gun school? My trusty Corporal Thompson hoisted the gun round and we began to prop it up to shoot at a high angle when—here he was again—diving at us and so close that I looked straight into his face—a florid young man with a little dark moustache. I picked up the gun and balanced it on the corporal's shoulder, and I fired a burst point-blank as the pilot fired a burst at me. We both missed. Then he was gone and out of ammunition, I suppose, as we saw him no more. That winter the Germans had got ahead of us in the technical air war, and often troubled us with attacks on ground targets. I used to fix a Lewis gun to a revolving bicycle wheel on a post as a protection for our billet, but I never shot it out with a German airman again.

(3)

Our battalion was in the forward zone, that is over the crest and always under enemy observation, from 9th to 14th November, from 24th November to 1st December, from 6th to 9th December, only fifteen days and nights, but enough to bring down the strength by one-third, from something over 500 to something less than 400. Fifty were battle casualties and the rest 'went sick'. We neither attacked nor were attacked and, excepting the young airman with whom I had fought a duel, I do not remember getting a glimpse of a German.

The killed and wounded were all lost by harassing fire, mostly on their way up or down the line. Once in position at Le Sars you could not show a finger by daylight, and by night every path by which you might be supposed to move was raked by machine-guns which had been trained on it by day. The entrance to the village, that is the gap in the ruins where the Bapaume Road passed through, the only way, by which you must pass, was under continuous shell-fire. If you could reach your funk-hole, and crouch in it, there was a fair chance of your coming out of it alive next day to run the gauntlet of the Bapaume

Road again. In your funk-hole, with no room to move, no hot food, and no chance of getting any, there was nothing worse to suffer than a steady drizzle of wintry rain and a temperature just above freezing-point. A little colder and the mud would have been more manageable. Life was entirely numbed; you could do nothing. There could be no fighting since the combatants could not get at one another, no improvement of the trenches since any new work would instantly be demolished by a storm of shell-fire. I don't remember that we had any 'wire' in front of us. We huddled and hid in piles of old brickwork and rafters, or behind hedgerows which once had bounded cottage gardens, scrabbling our way deeper down into mudholes, and painfully trying to keep our rifles clean, dragging out time until the relief came sneaking through the mud, exhausted before their tour of duty began. Then we must pluck up courage to escape, through the machine-gun fire, through the enemy barrage at the entrance to the village and away. To be clear of Le Sars and screened from the hideous Butte of Warlencourt by the ruins was something, yet not much. It was a three-mile trudge, carrying everything by the muddy track, on which you knew the enemy guns were registered, up the slope to Martinpuich, a name of evil omen to me. The first time I marched my men through it, picking our way among the ruins, I reached the centre of the village just as a thirty-centimetre shell (eleven-inch), the largest size the Germans used in trench warfare, landed fairly in the centre of a platoon of the Royal Sussex, killing fourteen of them outright and wounding I forget how many. Someone else had to mop up, I'm glad to say, after that incident. Our business was to march on with the comfortable feeling that a single shell was unlikely; another would shortly be on its way. It came. It approached with a noise like an aeroplane coming in to land and it thumped into the mud not twenty yards away from my marching column. It was a dud. Not everyone was so lucky; it was twenty months since our battalion had first landed in France and so slow was the leave-roster that there were still men at duty who had not been home on leave to England. When our last batch set out from Le Sars for 'Blighty' leave three were killed at the exit from the village.

Though some of these reminiscences are taken from a diary I kept intermittently in France, I have no written record of the Le Sars tour of duty, and much of the detail has now mercifully sunk out of my conscious memory. From the generalized picture of misery I recall one sharply defined detail—in the rain, by the light of a German flare, with the Butte looming up behind us, the face of my friend Oliver Sichel.[1] Older than me and senior in rank, he had just come out with a draft of reinforcements and was attached to my company, 'for instruction', on his first visit to the trenches. I was acting just then as company commander and it was my duty to induct him in command of a forward post—actually the most forward post of the British Army. Oliver was a literary man, a *bon viveur*, something of an aesthete, a comfortable figure who managed to look well dressed even in trench kit. Oh well! I can't say more, but I can't forget his face as I planted him for the December night, ankle deep in slime, exposed to the gun-fire and the rain. 'Is this it?' his eyes mutely asked me. 'Is this what I am to expect?' How unlike my own easy initiation at Gommecourt Wood a year ago, and how far away was that early enthusiasm!

(4)

What made the Le Sars sector intolerable to me was the glum discomfort of the camp at Contalmaison, the draughty huts standing in the mud, the ravaged landscape, the smell of battle, the batteries of heavies roaring away from their emplacements in Mametz Wood. Digging and roadmaking in these wretched circumstances were the only relief from Le Sars trenches and no mental relief. Everyone's health suffered until the doctor's sick parade assumed such proportions that higher command began to legislate against illness, like Canute against the tide. The care of feet was always a military idol in those days of marching armies. Every officer was accustomed to nursing his men's blistered toes, ensuring them clean socks, and attending to ritual washings, a routine that became more urgent as the winter drew on, because trench warfare had produced its characteristic variety of foot-rot. In winter trenches, when men stood for days and nights in mud, an affliction just short of frost-bite assailed them, 'Trench-foot'—I don't know what was its proper name—was endemic and almost everyone had a touch of it, though ideally it was an avoidable disease, if only you could wash and dry your feet, massage them daily with whale-oil, and change your socks. Neglected cases were extremely painful and could

1. Captain O. W. Sichel, killed 25th October 1918, when serving with the 2/6th R. Warwickshire Regt.

turn gangrenous. In the eyes of the higher command, therefore, the problem was soluble by disciplinary methods. An adequate supply of socks and whale-oil having been made available, orders were issued that every man should wash and dry and oil and re-sock his feet every day or pay the military penalty. Yet no one could explain how poor Oliver Sichel, standing in the rain with wet and muddy hands and no dry place to put anything, was to unwind his puttees, take off his boots, rub and dry his feet, so as to make himself clean and cosy. He didn't, and no more did anyone else in the Le Sars front line. Higher command fulminated emptily against the breach of discipline while trench-foot raged.

Then we were all 'chatty', a Hindustani soldiers' word which suggests that such conditions had been known in the Indian Army. Modern readers, I hope, are unacquainted with the body-louse (*pediculus vulgaris*), a notable carrier of disease, which lives in the folds and creases of sweaty, dirty old clothes. The louse or 'chat' is a whitish creature, about as large as a flea—perhaps the modern reader is unacquainted with fleas—but unlike it in its sluggish habits. Spot a louse and you can catch him without difficulty. I was never lousy in my life—didn't know what lice were—until I slept in a German officer's greatcoat during the Battle of the Somme. We used to say that when we captured German trenches we always came away lousy, and perhaps they said the same about us, for being lousy seems to be one of the hazards of active service when you are obliged to live dirty. De-lousing yourself was one of the pleasantest prospects of going out into rest. Only during the war was it discovered that lice carry a feverish infection which at first deceived the doctors, who called it P.U.O., 'pyrexia of unknown origin'. The soldiers called it trench-fever and it too prostrated its thousands every winter. When it was identified as carried by lice, the struggle for cleanliness was intensified, but there were as yet no bath-houses or brigade laundries at Contalmaison.

If not trench-foot or trench-fever there were other endemic diseases in the army camps. Since everyone was vaccinated and inoculated against typhoid—and against the resistant variety that the doctors called para-typhoid—and since it was forbidden to drink any water other than the chlorinated brew from the regimental water-cart, the soldiers escaped the greater plagues which had decimated armies of the past. This was the first war in which—to use the soldiers' grim phrase—

the butcher's bill was bigger than the doctor's bill. Not until 1918 did a new pestilence, the 'Spanish Influenza', break out with such virulence as to cause casualties on a battle-worthy scale. Yet everyone was debilitated by fatigue, by boredom, by the unclean air and poisoned earth, by the doped water, and the ill-cooked food. Minor ailments lingered, cuts festered, and diarrhoea became chronic. To my disgust I came out in boils for the first and last time in my life, and the barbed-wire scratches on my hands refused to heal. Taking one thing with another, the rifle-strength of the division, which should have been 12,000, and was 9,000 in October, had sunk to 6,000 by the end of the year.

At last, at last, we were relieved and took the light railway down to Albert, a little manufacturing town with no particular attraction for the peacetime tourist—but for us delight. Cleared of its inhabitants, it stood there still looking like a town, with roofs on most of the houses and glass in most of the windows, with pavements and drains and water from taps, with no 'civvy' shops but with canteens, bath-houses, and concert-parties. Here we were happy for Christmas.

11

Open fighting

THE winter of 1916–17 was the hardest for twenty years, wet and raw in December, snowy in January, and frosty for twenty-seven continuous days from 19th January until 17th February. In March the winter clamped down again with frequent falls of snow, the last and worst on 16th April, after which came a sudden mild warm spring. In January after a spell far out in rest, beyond Abbeville, our division took over trenches from the French Army on the south bank of the River Somme, which winds, as travellers by train from Calais to Paris may see, in a valley between low hills of chalk, sometimes narrowing under steep bluffs and sometimes opening out into a system of marshy pools and osier-beds. No longer fordable as it was in the days of Edward III and Henry V, its main stream is canalized and kept navigable for barges; so that it is a greater military obstacle now than then. During the Battle of the Somme the French had rapidly pushed forward on the south bank, from Frise to Biaches, while their comrades on the north bank had been less successful, getting no further forward than Clery. Between these villages was a gap in the trench lines for about three miles, where scattered outposts watched one another across the flooded marshes. Every morning flocks of wild duck rose from their nightly feeding ground, vainly pursued by a rain of machine-gun bullets from both armies. It was a pleasant war in the Somme Valley if only the weather was good, except that the loops and curves of the river allowed the enemy (and us too) to site guns which could snipe the unwary from an unexpected angle. The hard frost was no misfortune since it conquered the mud, and there was even a night when we slipped a patrol across the whole breadth of the valley on the ice, to range about in the villages behind the German lines. That was something to boast about in the 1914 War, though they didn't make any remarkable discoveries.[1]

Our sector on the hill-top above Biaches, a ruined village which the Germans clung to as a bridgehead on our side of the river, looked across to the pretty little market town of Peronne-la-Pucelle, the virgin fortress which was never taken in war until Wellington passed that way in his advance from Waterloo to Paris.[2] Above the town stood the high round hill of Mont St. Quentin, from which the Germans commanded the whole countryside and prevented us from approaching our front by daylight. The trench system was well sited and drained, with a communication trench three miles long for use in emergency, if ever one had the patience to struggle along it. A better plan was to conduct all our affairs by night, over the top. A four-mile trudge from the trenches back to 'The Dump', a general sorting and supplying and unloading place just out of sight of Mont St. Quentin; and then a further three-mile trudge in safety down the valley to Eclusier ('the lock gate') where there was a comfortable hutted camp with coke stoves and rows of bunks, as cushy a place as I remember, in a nook beside the canal, on which I skated in February, in which I swam in May. Many a time did we march up or down this seven-mile route, to go into the line, to come out into rest, on carrying-parties from the Dump to the front line, on digging-parties in the communication trenches, on wiring-parties in No Man's Land under fire. On two nights running, when the Boches were on the point of retiring, we marched back exhausted after a tough day in the trenches and were instantly turned round to march up again.

A few days after we moved into this sector the Boches made a determined raid on our sister battalion which repulsed it with loss. Whether they got the identification they wanted I do not know, but we identified them as the 1st Division of the Prussian Guard, commanded by the Kaiser's youngest son, whom one of our officers had met at winter sports in Switzerland three years back. No mean adver-

1. '*J'étais parmi les éclaireurs. Nous ne voyions rien. C'est une des grandes finesses de la guerre. On envoie pour reconnaitre l'ennemi des gens qui reviennent sans avoir rien reconnu, ni connu. Mais on en fait des rapports, après la bataille, et c'est la que triomphent les tacticiens*'.—Anatole France.

2. In 1923 when visiting this battlefield I found a trench still full of the flotsam and jetsam of war. I dug an old gun out of the mud and found to my surprise that it was not a modern rifle but a Brown Bess musket, dropped there by some British soldier during Wellington's last action against a French rearguard in 1815.

saries, they conducted the forthcoming operation very skilfully, but were not active in No Man's Land which we took into our possession. When we were the front-line company—three tours making seventeen days in all—one of the officers with a picked man went out on patrol every night for two or three hours to make sure that there was no Boche activity in front of their wire and that they still held their lines, since in February we began to suspect that they were planning a retirement. I noted seven such patrols in my diary, finding them very different from the easy-going Boy-Scout night operations at Gommecourt Wood a year earlier. Not only were the enemy more dangerous, the lines were much closer together, at one point less than fifty yards apart, hardly more than bomb-throwing range. To patrol here meant to belly-crawl every inch of the way moving one foot or one hand at a time, sliding over the mounds and pits of the shell-torn ground, either in the frost or in the mud, lying dead still for a quarter of an hour or more until you could hear your heart beating, advancing ten yards, twenty yards, until you were midway and could listen to the stealthy sounds of their sentries in front and your own sentries behind. Easy to lose your way in the dark among the shell-holes, unless under a clear sky you could navigate by the Pole star—east for Germany and west for 'Blighty'. You have a loaded cocked revolver in one hand and a bomb in your pocket, but dare you use them, however inviting the target, when the explosion will instantly raise up a sheaf of rockets and bring down a storm of fire from both sides? Better lie low and get exactly the information called for, that you have heard a German sentry coughing or whispering at such and such a point on your enlarged map, that you have seen a shadowy figure passing their wire by such and such a gap. Better get home alive with your scrap of news, and hope that your trigger-happy sentry won't shoot before you can whisper the password. If anybody's artillery should open fire when you are out in front, so much the worse for you, since no gunner can guarantee an accuracy of twenty or thirty yards. The 'effective beaten zone' of his shrapnel bullets will be much longer than that.

On 14th March, when we paraded to move up from Eclusier to the front line of Biaches, a communiqué from G.H.Q. was read out on parade. There had been a revolution in Russia and the Liberals had seized power. The news was applauded, since we supposed that Russia would now have a constitution like our own with the consequence that their war effort would be better managed. World politics faded out of our consciousness as we applied ourselves to the questions whether, and how the Boches would retire. The only way to find out was to send an officer to look. If they shot him dead we should know they were still there.

Early in the morning of 15th March I crept in from my patrol at Biaches with the information that I had not heard a sound; I thought they had gone. Not I, but the next subaltern for duty, took a fighting patrol and entered the German trench. He could find no one, but as he withdrew to report he was fired upon and lost a man. Evidently there were some scattered rearguards left behind and who could say in what strength. To break off and withdraw from a battlefield has always been regarded as the most difficult and dangerous operation of war, but at this point in military history the defensive was so much stronger than the offensive that disengagement was unusually easy, as had been shown at Le Cateau and at Gallipoli. It was now the Germans' turn and it would be suicide for us to advance without preparation, if even a few machine-guns had been left to hold us off. A local attack was hurriedly mounted against the key position, a farm called La Maisonnette, and meanwhile we kept patrols all night in No Man's Land. Next day the Boches showed their hand. Smoke and flames burst from the town of Peronne and from all the dozen villages which we could see from our hill-top. In fine frosty weather pillars of smoke rose to the sky right and left and far behind the lines. While this implied that they had withdrawn their main force they still pinned us down with long-range shell-fire and with rifle-fire from the front line. Next night we were relieved and marched back to the rest camp, but were instantly recalled to the front by another report that the rearguards had gone, and again I spent the night in No Man's Land. The following night, the same again. This time, the morning of 17th March, they really had gone. My captain went forward for orders and presently sent me back word to bring the company over the top, by daylight, from the Dump to the German front line.

I cannot explain the consternation caused by this order. For two years no one had raised a hand over the parapet by daylight unless in the stress of battle and covered by an artillery barrage. Tired as we were after two nights of marching and a week of trench duty, we were exhilarated. Open fighting had come. Were the Boches cracking up?

Had we got them on the run? With very mixed feelings and a good deal of nervousness I drew up the company in artillery formation (widely extended lines of sections in files) and manœuvred them across country for four miles, over the trenches, over No Man's Land, and into the German trenches at which I had so many times peered while lying on my belly in the mud.

During the day 'A' Company cleared Biaches after a fight between our leading patrol and a German rearguard; the 8th Battalion came up with pontoons from the bridging train and crossed the river un-opposed;[1] and next morning as soon as a bridge was built the cavalry went through. It was someone else's turn to lead now and we sat for two or three days in the German front line at Biaches, which will allow me an interval to discuss the retreat in general.

(2)

The spring of 1917 produced a whole series of unexpected crises, to which the German Army reacted rather sluggishly. Their new command, Hindenburg and Ludendorff, had again gone on the defensive in France, putting their main effort into the industrial mobilization of Germany and the submarine war against Britain. Though they knew, as everyone knew, that the Russian Empire was crumbling, they were not disposed to waste their effort in a march to Moscow. The submarine campaign reached its climax in April–June 1917, nearly bringing Britain to defeat; but 'nearly' is worth nothing in war, and after June our counter-measures began to reduce the monthly figures of loss. The failure of the submarines spelt inevitable ruin to Germany by bringing America into the war on 6th April, though more than a year was to pass before the Americans could make any contribution to the fighting front. In my letters and diaries the only allusion I find at this time to the submarine crisis was 'I think the Germans must be mad'.

In France their policy was to forestall the French who seemed likely to make a renewed attempt to bite off the Noyon salient by simultaneous attacks in Champagne and Artois. So likely was it that the Germans had dug the line (which they called the Siegfried Stellung

1. First across the Somme was Captain (afterwards Colonel) W. C. C. Gell, D.S.O., later my Commanding Officer. In the Second World War he became an air vice-marshal, commanding the Balloon Barrages.

and we the Hindenburg Line) across the base of the salient, with a switch-line or retrenchment, called the Wotan Line, to buttress the vital sector in Artois, but whether they would willingly retire to the Hindenburg Line was another question. It was most unlike them to give ground without fighting for it. What persuaded them to go was renewed pressure by Gough's Fifth Army on the Ancre front. Taking advantage of the frosty ground he reopened the Somme offensive in January and advanced four miles with slight losses. The German front seemed to be crumbling and we were indeed excited when we heard that Gommecourt Wood had been abandoned without a fight.

We knew, of course, that the Germans had more than one series of reserve lines roughed out on the ground far behind their front, just as they knew of our last ditch defending Calais and Boulogne. It was difficult to judge their intentions by air photography, because in the fluctuating air battle the enemy just then had superiority, and Richthofen's Red Squadron made every patrol over the Hindenburg Line a forlorn hope. Haig seems to have thought it unlikely that they would go, until they went. His published diaries at this time mention the German withdrawal as a possibility but not as likely enough to affect his plans for co-operating with the new French Commander-in-Chief, Nivelle.

Rather surprisingly, the German rearguards were instructed to avoid action and at first they gave us little trouble. A cavalry division which had been engaged in open fighting on the Rumanian front[1] was brought into action against us and we, who did not share the view so commonly held nowadays that cavalry were useless, were somewhat concerned about it. Once or twice I saw patrols of the famous Uhlans riding in the distance, keeping carefully out of range, and that is all. Our own cavalry, as I shall relate presently, were more effective. But if

---

1. My friend Arnold Hollriegel, the Austrian journalist who died at Auschwitz, used to tell me tales of the Rumanian campaign. One snowy night he and a colleague lost their way between the lines in open warfare and motored into an abandoned village. He described to me the pointed gables, thatched roofs, and half-timbered houses in the snow and the moonlight, silent and empty, like a scene from *Grimm's Fairy Tales*. They walked into the inn where dinner had been left on the table, ate and drank, and went to bed in the best bedroom, all alone. In the middle of the night my friend was woken by cries and tramplings. Looking out of the window he saw the market-square filled with Austrian and Rumanian cavalry on horseback fighting with swords in the moonlight.

you read memoirs or regimental histories of the German withdrawal to the Hindenburg Line you will find that British and Germans mutually accuse one another of being unenterprising. Both armies were physically and morally exhausted after the Somme fighting and the hard winter.

The main German forces had gone when we moved forward, having burnt every house, blown up every church, public building and ancient monument, broken every bridge and culvert, mined every crossroads, polluted every well. They had carried away all the able-bodied men and women into captivity, leaving the old and feeble concentrated in one or two villages; and—which seemed to distress the French most—they had even found time to ring-bark the apple-trees in the cider orchards. The country was dead, laid waste with a destructive fervour worse than anything in the Thirty Years War, a devastation that had no parallel since the wars of the Mongols. When we marched into Peronne, where the baroque façades of the houses in the market-place were blown down, and fires were still burning in the church, the old castle, and the public library, we saw a huge notice erected on the town hall: 'NICHT ARGERN NUR WUNDERN'. 'Don't be angry, only wonder!' Indeed it puzzled us a good deal. We were not angry but delighted that so large a region of France should be liberated and if we had any astonishment left it was at the ingenuities of German barbarity. What they had not destroyed they had defiled; and when one found a house or room unburned it looked as if it had been visited by a gang of those delinquent teenagers whose vandalism is reported from time to time in our newspapers. In those days we were less advanced in social decadence and could still be shocked. It is the first step that matters in the easy descent to hell and it is no defence to say that we were all to behave a great deal worse in the nineteen-forties.

(3)

On the first day we lost two officers from my mess, one shot by a German sniper when leading the advance guard, the other caught by a booby-trap. In a German dugout he had sat down in a chair and had drawn it up to the table, thus igniting the fuse of a concealed bomb with its starting mechanism tired to the chair-leg. We had been warned, and an order was given that no 'other ranks' were to be allowed into any house or dugout until an officer had searched it for booby-traps. We became rather expert at cautiously pulling every loop and pressing every loose board with a long stick from the best cover we could find, if any. This proved an insufficient precaution when, days and even weeks after the German retreat, large delayed-action mines exploded in most of the few houses still standing. The whole headquarters of the 4th Gloucesters, a regiment we knew well, was blown sky-high, and a particular success was gained at Bapaume, not far from us, where the two members of the Chamber of Deputies were caught by a mine while paying a ceremonial visit to their constituency. After a few such incidents the order came down from above that no one was to live in any house or dugout in the liberated area. This came a little late, in mid-April, but before the prolonged winter was over, and gave us several nights bivouacking in the frost. I recall, too, a memory of two or three evenings when we arrived in some shattered village, built hutches out of rafters and floorboards, and solaced ourselves beside blazing camp-fires since there was no shortage of fuel, like soldiers in the old wars.

Our General Fanshawe was now in his element. By a stroke of luck the Corps Commander (Pulteney—a quite good Corps Commander) was on leave and for a few days 'Fanny' took his place, while not relinquishing command of his own division. He bridged the Somme with two foot-bridges and two light traffic bridges built by our own engineers, while G.H.Q. built a main road-bridge within four days; and he sent a brigade of cavalry through. During the last ten days of March we all engaged in open fighting exactly as we had been taught at Aldershot and, some years later, 'Fanny' told me that it was very much like the early stages of the Battle of Ypres in 1914, when he had been a brigadier.

We were lucky to be working with the Canadian Cavalry Brigade, perhaps the most enterprising mounted troops in France, under Brigadier General 'Jack' Seely, who better exemplified the cavalry spirit than some more exalted generals. We hardly remembered that he was a civilian and a liberal politician, actually the Secretary of State who had come a cropper over the Curragh Incident just before the war. Having found the enemy disposing strong rearguards in a line of villages about five miles back, he pinned them down between 24th and 27th March, worked round their flanks, and eventually overran them in mounted charges with very slight loss. The famous Uhlans made no effort to intervene. Cavalry, properly handled under spirited leaders, proved that they could tackle infantry with machine-guns when the conditions were appropriate, as many times during the First World War in Poland, Rumania, and Palestine, but almost never in France. We much regretted it when Haig withdrew the cavalry division from our front for the Battle of Arras in which, as it turned out, cavalry had no chance at all.

Alas, I did not see the cavalry charge at Longavesnes, though I was only a mile or two away with my platoon, filling in the mine-crater at an important cross-road, when the brigadier reined in his horse as he rode by to tell me all about it. A day or two later we marched up to take over the outpost line. After reconnaissance we decided that only one outpost was necessary on our front, in a lonely thicket on a hill-top (which we called Capron Copse).[1] The Germans, who were falling back on their supports, could reach us with heavy artillery, while we, pushing forward, had to rely on the little short-ranged thirteen-pounders of the horse artillery, the pop-guns with which they now fire salutes in Hyde Park. I prowled about the lonely wood in the dusk and found a ditch that we could improve into a fire-trench with adequate command of the landscape. Uhlan patrols had been all about, but what worried me was that I was warned to retire upon the line of resistance if heavily attacked. Twenty times or more did I hold defensive positions which I was ordered to maintain to the last round of ammunition and that part of my instructions gave me no anxiety at all. Once only was I given leave to retire, with the consequence that I was looking over my shoulder all night and all day long. I went out into the night to explore, and got to know that 'they' were also out exploring all around me; luckily we missed one another.

In the morning there was General Fanshawe and an orderly with his pennon riding over the down with no apparent interest in an occasional shrapnel burst. His visit was followed by the arrival of our friends of the 241st field battery, who galloped up the slope, wheeled into action, unlimbered, and opened fire on the distant German post which the Uhlans were visiting, then limbered up and drove away, as gay and gallant as the Royal Military Tournament. We could see the Germans

---

1. I wrote an account of this incident for an anthology of war stories (*A Martial Medley*, Scholartis Press, 1930).

bolting like rabbits, but the corollary, as I feared, was that we were shelled all the afternoon by a long-range German gun from much further back. They didn't score a direct hit, but they tried.

When we were relieved after a wet cold day under fire with no hot food, we marched down in black darkness against a howling gale of wind and rain, losing our way and walking into a post of the Glouces-ters, who received us most efficiently with a smart burst of rifle-fire, wounding one of my men. Rather rashly I set off by myself to find our supporting party and found them—dead, a group of warm, fresh-killed corpses. It was not a happy day.

As we drew up to the Hindenburg Line the German resistance stiffened. Since the defences were not ready, their rearguards fought for every village and farm to gain time. We overran and destroyed one such rearguard in a brigade attack at Epehy, after which I was sent out on patrol to find how far they had retired. 'Take seven or eight men and locate the German Army.' Our outpost line ran along a railway cutting with a clear view over a wide grassy plain that rose to a blank skyline. My six men, the sergeant and I, arranged in a neat diamond pattern at discreet intervals, with our rifles and fixed bayonets slung, advanced into an empty landscape. When we were half a mile out, half a mile from anywhere, the Boches opened fire with a field-gun that must have been left with the rearguard. It pitched one shell in front of us, another behind, and would have scored on us with the third if I had not given the order to run for it. We had done our task by drawing fire. There they were! We ran and dodged, and I have vivid recollections of the shrapnel bullets hissing into the turf like hot hail. Home with one man wounded, and for the twentieth time I marvelled how much ammuni-tion can be spent without killing a man. We found the outpost line roaring with laughter and laying bets on our survival. It was the best example they had ever seen, they said, of 'indication and recognition of targets', a term of military art.

After many exacting days and freezing nights we finished with a night attack against two German outposts on 16th April, the date of Nivelle's offensive that was to have finished the war. Our petty skir-mish was for us as deadly as the great battle was for him. Again it was dark and wet, with a drizzle that turned to snow until before dawn a blizzard was blowing. Two of our companies blundered into one another and opened fire. The assaulting party ran into uncut wire which they could not even see. They dug themselves in and waited for dawn when the Germans cleverly slipped away. That night my horse, impressed for duty as a pack pony to carry ammunition to the front line, died of exposure and so, very nearly, did its master, to whom the whole episode was a half-conscious nightmare of fluttering trench-mortar bombs, the kind we called 'grey pigeons', coming down through driving snow. In the morning, when we advanced unopposed, I passed the corpse of a British sergeant, not of my regiment. He lay on his back holding a revolver in his hand, shot through the throat at such an angle that I wondered if it had been suicide. If I had been suicidally inclined that night would have driven me to it.

Suddenly everything changed. We went back to the Somme Valley, the weather turned mild, and slowly I recovered from what was the nadir of my morale. Never had I been so exhausted and dispirited. I even wrote to my mother that I was 'heartily sick of the whole affair', a flat statement as near as I ever came to defeatism. Theoretically, as a keen young soldier, I should have delighted in this month of open fighting and should have been proud of our exploits. Chiefly, I had been cold and frightened and I could not persuade myself it had been great fun.

May and June that year were warm and sunny. After our long hard winter campaign our division was in clover for many weeks, and I particularly lucky. We were put out to grass in quiet outposts looking across the empty landscape to the Hindenburg Line, which lay like a brown streak in the distance. No shelling to speak of, and the enemy unenterprising, so that we soon regained our health and spirits. I 'wangled' three days in Paris, hitch-hiking to Amiens, where I caught the mail-train, utterly unaware that the French Army was in a state of mutiny and the capital on the brink of revolution; my regular allowance of leave to England came round in July. Otherwise we lay in the sun doing nothing much more warlike than taking compass bearings on German gun-flashes when they did fire, so as to locate their batteries on the map.

It occurs to me that in this quiet interval our ears buzzed with the celebrated 'corpse-factory' rumour, which I then accepted as true. The form in which it reached us was that one of our divisional field ambulances—the fable was localized—wanted a corpse for some anatomical research and had no corpses, since none of us was just then getting

K

killed. So they dug up a German cemetery and found all the graves empty. Obviously the corpses had been taken away and melted down for glycerine with which to make nitro-glycerine, or soap. This sounds the kind of rumour inflated from some tiny bubble of fact. Perhaps someone, somewhere, had found an empty grave where there had been a token burial. Whatever the origin of the story, it proliferated, and we all indulged our morbid fancies with gruesome descriptions of corpses carried off to the glycerine factory by trainloads. Why it should be thought more reprehensible, if it had ever occurred, to convert dead men into soap than to convert live men into corpses I cannot say.

We were not altogether unenlightened. I asked my brother at Cambridge to send me out something worth reading and, with great discrimination, he selected *The Ring and the Book*, perfect for the purpose. The four of us in our company mess were far from being intellectuals, so that at first I was mocked by the others for my highbrow pretences, *La Vie Parisienne* being more to their taste. Presently I caught one of my messmates furtively peeping into Robert Browning and by the end of the tour we were fighting over my book and talking of nothing else at meals. To be contemporary I read the *Spoon River Anthology*, a forgotten book of the season at which the critics, some day, should take another look.

As far as I remember we were indifferent, perhaps ignorant, about the political convulsions of those months to which I shall allude shortly. December 1916 had seen great changes in London and in Paris. Lloyd George's success at the Ministry of Munitions had brought him such popularity as to enable him to overthrow Asquith's unstable coalition, with the help of the Tory leaders and the Press Lords. Determined as he was to fight the war through and to win by a 'knock-out blow', he had no confidence in Haig or Robertson, yet retained for some inscrutable reason a simple faith in the French generals who held similar views and were unshaken in their adherence to the Western Front strategy. We knew Lloyd George as the man who had provided the guns and the shells, and we applauded his emergence as Prime Minister, not knowing that he was conspiring with the French against the British command. When at the same moment a change of government in Paris led to the supersession of Joffre we saw no more in it than a repetition of what had happened to Sir John French Each of these good old generals had done well in his day and it was right that they should make way for younger men. As for the new man, Nivelle, we knew nothing except that he was one of the heroes of Verdun, a good reason for promoting him. Of course there would be a new spring offensive by both Allied armies and, since the German retreat which we thought was greatly to our advantage, it did not seem likely that we should strike straight at the Hindenburg Line, where there was no build-up of stores and communications, though our general, 'Fanny', wanted to do it. Allenby's offensive at Arras and Nivelle's on the Aisne seemed to make good sense and it was gratifying to see that we had profited by the lessons of 1916. It was disheartening but familiar that both offensives 'bogged down' after a few days. It was what always seemed to happen and, as on the Somme, phase two would probably be better than phase one. On 7th June the news of Plumer's victory at Messines, the most perfect attack with limited objective of the whole war, which was described to us with gusto by 'Fanny' as he visited us in the outposts one morning, changed the emphasis. We began to look north towards Flanders, a prospect I didn't much enjoy as, like a cat, I hated getting my feet wet. On 5th July we were transferred to the 18th Corps (Maxse), and began to train behind the lines for an attack which, we guessed, must be in the Ypres Salient.

Of the collapse of Nivelle's offensive, the fate of that unlucky general, the mutinies in the French Army, and Pétain's measures to restore morale we had not the slightest hint. We watched the news from Russia without apprehension since, as we supposed, Kerensky's Government was firm in its support of the alliance. We knew, of course, of the desperate condition to which Britain had been reduced by the U-Boats that spring and felt confident that America, which had entered the war on 6th April, would enable us to regain command of the sea. As for the American Army, we did not consider it at all. We assumed that the Americans would take as long to mobilize for war as Kitchener's Army had taken, and we should have won the war for ourselves before the American soldiers came.

12

Some random recollections

(i) ON THE MARCH

THOUGH the war on the Western Front seemed so immobile, the ceaseless interaction of trench reliefs implied that infantry units never stayed long in one place, not often for more than a week or ten days. In the year 1916, I find, I packed all my goods and moved house eighty times, of which fourteen removals were by train or bus and sixty-six by route march. Memory distinguishes little between these long days on the road except that some of them were in heat and dust, the others in cold and mud. They have faded into a recurrent pattern which I shall try to portray typically.

At first light the sentry from the quarter-guard wakes the orderly corporal, who goes round the barns to rouse the men where they lie sleeping in their clothes on straw. If there is still the peacetime frill of a bugler he is hounded out of bed to blow 'revally'. A book might be written on bugle-calls, those simple tunes arranged on five notes only which, the traditionalists say, Haydn composed for George III, though I think they are much older. The soldiers know them by the ribald words sung to them:

> 'Get oùt—o'bèd,
> Get oùt—o'bèd,
>   Yer làzy bùg-gers.'

In the half-light crowds of men pull on their boots, wind their puttees as if they were winding bandages, shave in their shirt-sleeves if there happens to be any water, and clean their rifles whatever and wherever the situation.

Here is the orderly corporal again, mustering two duty men from each billet to go to the cookhouse for 'dixies' of tea ('dixie' is another soldier's word from kitchen Hindustani). It comes boiling and syrupy, real 'sergeant-major's' brew that you could stand the spoon up in, and the dixie, an oblong-shaped cooking-pot, holds two gallons. Men line up by platoons to draw tea in their own mess-tins and look hopefully for bacon, of which there may be one fat greasy slice for each man. If not, breakfast is biscuits and jam, the hard tack that has always been the traditional food of soldiers and sailors, and the cheap tinned plum-and-apple that was a 1914 legend. Not much time for breakfast because everything must be packed, the blankets rolled and carted, billets cleaned, and fatigues done before we can march off. Those who cannot march must be sent to the Medical Officer's sick parade at the dressing station and what he will do with them, God knows.

Perhaps two hours after reveille the companies are on parade. If there's time, the turnout will be inspected by the company officers, and time must be found for rifle inspection on which lives depend. Now we march to the rendezvous which may be a mile or more away, so that another half-hour will be needed before the column is formed on the main road. Companies 'report present' to the adjutant; the orderly sergeant hands in the parade state, accounting for every man present or absent, and we move off by companies, a mounted officer at the head of each. We used to call the captain's horse a charger, but by 1916 it's more probably a pony impressed from a milk-float.

The morning is fine, we are all in good spirits and think nothing of the weight of our packs; every man has his personal property on his back, a rifle on his shoulder, bayonet and entrenching tool at his side, and a hundred rounds of ammunition in pouches strapped to his chest. In his pack is the iron ration, the emergency reserve of bully beef and biscuits which soldiers carry but must never touch. (Only once in the war do I remember orders coming down that we were to live on our iron rations for the day and it seemed like sacrilege.) We also carry a quart of water in a covered flask, and as this, too, may be drunk only with permission, for the present it is an extra burden. Sometimes there is a blanket to be rolled over the pack, or an additional bandolier of ammunition, and this is hell.

We step off briskly at a steady pace, which by its rhythm becomes automatic, almost hypnotic. On good ground, exactly thirty inches to the pace, exactly 108 paces to the minute, give you three miles to the hour, or two miles and a half in the hour, because ten minutes rest are allowed in every sixty. Whether you have been marching for fifty minutes or only for five, the whistle blows, at ten minutes to the hour, companies are halted, and everyone falls out on the right side of the road. Sit down, stretch your legs, put your feet up if you can. On the stroke of the hour, fall in by companies and march on.

The column starts with correct drill movements marching 'at attention'. As soon as the rhythm is established and the human cater-pillar acquires momentum the word is passed to march 'at ease'. Men sling their rifles, open their coat-collars, tilt back their caps—that is if we are lucky enough not to be wearing helmets—and become human again from the waist up. Talking is allowed and friends look over their shoulder to exchange a word with friends in the rank behind. A blue cloud of tobacco smoke rises and thickens, and before long someone begins to whistle, like the soldiers in the film of the River Kwai. This the sergeants encourage because it maintains the rhythm and ensures that the men still behave like automata from the waist down.

If we sing on the march in the morning, the songs are gay and ribald, and it's more than likely that the company humorist has composed some topical verses to that song about the idiosyncracies of the colonel. The nearest officer pretends not to hear, while he concentrates on memorizing it, so that he can give a spirited rendering of it in the mess that evening. Just when the language grows a little too free and the officer is wondering whether to take official cognizance of it, the word comes down the column—'March at attention!' We are passing through a village where another regiment has its headquarters, and its quarter-guard 'pays the proper compliment' by turning out and presenting arms, to which we reply, giving 'eyes right' by platoons. This is a bore, but it is only for a moment and is in a curious way enjoyable. This is our display of pride, our publicity, and we are ready to show them what good soldiers look like. If their guard is slack or untidy it is not only the colonel and the sergeant-major who will take notice. The company humorist has seen it too and is already improvis-ing a new verse about this 'pretty rotten lot'.

But this time we like the look of these strange soldiers who come flocking out of their billets to watch us pass. We are all connoisseurs of regiments and divisions, so that we quickly see by the Lamb on their badges that they are the 'Queen's', and by the domino sign of the 'double three' on their notice-board that they are the 33rd Division. 'We took over trenches from them on the Somme,' says somebody. 'Cushy trenches too. The Boches daren't show a finger.'

The days wears on; three spells of marching have brought us seven or eight miles and we halt for our dinners. A battalion of 800 men makes a column a quarter of a mile long, not counting the transport, sixteen limbered wagons, and two smaller vehicles called Maltese carts which trail behind. All these are loaded to overflowing with the official stores of the battalion and with everything that the quartermaster has been able to scrounge in addition. With the transport are four cooking-stoves on wheels, the field kitchens, in which dinners are being stewed in dixies as we go along. Behind them march the company cooks, stoking or stirring as they go, the only men in the battalion whose clothes can never by any force of discipline be kept clean.

At the midday halt the 'cookers' come trundling up from the rear and are greeted with cheers. Again the orderlies for the day are called out, the dixies, now full of stew, are carried to platoons while the men line up to fill their mess-tins, and each produces his own knife and fork. There may be green vegetables in the stew and there may be half a loaf of bread for each man, or 'two between five', and what is left he will keep for his tea. Every officer sees that his men are fed before going to his own mess, a picnic-party set out under a tree by the officers' servants.

There are still three spells of marching to the next billeting area, to be accomplished without the morning's gaiety. Some, who were on duty last night, are tired out; some are footsore; and almost everyone is bored. It comes on to rain. We get into a run of heavy traffic and the Divisional Supply Column, with its three-ton lorries comes by too fast, forcing the marching men into the ditch and splashing them with mud. Wet puttees are abominable. Too late when tunics are already damp the company commander says: 'Get out your groundsheets'; and when you've draped them over your shoulders the rain still drenches the baggy turnover of your trousers, infiltrates down your neck, brings out rust-spots on your iron-ware, which now weighs heavier than this morning.

The optimists and the morale-raisers of all ranks start up a song to keep things going. Oh yes, we sing, but now it is deadly sentimental:

> 'A long, long trail a-winding
> into the land of my dreams.'

We drool away, and wish there more verses to drag out time as we count the trees that line the road, the 100-metre stones that the French Government so efficiently provides, up to the kilometre post that brings us near the next ten-minute halt. At any cost, keep up the rhythmical movement; break step and the column would disintegrate. 'Boots, boots, boots, boots, moving up and down again', by this we are hypnotized into continuance, and the morale-raisers are now reduced to doggerel which has no merit but length, the non-stop songs:

> 'Eight men went to mow, went to mow a meadow,
> Eight men, seven men, six men, five men, four men, three men,
>   two men, one man—*and his dog*,
> Went to mow a meadow!'

The road surface is or seems worse, so that march discipline falters. The sergeant-major yelps his 'left-right, left-right' in vain, and officious subalterns stepping out of the column to cruise up and down looking for the weaker brothers make less impact. No one now cares, and only tea and billets ahead draw the men forward. At the rear, a new phenomenon occurs. At every check in front the column draws out like elastic so that the pace seems to vary. In front they are marching steadily and keeping time; behind they are breaking into a run to make up lost ground. 'Step short in front,' the word is passed forward; 'Step out in rear,' is the reply. Mounted officers ride back, making themselves unpopular by splashing the footsloggers who envy them as they pass, but nothing can prevent this tendency. They step short in front and, having given this slight relief, step off briskly again, while the rear which has hurried to catch up must now hurry again to keep up.

There may be stragglers, or men who are about to straggle. That man who reported sick this morning but was sent by the doctor to 'light duty' looks as if he is going to faint. Though his mate on one side carries his rifle and his mate on the other holds his arm, he breaks step and throws everyone behind him out of step. 'Left-right, left-right' bellows the sergeant. 'Pick it up there.' The subaltern, not so heavily loaded as his men, carries someone's rifle—out of bravado carries two rifles—and the captain is just about to put the sick man on the 'company horse' when he is sent for and has to ride away to the head of the column. Everyone consults to get the sick man along because 'falling out on the march' is a military offence as well as a disgrace to the platoon. And if he falls out what will become of him? If not this, then some other trouble at the rear of the column where everyone seems to be footsore. When at last we reach the billeting area in the dusk, no one notices that our rifles just slide off our shoulders as we order arms. Six hours marching has brought us only fifteen miles, but we were up two hours before the march began and there is much more to be done now we have arrived.

Here is the billeting officer who was sent ahead this morning with a sergeant from each company. The column breaks up and our guide leads us off to billets in a hamlet a mile farther on. One platoon goes on again along a dark dirty lane to a solitary farmhouse. Once there they must send orderlies back to the cookers, comfortably established in some farmyard and now making tea in their dixies with a powerful taste of stew. Tired men must manhandle those dixies back along the lane. With the arrival of the 'char' (the Hindustani word that has been used for tea since the days of Cromwell's Ironsides) life becomes bearable, and when the soldiers get their boots and puttees off and snuggle down in the straw with one or two candle-ends to light a barnful, they even begin to sing again—very sentimental songs:

> 'Take me over the sea,
>   Where the Allemans can't get at me.
>   Oh My! I don't want to die;
>   I want to go 'ome.'

Even this is not the end of the day. The men are routed out to wash and tend their feet, pricking blisters and rubbing in oil, before foot inspection by an officer. If a man goes lame through neglecting his feet he will be 'crimed' as certainly as if his rifle was dirty. And after foot inspection, if it is a lucky day, comes the rum issue. In a good regiment the rum, in its jars of earthenware, is always kept under the care of an officer and is given out, in strict allowance, only in his presence, '1/64th of a gallon per man, per day, perhaps.' The orderly officer visits all the billets in turn with a sergeant carrying the jar. Some men pour it into their tea, but most take their tot in an enamelled mug and toss it down with a 'Good health, sir'. It's strong enough to bring tears to a recruit's eye, and we think the less of the Navy who take their rum ration watered down into grog. Rum issue is a privileged occasion and no one minds that the end of the queue is singing a parody of that tear-jerking song of Gertie Gitana's:

> 'If the sergeant's pinched yer rum—never mind;
> If the sergeant's pinched yer rum—never mind;
> . He's entitled to his tot, but he's scoffed the bloody lot.
> Well, yer get yer bob a day—never mind.'

Rum, not every day. And if there is a combination of no rum ration, no soft bread, and no delivery of mail, the men will be near mutiny. It makes no difference. The orderly sergeant gives out tomorrow's orders which he has just got from headquarters; a sentry is mounted; and the billet sleeps. Tomorrow, the same again.

(ii) TRENCH KIT

Why do soldiers in all ages wear fantastic headgear? The Germans went to the war in helmets of black patent leather with brass spikes on top and brass spread-eagle badges in front. They called them *pickel-haubes* (spiky-tops), and must have set store by them, as they went on wearing them under grey canvas covers long after the war had ceased to look like a parade. No trophy was so highly valued as a *pickelhaube*, and proud was I when I captured one on the Somme; sorry, too, when I gave it to my girl-friend of the moment who didn't seem to care for it. About that time the Germans were moving into steel helmets, the coal-scuttle kind that fitted down over your ears, and there were no more spiky-tops to be seen in the trenches. The British went to the war in what used to be called, after a forgotten Secretary of State, Brodrick Caps, which had few merits except a peak in front to shade your eyes when shooting. They were stiff and uncomfortable, shook off or fell off if touched, and gave no protection to the back of your neck. It was soon discovered that their flat disc tops were conspicuous from the air and in the first war winter the soldiers learned to pull out the wire stiffeners, making the caps more comfortable and less easily observed. A soft cap became the mark of a front-line soldier and was imitated by those who wanted to cultivate a front-line look. Hatters in London obliged by producing floppy caps which you might dare to wear in the trenches, or out of the colonel's sight, or in London unless the provost-marshal pulled you up. Strict senior officers were horrified at this new vulgarity.

In those days overdressed young men were called by the curious slang name of 'Nuts', or, more oddly still, ' 'K'nuts', and the matinee idol Basil Hallam (who lost his life as a balloon observer over the Somme Battle) was the 'Kernel of the Nuts', as he used to declare in his song, 'Gilbert the Filbert'. I heard him sing it once during an air-raid at a camp concert in France, wearing clothes which made me sick with envy. He had just come off duty and was, so to speak, in khaki service-dress uniform but with a suit of so exquisite a cut and a colour-scheme so delicately varied from the official drab, that his clothes, somehow, did not resemble mine. He wore a hunting stock in a shade of pearl-grey, instead of a collar-and-tie, dove-coloured riding breeches, yellow 'chammy' gloves, puttees that were almost lemon-coloured and a floppy cap arranged over one ear. Good colonels strove to prevent the likes of me from imitating the likes of him. Though the other ranks could not vary their coloration as completely as the officers they could do a good deal with floppy hats. Every soldier was given—I should say was 'issued with'—a knitted 'cardigan', that is a sleeved waistcoat and an object called a cap-comforter, a knitted muffler which you could wear round your neck or compose into a sort of woollen turban, very comforting indeed when sleeping out in winter. Some men managed to give a jaunty air to a cap-comforter and to wear it night and day, unless positively obliged to put on the official service-dress cap. There were many private variants of the cap-comforter knitted by loving hands, particularly the 'Balaclava' (like the 'Cardigan' a survival from Crimean winters), a hood that pulled down over your ears and throat with a window in front to breathe and look through.

In those horse-riding days about one man in ten of even an infantry battalion was on a job that required horsemanship and therefore riding breeches, which favoured the well-made leg more than did the slacks worn by foot-sloggers. When wearing breeches you rolled your puttees downwards from the knee, fastening them with a tape round the ankle which, again, was thought more elegant than the marching soldier's method of rolling his puttees upwards from the ankle and concealing the tape under the knee, beneath the 'plus-four' turn-over of the loose trouser. Once a horseman always a horseman, and it was surprising how many soldiers managed to dress like cavaliers. Then there was the question of riding boots, about which martinets had strict opinions. The guns, the ammunition wagons, and the transport-wagons of the infantry were drawn by pairs, or fours, or sixes, of horses or mules, with a driver to each pair. He was, more properly, a ride-and-driver, like the postilion of the old mail-coach, riding one horse and leading the other, a job which needed heavy boots and a leg-guard on the near-side to save his leg from being crushed between the two beasts. Drivers' knee-high boots were much sought-after in the trenches though, from my experience, I never found them mud-proof. Nothing was! High boots have a fetishistic value that I cannot assess, and in 1915 trench boots were all the rage, transport-drivers' boots, if you could scrounge them, or hunting boots from England if you could afford them. I preferred marching boots and puttees, with rubber waders if it was wet enough and if they were to be had. Part of the ritual of regular trench warfare was the inventory of trench-stores, solemnly checked and handed over at every relief: so many picks and shovels, gas-blankets to screen dug-out doors, gongs to give warning of a gas attack, bombs and small arms ammunition, Very-pistols and flares, and so many pairs of 'Boots, gum, thigh', the heading under which they were indexed. It was part of the jargon to refer to military stores by their reversed titles: 'Coats, British Warm', and so on.

Pre-war military greatcoats were too long in the skirt for trench work. Officers, and mounted men, wore the short coats known as 'British Warms', which were in vogue on the North-West Frontier and which all who could acquired. A trench issue of the first winter was a long-haired sleeveless jerkin of goat-skin, much fancied by the dressy. They came in all colours like Laban's sheep and, while some were ring-straked, an occasional prize was all-white or all-black. In the second winter they were mostly replaced by jerkins of soft leather, but some connoisseurs preserved their hairy Robinson Crusoe goat-skins until the war's end.

When we came out of the line an eagerly awaited pleasure was a visit to the Divisional bath house. Platoon by platoon at intervals we marched, comfortably and unarmed, in 'clean fatigue dress'—that is without belts or puttees—to the village where it was established.

Everyone undressed, and forty naked men boiled themselves shrimp-pink under a hot shower, while their uniforms were put through the de-lousing machine which destroyed lice and their eggs by heat. Every man's flannel shirt and woollen underpants were reft away to be cast into the laundry in exchange for clean underpants and a shirt off the pile. It was Hobson's choice; take the next and be thankful, whatever the size and cut. Dirty and lousy though we often were, I think we were the cleanest army in history.

Shirts may be common property, but tunics are strongly individual. Soldiers of all countries are much addicted to distinguishing badges which no system of security overcomes. While higher authority suppresses numerals and crests which might reveal troop dispositions to an enemy spy, local pride replaces them with new distinguishing marks. The old regimental badges of the British Regular Army gave little information to the enemy, since the battalions of a regiment rarely served together (our Warwickshire Brigade being an exception). There were a dozen Divisions in which you might see the Warwick-shire Antelope or the 'Cat-and-cabbage' of the York and Lancasters. It was divisions, not regiments, that enemy Intelligence was searching for, and at an early stage divisions began to use signs meant to be secret, though surely not very secret, instead of numbers. Ours was a white diamond on a black ground.

Some divisions, some brigades, introduced coloured flashes and patches worn on the collar or shoulder-strap to identify units, or even companies within units, so that by the end of the war we were all considerably striped and spotted, another mark of the front-line soldier; not, however, with medal ribbons, which were not so widespread then as now. Middle-aged soldiers frequently wore the two South African ribbons and if they could put beside them one other Indian or African ribbon they counted as great campaigners. Your Divisional Commander might have five or six medals and even Haig or Kitchener no more than two rows. We rather despised the French and Italians for handing out campaign medals and minor decorations so liberally; that is, until towards the end of the war we began to do the same. The 1914 Star, awarded to soldiers who had fought in France in the first campaign, was rare enough to be highly regarded. Two new minor decorations were instituted in 1916. A man might put a blue chevron on his sleeve when he went on active service (red if before

1915) and might add another for each completed year overseas. Beneath the chevron he might place a stripe of gold braid if he had been wounded. Experts in the lore of the B.E.F. could make an accurate judgment of a man's fighting record by considering all the factors. Look at a man you meet on the leave-train: his cap-badge tells you he belongs to a good fighting regiment, but since he has four blue chevrons and no wound-stripe you may be confident he has a safe job down the line. His neighbour who has one chevron and two wound-stripes has had a very different war.

Steel helmets of the British type were tried experimentally by front-line units in the winter of 1915–16. Issued at first as trench-stores, they were handed over from sentry to sentry. Even in the Somme Battle they were still so scarce that they were eagerly collected from the corpses after an action. Helmets were popular with the troops, not only because they gave a sense of security but because the broad brim fended off the rain. With their round dish-shaped helmets, leather jerkins, and long boots British soldiers had a fifteenth-century look, and from helmets to body-armour seemed a natural step. Several styles of breast-plate were tried both by the Army and by amateurs. It was not uncommon in the trench-warfare days for us to make our own experiments. I once carried about a cuirass of stiffened fabric which was designed to stop shrapnel bullets, but got tired of it as I never seemed to be inside it when the sudden emergency came, and I couldn't wear it permanently. One of my friends was killed on 1st July 1916 while wearing a breastplate of light steel under his tunic. A shrapnel bullet struck him on the shoulder, driving a sliver of steel into his lung and thus converting what might have been a slight wound into a deadly one. Such fads as these belonged to the sedentary war of positions, when there was time to consider devices and gadgets which you discarded in more exacting days. Body-armour could not cover every vital spot and when advancing under fire I always felt a strong genetic urge to snatch the helmet off my head and hold it in front of another part of my person which might yet do more for humanity than my brains.

(iii) CENSORING LETTERS

In the evenings all officers had a task to do, whether in rest billets or in the line, the censoring of letters. At the base there was a staff of security officers who sampled all correspondence, destroying letters which revealed military secrets, blacking out indiscreet phrases, and occasionally taking steps to punish babblers. Assuming that every unit maintained its own security, the censors merely exercised a general supervision. Letters from the front, which travelled unstamped and post-free, were of three kinds. At critical times, when a movement was afoot that must at all costs be kept secret, no correspondence was allowed except by field postcards bearing a printed formula in which you struck out the sentences you did not want ('I am quite well', 'I am coming home on leave', 'I have been wounded', etc.). In very quiet times, as a privilege, a ration of 'green envelopes' was issued at the rate of one or even two a week. The writer signed a certificate on the green envelope that it contained no military secrets and it was then subject only to the selective censorship at the base. Between the stringency of the field postcard and the laxity of the green envelope, lay the common form of regimental censorship. Every ordinary letter had to bear the signature of an officer, who was then responsible if the base censors discovered a breach of security. Accordingly letters were read and countersigned by the company officers before they were despatched and, in retrospect, this seems one of the most intolerable intrusions into privacy that the military life demanded. It was also a great burden to the company officers to read a hundred ill-written letters every evening.

'Ill-written', I say, but I am inclined to think that in those days when the compulsory school-leaving age was twelve, and when almost all who attained to secondary education were officers, handwriting was better and composition no worse than among those who leave school at fourteen or fifteen today. I remember much calligraphy in good round 'copperplate', and many formal sentiments correctly expressed. ('I now take pen in hand to write this, hoping it finds you in the pink as it leaves me at present.') Illiterates were rare, and whatever may have been the faults of the old 'board schools', they did in fact teach 'the three Rs'.

Naturally enough, the knowledge that your letter would be read by your platoon commander put some restraint on your literary style, though not always. As we sat round the dugout table, reading piles of letters by the light of one candle-end, we got to know our men with a new intimacy, not because they opened their hearts in letters which would be so public, but because they revealed their characters. Whatever else, this sharing of privacy tightened the bond between officers and men. Of course, if there were no green envelopes and a reliable man came to me with a letter in which he wanted to be private, I would sign it unread. But if you were down at the base, a casual passer-by among thousands of others, censoring letters was no more than a tiresome fatigue, and submitting your letters to censorship by an indifferent stranger was a lesser indignity.

(iv) SEX-LIFE OF THE SOLDIER

When writing for readers in the nineteen-sixties there is one topic I dare not shirk, though for 1914 readers it would have been a topic I dared not face—the sexual conduct of the young soldier. In that period of fifty years the class-structure of English society (and when I say English I mean English) has been relaxed almost as essentially as the structure of taboos which once restrained the relation of the sexes and restrain them no longer. Throughout the solid core of English society, fifty years ago, there was one moral code for men and another for women. Propriety, decency, were the outworks and the safeguards of virtue for both sexes, but private lapses from the high standard maintained in public might be overlooked in men, whereas in women they were unpardonable. In the world where I was brought up, the female sex was permanently divided into two classes: those who 'did' and those who 'didn't'. It was assumed that the women one met in 'decent society' lived on a plane of such exalted virtue that the slightest allusion, however obscure or oblique, to the functions of the body was an insult; and it was equally assumed that elsewhere, on another plane, was a class of women who were not so ethereal and not so restricted in their conversation. It might be reprehensible for a man to consort with women of both classes on distinct occasions, but everyone knew it sometimes happened, and only the strait-laced would reject a man's acquaintance because he was known to be a libertine. On the other hand, no woman could move freely across the barrier; a single sexual lapse consigned her irrevocably to the class that 'one could not possibly meet in decent society'.

My friends in 1914 belonged to the professional middle class, the families of lawyers, doctors, clergy, schoolmasters, army officers, and the like. They went to the parish church on Sunday mornings, sent their children to public schools—sometimes to Oxford and Cambridge; they were emphatically, self-consciously 'gentry', dressed for dinner in the evenings or at least apologized for not doing so, and thought it impossible to live in a house without two resident maids, who wore caps and aprons, and were treated with patronizing benevolence. Everyone in this class seemed to be comfortably off, even prosperous, but few were rich and none very rich. Throughout three or four generations, from the era described by Jane Austen to the era described in its death-throes by John Betjeman, there was little change in their way of life, and for these hundred years they were the real governing class of England. They provided the bishops, the judges, the high civil servants, the generals, the admirals, the colonial governors, but not the millionaires whom they affected to despise as vulgar upstarts. At its top end, the professional middle-class shaded off into the aristocracy, which it imitated, envied, and slightly disapproved of. 'Society people', it was felt, were cosmopolitan and raffish, corrupted by money, and in danger of growing un-English. But it was hard to resist a glow of pride when they did ask you to dine, and so admitted your claim to gentility. The stratification downwards in the social scale was more rigid. An invisible barrier separated the professional from the commercial class. To be 'in trade' was a bar to admission into good society, with the exceptions, by whom made no one could say, that publishers, wine-merchants and one or two more varieties of salesmen were held to be presentable persons. Tradesmen were likely to be radical in politics and nonconformist in religion, and fortunately they could be recognized in a moment by their lack of a public-school accent.

At the beginning of the war officers were selected almost exclusively from the gentry, that is to say from the aristocracy and the professional class. By the end of the war the barrier between the professional and commercial classes had vanished, never to be restored. The 'temporary gentlemen' who became temporary officers in Kitchener's Army proved the worth of their grammar-school educations by revealing their talent for responsible leadership even though their accents were not refined. But I am discussing sexual conduct and here the taboos ran true through the whole middle section of the nation. The daughters of tradesmen, too, were put in moral purdah by their menfolk, and screened from contact with those other women who 'did'. If I had lived a little higher in the social scale I might have met promiscuous

L

groups in the fashionable world, but at seventeen I hardly knew that such groups existed. If lower, I think I should have found in the working class a healthier, more natural, approach to sexual conduct. What I have to offer is a single case-study with the suggestion, made after a varied life, that it was typical of Englishmen in the middle ranks of society.

Part of the attraction of soldiering was the unspoken assumption that on active service soldiers were released from the taboos of civil life. By accepting a new social discipline they passed into a world where property and life would no longer be sacred, where the reward of victory was—well, what was it? We no longer lived in an age when soldiers fought for plunder. They still fought for glory and, whatever else that might imply, it surely meant the favour of women. The stake was your own life; the cause was one for which you thought your life worth staking: the prize certainly was not wealth, but there must be a prize, and some women made part of it plain by offering white feathers to men who were not willing to take the risk. One of the oldest jokes that British soldiers make about themselves is to refute the accusation that they are 'brutal and licentious'. 'No inclination to be one and no opportunity to be the other', they say, and so the truth slips out.

Now I must return to my case-study, to this greenhorn of eighteen who wanted to be a soldier, and to fight in France, and to relish all the flavours of the military life. According to the custom of his generation and class, he had received no instruction of any kind from parents or teachers upon what are called the facts of life, nothing but a clear conviction that they must never be mentioned in the company of respectable women. Not that he was uninformed, in a way, since boys habitually instruct one another, in most societies as I suppose, by talking smut which conveys a confused and sullied impression of what sex is all about. A combination of the taboos which limited conversation in mixed society, and the vulgarities which seemed so amusing when the boys were segregated, meant that a sensitive young man was deeply frustrated in the company of girls. He had not much small talk and, since more than anything else he was interested in girls, it inhibited him to find that he had nothing to say to them. He was tongue-tied and shy. But, once a soldier, things would be different. Girls, he supposed, would be fascinated by a soldier and, in a measure, he found this to be true.

He cut a rather better figure with his girl cousins in uniform, and the assistant in the baker's shop at Sutton Coldfield, with whom he dutifully walked out on her free afternoons, was visibly impressed. All this was far removed from the licentious life of the traditional soldier, and she successfully repulsed his advances when he tried to proceed beyond a modest kiss. He got no farther in the path of lovemaking than, a year earlier when at teen-age parties—'flapper dances' they were vulgarly called in those days—he had once or twice kissed the daughter of some respectable neighbour in the conservatory.

For a soldier the taboos no longer existed. Nothing prevented an approach to the other world of the women who 'did', except a fastidious timidity. In France, as we well knew, there was a different system of taboos about sex, so that it was no surprise to find the town of Le Havre wide open. It had a red-light district with well-advertised brothels on two scales of payment, first-class for officers and second-class for other ranks. I have never discovered the official attitude of G.H.Q. towards licensed prostitution, which had been the subject of much controversy in late Victorian England. The impression I formed was that it was accepted as inevitable in the first years of the war but driven underground in the later, grimmer, days. It seemed to me—and this may be only a measure of my growing sophistication—that the luxury and glamour of the Rue des Galions as I saw it in the winter of 1915 had become drab and clandestine when I found myself again at the base three years later. While there were licensed brothels in all the towns of the back areas, where the French civil authorities retained control, I do not recall their existence in the forward zone, where the British Military Authority administered through officers known as 'town majors'. Since we were not an occupying army like the Germans, our status was hedged around, quite rightly, by the French local governments. (But it was not true, though the soldiers all said so, that they made us pay rent for the trenches.)

Front-line soldiers rarely got farther from their units than walking distance. The art of hitch-hiking (which in those days we called 'lorry-hopping') grew up rapidly during the war with the limitations that motor-lorries were still scarce and that they shuttled up and down between railhead and the forward units, which was not likely to be the way you wanted to go for fun. There was no regular leave for the day or for the week-end in France, so that visits to the towns were rare pleasures. Yet they occurred: occasionally, once or twice a year when you were out in rest, brigade might get the loan of a few lorries and run an excursion to Amiens or Boulogne, from which the lucky ones returned at midnight, not too drunk, and boasting of their sexual adventures. I remember the envy with which we heard of one brigadier who brought his brigade out of the Somme Battle, promising every man a day in Amiens and every officer a week-end in Paris, which was unheard-of liberality. Going on leave meant escaping from the man's to the woman's world and was described in terms of conventional ribaldry.

There were other methods of escape, for officers and sergeants mainly, but for technicians too, when detached for special duty or sent on courses of instruction. Walk to the transport; lorry-hop to rail-head; travel all day in a slow supply train that was side-tracked at every station to let priority traffic through; change trains and wait twelve hours for your connection; it was bad management if you could not dodge the column at some likely town, at least long enough for a good dinner. As soldiers were mostly sex-starved, th mere sight of a waitress was part of the delight. Amiens and Boulogne swarmed with prosti-tutes and semi-prostitutes, some of them refugee girls from the devastated area, and some the riff-raff that is always to be found at the heels of an army. They did not lack custom from men who had not seen a woman's face for months, with the consequence that venereal disease was endemic in the armies. Eighteen cases per thousand of the soldiers were admitted to hospital in 1917. Early Treatment Centres, at which instruction was given in the use of prophylactics and remedies, were instituted in the later part of the war.

Again, the comment must be made that the armies were so young. I think of Chaucer's Squire,

> 'A lover and a lusty bachelor . . .
> Of twenty year of age he was, I guess.
> And he had been some time in *chivachye*
> In Flanders, in Artois, and Picardie',

the three regions of the old front line. A large proportion of the soldiers were lusty bachelors, who lacked the grace to recognize that the hard-ships and deprivations they suffered were worse for the married men.

It happened by chance that I was one of four young officers who survived for more than six months together without a casualty, while our friends were being cut down left and right. Three of us were unmarried and could carry our burden with high spirits; the fourth (I'm glad to think he survived the war) was a newly married man, who spent every evening, whatever the danger or discomfort, writing a long letter to his wife, and I (God forgive me!) regarded him as a spoilsport for not joining in whatever pastime we had.

There were fastidious soldiers and strait-laced soldiers; there were faithful as well as unfaithful husbands; there were middle-aged men who regulated their conduct; but the popular line the Army followed, at every grade, was the pursuit of sex, on the rare days when opportunity offered. A compensation was found for sex-starvation in the recourse to bawdy jokes and rhymes, of which there was a never-failing supply. I rather think that young men nowadays are freer from this curious obsession.

In the forward zone there were few towns and those there were had few inhabitants. Ypres was completely evacuated, Arras was maintained by a handful of persistent residents, Albert was twice evacuated and reoccupied. So far as these towns survived, they were populated by soldiers making themselves at home in empty houses, while a few wretched shops and cafés hung on in the main streets to live on them. While the towns withered away, the countryside with its large scattered villages was kept under cultivation as near to the line as was safe. Rural France, like rural England, had been feudal with a *curé* to every church and a *seigneur* to almost every château. In these days brigade headquarters had taken over the château and only those peasants stayed on in the village who actually worked the land. While the young men were away in the Army, the heavy farming was done by old folk and young women, who crowded up into two or three rooms of their picturesque old houses, leaving the best bedroom for three or four British officers, the parlour for an officers' mess, and the farm offices for the sergeants. Soldiers slept on straw in the barns, cookhouses smoked in the farmyard, and mules were tethered in lines among the orchard trees. There might be two hundred men to the three or four women, who had stayed behind with great confidence in their own ability to look after themselves. I do not think that the males won easy victories in the sexual contest.

The village of Toutencourt, not far from Sir Douglas Haig's advanced headquarters, had about two hundred inhabitants, of whom five or six were buxom young peasant women, quite accustomed to grubbing up sugar-beet. Every month, a hundred sex-hungry officers descended upon Toutencourt to attend a refresher course at the Fifth Army Infantry School, and by the third day it was generally known that one of the five or six girls was remarkably pretty, a slim, black-eyed darling called Yvonne, with well-shaped hands and feet, and a *chic* that showed itself even through her working clothes. The rumour ran that she had been a parlourmaid in Paris before coming back to the farm. At least thirty officers a month, many of them more skilful hunters than the present writer, gave as much concentrated attention to the pursuit of Yvonne as they did to the study of tactics, yet I never heard that any of them got further than:

'*Bonjour, Mademoiselle Yvonne,*' to which she replied with a smile that wiped away the memory of the trenches:

'*Bonjour, Monsieur le Capitaine.*'

How grateful one was for that! But of Yvonne's real life I know nothing.

While we were waiting to go into one of the Passchendaele attacks, camping in the oakwoods of Vlamertinghe, another subaltern and I were given the unusual privilege of an evening off. We lorry-hopped down the main road to Poperinghe and were damnably bombed by low-flying German aircraft on the way. Poperinghe was a pleasant little market town, as it might be Ware or Stevenage, and already familiar to British soldiers when Chaucer mentioned it in the *Canterbury Tales*, a malting town set among hop-gardens. In 1917 it was packed with troops, using the clubs and canteens that had been fixed there for almost three years, as well as the billets through which they passed in succession week by week. We looked in at the famous soldiers' club called Talbot House ('Toc H') and were somewhat mystified by its masonic air of guarding a secret that we did not share; and we accomplished our intention of dining at La Poupée, not so much for the food, though it was good, as for the privilege of being served by the two pretty daughters of the landlady, almost the only Flemish girls left in the town. This I remember well but even better—pray don't misunderstand me—the beautiful female impersonator who sang and danced in the 'Red Roses', the concert-party of the 55th (Lancashire) Division.

These occasional raids into the territory of the other sex were distractions from the routine of an all-male society. As the intensity of war increased, absorbing more people more deeply in its soulless mechanism, the battle-zone from which all civilians were excluded spread wider, and the kindly processes of common life died away. When the Germans retreated to the Hindenburg Line they took the inhabitants with them and laid waste the country, leaving behind a wilderness as void as the Somme battlefield from which they had withdrawn. For the last two years of the war, half the British Army was living in the devastated area, an uninhabited prairie about as large as the county of Sussex, within which there was no activity other than military activity, and there were no women at all. Even the nurses were not allowed further forward than the casualty clearing stations at corps headquarters. (I have heard tell of a voluntary canteen worker who disguised herself as an officer and spent a night in the trenches, but that is another story.)

From February to June 1917 my battalion was in the devastated area, at first in the line in harsh conditions but later enjoying a sunny springtime in outpost positions, so quiet and rural that resilient young soldiers renewed their strength. Those who did not have the good fortune to go on leave or on a course during these five months never saw a street, a shop window, a civilian, or a woman of any class. I am now bound to ask myself the question, what was the character of our sex-life? I believe that hardships shared by men with a common purpose sublimate the sex-instinct, that *esprit de corps* provides a temporary substitute for a sexual urge which may reappear later. And from that assumption I must go on to ask whether there is a homosexual element in *esprit de corps*? Was there a tendency to reject the notion of women's society, to derive an emotional satisfaction from a world of men only?

This is a subject that it would have been impossible to mention, fifty or even thirty years ago, except in a scientific journal. To such a discussion I can offer only my own case-study—what I recall of my own experience. I was young and strong and, after all these years, I think I may admit that I was a handsome boy. No one, I'm sure, was more passionately devoted to his men, to the life of the regiment. In such circumstances we might have expected one of those emotional upsurges of homosexual conduct that occur in boarding schools and, I'm told, in ships. I remember no such thing. Racking my memory I can drag up one or two minor incidents which, to a maturer judgment, suggest sexual abnormalities. I never heard of the exposure of a scandal and I never found myself on the fringe of one of those secret rings of homosexuals, which one cannot overlook in the city-life of the nineteen-sixties. Such phenomena may have appeared in the British armies as they did, I think, in the German armies and, certainly, in the Turkish armies, but not within my range of observation. I must, however, relate, if I am to be honest, a change in my own mental make-up towards the end of the war.

I can describe this best in relation to 'Blighty' leave. In every unit in France an almost sacred document was the leave-roster arranged in priority in two columns, for officers and other ranks. My turn came round four times, which was twice what I should have got if I had been a private soldier.

When first I came back on leave in April 1916 I happily resumed my family life like a schoolboy home for the holidays. By my third leave, in July 1917, my uncle was no longer at the Hampshire vicarage which I thought of as my English home, and my cousins had dispersed to war work or war marriages. I spent this leave mostly racketing round theatres and restaurants with soldier friends in London where—so far as I could see—the old taboos still prevailed. No doubt the social disruption of wartime had encouraged promiscuity, but not in my quiet circle of friends. 'Women who did' were still sharply divided from 'women who didn't'. The change had taken place in me, not in them, with the consequence that I found myself leading a double life. The quiet respectability of my family with its unaltered moral standards could in no way be related to the all-male society of the regiment, with its acceptance of death and bloodshed as commonplace events, and its uninhibited approach to women. If this estrangement touched me, who had no experience of love, what must it have meant to happily married men? Leave periods late in the war could bring misunderstandings even to lovers. Life in England in 1918 I shall reserve for a later chapter'

(v) MILITARY LAW

A time-honoured ritual of the Old Army was the annual reading on parade of those sections of the Army Act which imposed a code of military law upon serving soldiers. Martial law, superseding the common law of England, was never enforced during the First World War and soldiers remained citizens, with the privileges and obligations of other British subjects, except that certain military crimes and misdemeanours prescribed in the Act were punishable by process of military discipline. Soldiers were British subjects with additional obligations and with no compensating privileges or exemptions. Accordingly, the British military code was exacting, and by the letter of the law more severe than that of the French or German armies. On the other hand, British commanders were also subject to the ordinary processes of law and had no authority beyond what was conveyed to them by the Army Act. It would have been inconceivable for a British general to execute spies or mutineers by his own summary authority, as French generals seem to have done, much less to order the execution of hostages as many German generals did. The process of British military law was slow and formal and strictly prescribed by the King's Regulations, so as to carry out the provisions of the Army Act, a very old-fashioned statute, expressed in the sonorous language of the eighteenth century!

'Every person subject to military law who, on active service, commits any of the following offences, that is to say: By discharging firearms, drawing swords, beating drums, making signals, using words, or by any means whatever intentionally occasions false alarms in action, or treacherously makes known the watchword or countersign shall, on conviction by court martial, be liable to suffer death, or such less punishment as is in this Act mentioned.'

Such picturesque phrases as these, when read aloud on parade, were likely to provoke ill-concealed laughter in the rear ranks, which was not to be construed as implying that the provisions of the Act were anything but deadly serious.

Let us look at the pains and penalties of military discipline from their milder beginnings. Every day when routine permitted, the company commander held his conference, usually known as company orders. Here he interviewed the sergeant-major, sent for N.C.O.s or men to whom he wished to give special instructions, received men who wanted advice, heard complaints, and held a court for dealing with misdemeanours. The first threat to an offending soldier was: 'Take his name. Put him on a charge. Bring him up to company orders!' To be unpunctual, unshaven, idle, neglectful, insolent—or, worse than that, to have a dirty rifle, brought you hatless—which was the sign of military disgrace—before the company commander's table, with your sergeant giving evidence against you. In England the normal punishment for minor offences was confinement to barracks (CB), but in France anywhere near the front you were confined already. There was little the company commander could do except give you the rough side of his tongue and tell the sergeant-major to find some fatigues for you. There were always some dirty or unpleasant jobs to be done by somebody and it was convenient to allot them to the 'defaulters'. The severe punishments that your captain could inflict were to make an entry in your conduct-sheet which stood as a black mark against you for the rest of your military life, or to remand you for C.O.'s orders, an alarming prospect, for the colonel had formidable powers. He could take away acting rank or privilege, he could impose stoppages of pay, and he could inflict the humiliating penalty of field punishment for as long as twenty-eight days.

In its aggravated form 'Field Punishment, Number One' was a relic of older, more barbarous times and was already looked on with disfavour by military reformers. When inflicted by old-fashioned disciplinarians it could be brutal, as many old soldiers will recall; in a well-ordered unit with a good-natured sergeant-major, the degrading features might be much diminished. Fifty years ago the retributive element in penal sentences was more generally accepted as socially necessary than it is today, and in the services the old custom of making a public example of the offender was regarded as normal. The Germans massacred hostages in order to create a moral effect on other civilians. We shot one of our own men now and then, by due process of law, in order to encourage the others. But I have not yet come to that. Soldiers condemned to field punishment were publicly humiliated, as a warning. For a beginning they were obliged to do all their military duties in the front line or out of it, under observation and, on coming off parade, were at once taken in charge by the regimental police. They were on call at any time for such dirty or dangerous fatigues as should come up, and were deprived of all privileges, such as green envelopes and the rum ration. They slept under guard, their pay was forfeited; and worst of all, their names were put down to the bottom of the leave-roster.

None of these inflictions gave one half the humiliation that came from the punishment often called 'crucifixion'. A man under field punishment was publicly exposed for an hour or two hours a day, with his hands behind his back handcuffed to a wagon-wheel; or that is how I have seen it done. I have heard tales of more cruel methods, when men were actually spreadeagled against a grating with their wrists and ankles made fast. This I never saw in the Army, though I have known a merchant captain punish mutineers at sea by spread-eagling them on the upper deck in a storm. The survival of 'crucifixion' to so recent a time reminds us that the agitation against corporal punishment and against the punishment of death is modern. I am writing of what happened fifty years ago, and I could then discuss such questions with men, no older than I am now, who thought in terms of what happened one hundred years ago. In the year 1864 hangings were still public; soldiers and sailors were flogged for service offences until their backs were bloody; minor misdemeanants were set in the stocks. I have spoken to old soldiers who remembered the days of military flogging, and 'Field Punishment, Number One' comes midway between the penal codes of those days and these. The sentence was not given except for a serious military offence, such as a neglect of duty that endangered the line, and on this notion of military crime and punishment I shall have a further observation to make.

Very serious offences were sent to a field general court martial which was convened when necessary by the brigadier. All officers expected to sit on a court martial occasionally and my turn came perhaps twelve or fifteen times, often with two or three cases to try. The proceedings, all taken down in long-hand, were scrupulously formal and deliberate. On active service the court consisted of a major, a captain, and a lieutenant, unless a prisoner of higher rank required a court of senior officers. Usually the adjutant of the prisoner's unit acted as prosecutor, and the prisoner, who was entitled to the aid of counsel if it were available (which it rarely was on active service), brought an adviser into court, often one of his company officers, as 'prisoner's friend'. The rules of evidence were strictly enforced and the prisoner's interest was protected by the same provisions as at common law. When the case was concluded, the prisoner was withdrawn and the court considered its verdict, the junior member giving his opinion first, no small responsibility for a subaltern of nineteen when a death-sentence was involved. If the prisoner was acquitted he was at once released; if found guilty he was detained in custody until the sentence was confirmed by the convening authority, which meant a delay of two or three weeks. Court-martial proceedings were referred to the Judge Advocate General, the legal adviser to the Army Commander, who scrutinized and, not infrequently, quashed them for some technical irregularity on a point of law.

A man might be court-martialled for any crime committed on active service, not only for a military offence. I have sat on a court which tried a man for murder, and I'm glad to say we brought it in as manslaughter. I have tried a man for striking his superior officer, which might have led to a death-sentence had we not ourselves stopped the proceedings on a technicality. A large number of field general courts martial sat to try military crimes which would be no crime at common law, and imposed sentences which seem shocking in retrospect. When under instruction, young officers were taught that in the conduct of proceedings the first duty of the court was to ensure that the prisoner had every advantage to which he was legally entitled, that every member of the court was to consider himself the prisoner's friend; but that the prerogative of mercy was no concern of theirs. The court should not hesitate to pronounce a heavy sentence if the case was proved; and there were many military crimes for which the normal penalty was death.

A memory that disturbs me when I look back on it is the hint or warning that came down from above, now and then, that morale needed a sharp jolt, that a few severe sentences might have a good effect. It was expedient that some man who deserted his post under fire should die to encourage the others. Sometimes discipline would be screwed up a couple of turns; death-sentences would be confirmed and executed; and at the colonel's level, field punishment would be rather lavishly imposed and harshly administered.

The military executions in France, few indeed when compared with the dreadful daily death-roll, gave a shock which seems to have increased its effect with time. They exercise a fascination which horrifies the writers of war-books, as if they had been a major factor in building up the war neurosis. A well-known evangelical bishop once described to me how, as a young chaplain, he had interviewed a deserter on the night before his execution, and had persuaded him to take his fate like a hero who now had the opportunity to die for his comrades. I could not quite accept this thesis but, I thought, in the insane morality of war, what difference is there between sacrificing a man by sending him out on patrol, 'to draw fire', and sacrificing him to a firing-party for the good of the general morale. Either may be no more than a wasted life even in the arithmetic of attrition. The competent military authority may or may not get the desired result.

No less than 3,080 death-sentences were pronounced by British courts martial during the First World War, but only 346 of the sentences were carried out, 322 of them in France or Flanders. Out of this number three officers and 291 other ranks were British soldiers. By far the largest number, 240, were condemned for deserting their posts under fire and of these forty were second offenders. Fifteen out of the 291, including one officer, were executed for murder, which we may assume was something like the normal homicide rate. Twenty-five civilians were executed in the United Kingdom for military offences.

Three hundred and twenty-two military executions meant that about once a week during the war a notice was read out on parade that an unnamed soldier had been shot for desertion or for cowardice.[1] Nine times as many men were sentenced but reprieved. At the beginning of the war death-sentences were often commuted to terms of imprisonment which served no purpose except to gratify the wretched victims, whose act of desertion thus achieved its object. When Haig became C.-in-C. he released the prisoners on ticket-of-leave, sending them back to their units to try again. Thereafter, when death-sentences were commuted, it was often for a long term of field punishment. It was once my duty to promulgate the sentence of a court on three deserters, on parade, in a hollow square of soldiers. 'The sentence of the court was that the accused should suffer—death!... Commuted by the Army Commander to three months' field punishment.' No one was supposed to know of the Army Commander's mercy until it was announced, but I think they knew.

Executions were carried out in a private place, but in front of a witnessing party from the victim's unit, who saw him tied to a post, blindfolded, and shot by twelve men chosen at random from another regiment. The death was recorded simply as a casualty on active service.

1. In the quietest times the weekly death-rate never fell below 2,000 and over the whole war averaged about 4,000.

(vi) TACTICS

We were much concerned with tactics in the spring of 1917, and after our month of open fighting we gave ourselves credit for knowing a thing or two in the 48th Division. During the eighteen months of trench warfare, when battles had been conducted like sieges, much heresy had been preached and almost everyone had lapsed into heretical practices. All that was now discredited and we, at least, believed that salvation would come from the pure doctrine of the pre-war Field Service Regulations. We had been among the first to revert to the orthodox principle of holding our front with only a few well-sited posts, and we had noticed that on 1st July the Kensingtons, who held a continuous front, lost three times as many men as we did. Defence in depth was our rule and we never in the war lost a trench without regaining it by an immediate counter-attack. This implied fighting with rifle and bayonet over the top, not with bomb and bayonet along the trench, and before the end of the Somme Battle we had rejected the 1915 love of trench-fighting. It was my experience, after four bombing operations, that bomb and bayonet rarely got you anywhere. The chief exponents of trench-fighting were the instructors at the 'Bull-rings', the assault-courses in the Base Camps at Etaples, Le Havre and Rouen.

We used one type of bomb only, to replace the suicidal home-made jam-tin grenades of the first winter. The Mills grenade, the size and shape of a large grape-fruit, could be bowled like a full-pitched cricket-ball, with a range of thirty yards. A strong man might reach forty yards, the length of two cricket pitches and, out of the line, the nation of cricketers rather enjoyed their sessions of bowling practice. Holding the bomb with a firm grip in your right hand, you pulled out the safety pin with your left, and were then committed, since it was difficult to put the pin back. As you threw, by releasing your hand-hold, you allowed a lever to fly up which ignited the fuse. The bomb burst three and a half seconds later, at a safe distance from you, or so you hoped. It was a killing bomb which broke up into black slugs of iron the size and shape of sugar-lumps. I have had a Mills bomb picked up and thrown back at me, by a German who was either a very brave and quick or a very foolish man.

Their stick-bomb was a different article, a round tin of explosive mounted on a handle like that of a tennis racket and ignited by pulling a loop of string. It was thrown, not bowled, to a longer range than our Mills bomb, with less accuracy and with much less killing-power when it arrived, though it made a loud intimidating noise. It was safe and easy to operate but large and clumsy, and the Boches were denied the advantage we had of tucking a Mills bomb into a side-pocket where you could forget about it till it was wanted.

A neat pattern of drill for bombing parties was devised in 1915 and was not to be rejected because, like all forms of battle-drill it omitted to tell you what to do in the hideous crisis of a bomb-fight which was determined in a few seconds of panic. At the moment of truth what matters in a battle is to produce men who will fight, not men who hold a certificate for proficiency in a sham fight, and the best bomber I ever saw in action was a rather loutish corporal who failed in the simplest test at bombing practice, out of the line. If you had the right men, and time to organize them, and if they were up to it, you started your bombing party along the trench in single file: two bayonet-men, two bomb-throwers, officer with a periscope, and then a tail of under-studies and bomb-carriers. When you find the enemy behind a traverse, the throwers throw, the bayonet-men dash forward, and every-one moves up by the length of one firebay. So you bomb your way along from traverse to traverse.

The weakness of this system is that it makes no provision for what you do when the Boche lands two or three bombs in the midst of you. There may be a second, or at most two seconds, for action. Very rash to run forward when you don't know what is round the corner and have no time to clear a path by throwing your own bomb; so you run back. Then everyone runs and you're at your starting-point again. Very cautiously they creep up on you. This time you're ready and land two or three bombs in the midst of them, whereupon they run back. You can go on playing this game of alarums and excursions all the afternoon if your nerve will stand it, losing a man or two at every rally. All depends on anchoring your little force to a good 'bomb-stop'. Choose a place in the trench where by digging you can plant a Lewis gun or two riflemen to shoot down a straight length, behind a barricade with some sort of overhead cover. Then you can dispense with bombs and bombers, and can hold your trench with rifle-fire. No use, as I thought, for attack or defence, a Mills bomb was a handy weapon for mopping up a captured trench or to give you aid and comfort on patrol. The Germans were more devoted to the cult of the hand-grenade than we were and, even at Passchendaele, I have had a stick-bomb thrown at me in the open. Their rank and file never reached the proficiency of ours with rifle and bayonet; indeed, though I have several times confronted German soldiers carrying bomb or rifle, I never remember seeing a German with his bayonet fixed.[1]

British soldiers, and sometimes their officers too, went into action with the short rifle and long sword-bayonet, a more formidable weapon than the little spike which our soldiers fit on their rifles to day. The *arme blanche* is carried chiefly for moral effect, as even the French tacticians knew in 1914. It is the appearance of a bayonet-charge, resolutely delivered, that gives it decisive force. Rare indeed are the soldiers who will face it and I have always doubted whether our pictures of lines of men standing fast to hack and thrust at one another in the Middle Ages had any reality. When the charge is driven home, one side or the other will break and most of those killed by the bayonet have their wounds behind. In the 1914 War the sword-bayonet was an essential part of our armament even though the deaths it inflicted were few. I never knew the enemy to stand if your men with their long gleaming blades could get to charging distance. Again, the sword-bayonet gave confidence to the man who carried it, out of the line as well as in the line. In civil troubles soldiers felt secure, and imposed respect, by carrying side-arms. A big knife, which would be called a *panga* in East Africa, can be used for many purposes as well as for chopping wood.

Our infantry tactics in 1917, putting the Mills bomb aside as a secondary weapon, depended on the rifleman and the Lewis light auto-matic gun. We were always told that its English inventor, having failed to sell it to the War Office before the war, had sold it to the Belgians who let us have it in 1914. I learned the rudiments of its management at Bordon Camp where we had one precious specimen in July 1915. Since the contracts for heavy machine-guns had broken down, the infantry battalions were to be supplied with Lewis automatics, at the old rate of two per battalion, while the heavy machine-guns were to be brigaded, as a Machine Gun Corps (best known to the present generation, perhaps,

1. But one of my N.C.O.s, Lance-Corporal Phillips, with only a bomb in his hand, was charged by a German bayonet man. Using the technique of unarmed combat he fended off the blade with his bare hand and killed his man.

by its elegant memorial at Hyde Park Corner). When I got to France in December 1915, our battalion had just received two Lewis guns and didn't know what to do with them. Thus I found myself regarded as an expert, was appointed the Battalion Lewis Gun Officer and, I suppose, became about as expert as any other amateur finding out for himself how to use a new machine. It was an ingenious toy which you could take to pieces and put together again in two minutes, and which never gave serious trouble except from wet dirt—of which there was no lack on the battlefields. What puzzled us was the ammunition supply, made up in circular pans holding fifty rounds, which were difficult to re-fill and devilish heavy to carry about. Put a pan on the gun, press the trigger, and brrrrr . . . it was empty in five or six seconds. One man fired the gun and four or five tried to keep it fed. A commonplace experience in battle was to get your gun to a position where you could shoot to some purpose, only to find that the unfortunates toiling with the canvas buckets in which the pans were carried had fallen behind or had let the ammunition get muddy. Lewis-gunners spent long hours unloading pans, cleaning the cartridges, and re-loading; and I spent long hours instructing in these mechanical mysteries. The guns multiplied until by the summer of 1917 we had sixteen to the battalion, one for each platoon, and there was even a time, our strength being very low, when I put every man in the battalion through a Lewis-gun course. The light automatic, we thought, was the weapon of the future and the heavy machine-guns, to which the Germans were faithful, ceased to intimidate us. I have seen my company commander (Major A. S. Alabaster) engage a machine-gun with his single rifle, and silence it by accurate shooting.

The tactics, which good divisions had worked out for themselves after the Somme fighting, explain why the Battle of Arras was never regarded with the same gloomy horror. At my level the principles we accepted as relevant to our own experience were flexibility and depth. In defence, we sited our posts in chequer-board patterns to support one another with crossfire; in the attack we manœuvred, not in lines but in groups arranged in diamond formation. Each platoon with its own Lewis-gun section was a tactical unit which could provide covering fire for its own movements and could change front to act in any direction. Instead of continuous trench lines we now dug 'cruciform posts' with a section in each arm of the cross for all-round defence. The

M

system was codified and rationalized in simple well-written pamphlets, the work, I believe, of a young staff officer named Liddell Hart. It tallied very well with our experience and, in fact, I thought I understood it rather better than the instructors at Toutencourt, where I was a restless insubordinate student.

(vii) MANPOWER[1]

The greatest number of mouths fed in the British armies in France, as far as the published figures show, was 2,077,000 in December 1917, of whom 1,678,000 had been recruited in the United Kingdom and the others in the Empire overseas. There were also with the armies 360,000 horses and 80,000 mules. Nothing much can be derived from the crude totals except the consideration that Haig, in addition to his other duties, was responsible for a population much larger than that of Liverpool and Manchester added together. While all were subject to military law, by no means all were soldiers, and a first rough classification distinguishes them as about 1,250,000 combatants and 750,000 non-combatants, the latter class including nurses, the Women's Auxiliary Army Corps (introduced in 1917), the Royal Army Medical Corps, various welfare workers, and a great and growing force of unarmed labourers, some of them Asians and Africans. Many deductions must also be made from the gross figure of combatants before a real account can be given of the number available to fight on any one day. In normal times 5,000 men were despatched to Britain every day for a fortnight's leave, with the consequence that the effective strength was always less by 70,000 than the nominal strength. An incalculable number, much higher in the winter months, were at all times absent, lightly wounded, sick, or convalescent, but not so thoroughly invalided as to be sent home and 'struck off the strength'. All the safe secluded areas of the war zone were populated with rest camps, schools of instruction, technical departments, and experimental stations, which proliferated as the war intensified, and all these establishments were manned from the fighting units. Every battalion had men on the nominal roll who resided permanently at G.H.Q. as clerks, at the army school as instructors, at the divisional concert-party as

1. All figures, unless otherwise authenticated, are from *Statistics of the Military Effort of the British Empire . . . 1914–1920* (War Office, H.M.S.O., 1922).

entertainers, or what not, but were never available for duty in the line. While strict administration always implied a necessity to comb out the back areas and to return superfluous trench-dodgers to regimental duty, it will not be supposed that such efforts succeeded. Human beings are skilful at hiding themselves away in crannies where they can avoid unpleasantness, soldiers not less than other men, and four years' campaigning with little movement enabled many hermit crabs to ensconce themselves in comfortable retreats, so numerous and various that they do not allow statistical analysis, but may be better described fictionally.

Look, now, at jolly old Colonel Falstaff who commands our Infantry Base Depot, so familiar with the young officers in the mess, especially with the ones who pay for his glass of dry sherry, and not quite so popular with Privates Shadow and Wart who are pushed into the draft to make up the number, whatever their condition. The colonel already has the new-fangled C.B.E. ribbon on his chest and is playing for a 'K.' at the end of the war, if only he can be made Base Commandant and a major-general, if only his credit with the grand friends he talks about is as secure as he pretends it is. A better soldier is that sardonic Major Jago with his well-earned D.S.O. from the Battle of the Aisne, a disappointed man whom one would expect to have got a higher place than Camp Commandant at corps headquarters, especially as he has the general's ear. On the make in some other direction, you feel sure, he has business with French civilians and is up to something—you can't say what—with the *sous-prefet*'s wife. The town major of Miraucourt,[1] Captain Pistol is a simpler type, with a posh super-regimental style that no one believes in, not even himself. With his puce riding-breeches, though he never mounts a horse, and the loaded revolver which he wears twenty miles behind the line, and his big talk about Spion Kop and Colenso, though everyone knows that in that war he had been town major of Stellenbosch, he aims lower than Major Jago and is content to maintain a sleeping partnership with the landlady at the *estaminet*, where he can sometimes persuade the company to listen to his brag. One who is not impressed by the town major's talk is young Mr. Poins, a colourless fellow with no advantage except that of being an old Etonian, which hardly seems to justify his selection as bearleader to the Prince of Wales. Bardolph, the Canteen Sergeant, has other ways of making life worth while in the back areas, but must have

1. With apologies to Mr. J. B. Priestley.

been more than regularly drunk when he was caught in the *mont-de-piété* at Abbeville trying to flog the communion plate that he had pinched from the Chaplain-General. Corporal Nym knows better than that. A man of few words, he looks so impressive that no one notices he is bone-idle and still draws pay as storeman in charge of an ammunition dump that was emptied nine months ago. It will be a ruthless comb-out that gets him back to duty.

The 1,250,000 combatants, so-called, were disposed in sixty infantry divisions, each with an establishment of about 18,000 men, and three cavalry divisions of smaller size, under the umbrellas of eighteen corps H.Q.s, five army H.Q.s, G.H.Q. and the line of communications. A division should have mustered 12,000 infantrymen and 3,000 artillerymen if up to strength, as well as Engineers, Army Service Corps, and Army Medical Corps. I have already mentioned that in January 1918 the establishment of infantry divisions was cut by one quarter because of the shortage of men. In my experience, certainly in the territorial units, battalions had never been up to strength since first they arrived in France. Drafts of new men from the base camps always lagged far behind losses in battle, and the nominal strength bore little relation to the actual fighting strength because of the large numbers of men 'on detachment', that is to say posted away to special duties. Long before Sir Douglas Haig reduced the number of battalions in each division from thirteen to ten, I had been obliged to reduce the number of sections in my company from sixteen to twelve. When we moved into battle our strength, after 1916, was further reduced by a cadre of 10 per cent of each rank, held back to reconstitute the battalion if it should be destroyed.

Even to estimate the manpower of the B.E.F. by divisions is inadequate because, as the war grew more mechanized, the effective fighting strength became dependent on tanks, heavy guns and aircraft which were not allotted to divisions but to corps or army headquarters. The elaboration of the army system always took the form of drawing men back from the fighting front into the essential but often non-combatant duties behind the line. The shortage was in front where, in March 1918, the infantry battalions were 10 per cent below strength even on the reduced establishment. It was by juggling with gross figures of combatants and non-combatants, soldiers actually with fighting units and soldiers in administrative posts behind the lines, that Lloyd

George persuaded the House of Commons to accept his assurances of the strength of the Armies.

The quality of the troops was no less vital than their quantity in gross numbers. Demands from the fighting units upon the base depots had an effect which has not been much noticed. Requirements were sometimes met by despatching up the line convalescents not yet fit for hard service and men of low medical category who ought to have been kept at light duty. From the middle of the war onwards we were plagued with recruits who could never become efficient front-line soldiers, and we had to use some ingenuity in getting rid of them. My Colonel Sladen solved one such problem in his own way. We had three men with whom nothing could be done; one mentally deficient, another with such an impediment in his speech as to be almost dumb, and the third a foreigner, a Danish volunteer who could not speak English. The third was the most difficult since his platoon were convinced that he was a German spy and threatened mutiny if put on trench duty with him. On the day before a battle we sent for the three men and ordered them to proceed by train to the base at Havre. We put the dumb man in charge of the party because he could not explain himself, and we handed him an impressive envelope, sealed but empty, addressed to the Base Commandant. With these non-instructions they departed out of our life and we never heard of them again. The confusion of next day's battle hid their traces.

Statistics of battle losses, which at first sight seem straightforward, are remarkably elusive. Most popular writers on the First World War make use of the tables of comparative losses given by Sir Winston Churchill in his classic work, *The World Crisis*. While I acknowledge the superlative merit of this book, which is worthy to stand beside Clarendon or *Thucydides*, it is necessary to add that these comparative tables have been completely demolished by later research, notably by the work of Sir Charles Oman, so that careful students will be well-advised to use the very different figures given, with caution and with many reservations, by the official historian. When Churchill wrote, he used the information then available, comparing accurate figures analytically arranged by the British War Office with round figures put out by the German propaganda during the War, a genuine maximum compared with an unreliable minimum. No analysis like that issued by the War Office has ever been made of the German losses. In their published tables there are many gaps and where it has been possible to examine the actual losses of particular units they usually present a figure much larger than is indicated by the propaganda totals. Several discrepancies in the mode of calculation make direct comparison impossible, one being that the British figures include all lightly wounded men who received first-aid treatment at the dressing-stations, while the German figures record only severely wounded men who were detained in hospital.

In a battle on the Western Front it was unlikely that an attacking formation would confront a similar defending formation, since one of the commonplaces of tactics is that the joint between two armies is the weak spot. As a rule, one army attacks part of two, while a diversion is often made by a neighbouring army on a flank. It is rare for the whole force of an army to be engaged in battle on one day. At the end of the day's fighting every unit reports its casualties, often a rough estimate including numbers of men reported 'missing' which may mean dead, or wounded and taken prisoner, or unwounded and taken prisoner, or merely lost and likely to rejoin in a day or two. Long before these figures can be corrected, the reports of all the units will have been collated, at brigade, division, and corps, together with the routine reports from other units which have not been in the main action, and may have been issued to the Press as a rough estimate covering the whole army front, though a part only of the front was fought over. A similar process went on behind the German lines, but for a different frontage and perhaps for a different period of time. To estimate the relative losses in the battle by comparing these two gross figures is wholly unreal. The only way to compare the figures is to identify troops who were actually engaged and to tabulate their corrected casualties. I have elaborated this point merely to demonstrate the complexity of the problem and to warn readers against too ready an acceptance of alarming totals. The war—heaven knows—produced its spectacular massacres, like the French Battle of the Frontiers in August 1914 and like the first day of the Battle of the Somme. In the long run, the heaviest losses were inflicted day by day and week by week in the battles of attrition, and it was the stubborn German counter-attacks that cost them the highest price.

(viii) THE ETHICS OF SCROUNGING

To be a soldier on active service means to reject the sanctity of life and property. Your end in battle is to compel your enemy to submit and if you succeed his body and his possessions are at your disposal. Though in the heart of a fight he may throw down his weapons and ask for mercy, if he leaves that moment of surrender too late he is likely to be bayoneted in hot blood. No soldier can claim a right to 'quarter' if he fights to the extremity. But if in a lull of the battle the enemy show a white flag, and come out of their firing positions, unarmed, with raised hands, crying out *Kamarad, Kamarad*—the German slogan of surrender in the First World War—then by the conventional Law of Arms they are entitled to mercy. Their lives and personal property are no longer forfeit.

In the heat of the battle quarter may be refused, weapons may be taken from the enemy and used against their comrades. The captors may live on enemy rations, make free with their comforts, and seize badges, crests, helmets as trophies. I knew an officer who in every action, or so he said, began by seizing a German Mauser rifle, which—oddly enough—he preferred to ours; and I long coveted and at last won a German officer's pistol. In attacks we lived on captured food, drank German brandy, if we could find it, slept in German blankets, but there was rarely any loot to be had of greater value. Men did not bring jewelry or negotiable securities into the trenches. Further back, when the disconsolate bands of *'Kamarads'* were shepherded to some collecting point, they were systematically 'frisked' for concealed weapons, or for papers that might be useful to the Intelligence. At this stage, as everyone well knew, the unscrupulous might also deprive them of their wrist-watches and petty cash. Such things will be, after a famous victory, but we should have scorned to behave so in the front line. And we were otherwise employed.

There was little opportunity for systematic looting on the Western Front, except in 1914 when the Germans had opportunities which they did not neglect. Real looting occurs in a rapid advance when whole populations abandon their homes and civil authority breaks down. Movement in the First World War was usually so slow that towns were not captured until they had been evacuated and destroyed. In the Second World War the tempo was so much faster that most soldiers, on one occasion or another, found themselves moving into half-empty cities and deserted farms, where the people had merely fled and had left their belongings unguarded. Everyone could tell tales of looting in 1940 and again in 1944, when the conventional picture of warfare was displayed. Where does a commonly honest man draw the line? You seize a château to 'put it in a state of defence' by knocking holes in the walls, by digging trenches across the tennis-court, by barricading windows with mattresses, by piling the furniture in barricades. When you are hungry and thirsty, are you to leave the food in the pantry and the wine in the cellar? When the order comes to retire, are you to relinquish Milord's cash-box and Milady's jewels for the Germans who will be there in half an hour? Ask yourself what you would do. Horses and fodder in the First War, automobiles and petrol in the Second, were fair game if you could find them. But what is a hard-shelled forager to make of bulkier treasures? What could we do with the dinner service of magnificent Sèvres porcelain which we found hidden in a village pond! Or the folio first edition of Molière in that villa at Peronne? Too heavy to carry, they remained, the china to be broken piece by piece in some company mess, and the folio pages to be used for lighting fires.

In short, there was little looting in the First World War. On the other hand there was a vast amount of 'scrounging' which implied a local code of ethics. To be 'on the make', to 'win' more than you were entitled to, was in some strange sense a meritorious form of conduct, but only on condition that it was socially directed. A man who stole rations of rum, or—worst of all—the contents of a private food parcel —from his own section was lucky if not severely beaten up. In no respect did the small-scale *esprit de corps* of each section or platoon operate more strongly than in the ethics of scrounging. The further away from your own group your victim belonged, the less was the moral blame attaching to your theft; with the extreme case that to deprive the enemy of any form of property was positively virtuous; and to acquire some trifling luxury or convenience for your group excused any minor delinquency. To steal a bottle of rum from the company that relieved you in the trenches might be thought rather near the limit of decent behaviour, but a bottle lifted off the dump at divisional railhead was a famous achievement.

At the end of my random recollections I pause to consider how little

they tell of a soldier's life in France. I have said nothing of the villages
with their impoverished shops that sold nothing but greetings cards and
bars of chocolate, the estaminets with their 'van-blong' and fried
potatoes; of the soldier's jargon, half kitchen-French and half kitchen-
Hindustani; of the quarter-master's stores and the Expeditionary Forc-
Canteen which between them could furnish most of the wants of a
simple life; of the endless games of 'Housey-housey', which is now
called Bingo; of the concert-parties (now made more familiar by Joan
Littlewood's musical play, *Oh What a Lovely War*) with their privileged
place as recognised jesters and their treacly sentiment that satisfied
another mood; of church parade conducted most seriously before the
whole brigade in hollow square, and the communion administered
after the service to a devout group in the corner of a field; of long lazy
afternoons in summer to offset against the wintry nights on working-
party; of the timeless quality of army life which knew neither hours
nor weeks but only such periods as next spring offensive, or when we
go out into rest, or when I go 'on leaf'; of the ebb and flow of life
through the battalion: the faces that you did not see when the companies came down from the line, faces that were too soon forgotten
since death was common, the newcomers of whom at first you were
resentful, who so soon were absorbed into your little world; of the
existential sense which made each moment actual and immediate. We
knew we were alive. But I shall have to tell that I came to have doubts
about it.

13

Passchendaele

WHY did Haig select the Ypres Salient as the field for his chosen battle? Through three campaigns he had conformed to the wishes of the French, had supported them loyally, and had shouldered the blame for the failures which had been partly due to the miscalculations of Joffre, Foch, and Nivelle. During the spring of 1917 he had several times proposed to the French that his effort should be transferred to Flanders, without evoking the least sign of their approval or interest.

Throughout the war the conflict between French and British strategic thinking turned upon the axis of advance or retreat, as it did again during the Battle of France in 1940. In extremity, the French regarded the defence of Paris as their main object, while the British gave priority to the Channel ports. In 1914 Joffre had blamed Sir John French for threatening to withdraw on his Channel bases; in 1918 Haig was to blame Pétain for threatening to withdraw towards Paris. When they advanced, Joffre—and Foch after him—was for driving the enemy back from Champagne and Artois; Haig was for clearing the Flanders Coast so as to make full use of British seapower. At the Admiralty, Jellicoe had long been urging Haig to take this course not only, as has been suggested, because of the supposed use of Zeebrugge and Ostend by U-boats, but for the much greater reasons that had led Kitchener and Churchill to fight for Antwerp in 1914, the reasons that were to make Montgomery fight for Antwerp in 1944. With the whole Flanders Coast in allied hands we should be half-way to achieving our war aims. Strategically, the key to Flanders was the railway behind the German front through Roulers, only twelve miles from Ypres. If this small advance could be made, with or without the aid of a coastal landing, the Germans would be unable to supply their troops in West Flanders and must retire at least from Ostend. This was the picture painted by Haig, and here was his intention as soon as he should be free of the entanglement with Nivelle's abortive battle. His own share, the Battle of Arras, had been useful in its way, a successful battle of attrition but irrelevant to his own plan, an eccentric stroke in the wrong direction from his point of view.

Haig's diaries make it clear that, whether he knew of the French mutinies or not, he was quite sure by June that the French generals would do no more fighting that year, so that the British must take the whole of the strain. It was the chance for which he had been waiting and he was completely confident, even though half the campaigning season had gone before the successful opening move at Messines cleared his right flank. To begin the build up for the main battle in mid-June would still leave time if the weather was favourable. Haig would have been more than human if he had not been influenced by his recollections of the autumn campaign in Flanders three years earlier. First Ypres had been his battle, fought and won against odds that seemed to leave little room for hope; now he was in great strength, commanding two million men, with adequate munitions at last, and enjoying a temporary superiority. In 1914 the fighting had continued far into the autumn, the crowning defeat of the enemy having been as late in the year as 11th November, and the same month in 1916 had seen victory on the Ancre. This self-assured, stubborn, experienced man could face the future with his quiet customary optimism. But in 1914 there had been a dry autumn and in 1917 there was to be a wet autumn.

A factor hard to calculate in any war is the extent to which a commander, even a Napoleon, is limited by dependence upon his staff. Everyone has heard of Colonel Hentsch from headquarters who persuaded the German Army Commanders that they had lost the Battle of the Marne, and all the evidence now makes it plain that the grandees whose names appeared at the head of German Armies were sometimes not much more than puppets dancing to strings pulled by the Great General Staff. While no such secret trade union of staff officers existed in the British Army there were, inevitably, occasions when commanders were unable to override technical objections or when they were misled by advice given in good faith. What else would anyone who knows the world expect?

Plumer and his chief staff officer, Harington, made a team of outstanding efficiency, within the narrow limits of what was possible on the Western Front in 1917. For all his thrusting energy—he was thirteen years younger than Plumer—Gough never attained the same sureness of touch in managing a battle or in winning the confidence of his Corps Commanders. Even in 1916, Haig's diary contains a guarded criticism of Gough's chief staff officer, Malcolm, who drove the divisions too hard. The hostile criticism of Gough, which is a feature of so many recent war books is, however, a matter of hindsight. We knew nothing of it at our level when we served in his Army in 1917. The delay, caused by transferring artillery from Plumer's front to Gough's, used up more of the precious summer weather but made it necessary that the divisions should be driven harder. This is one of the familiar dilemmas of war—whether to 'change the bowling'. Haig had decided for Gough the fast bowler against Plumer the slow bowler, which proved to be an error of tactics. At G.H.Q. the man who had the C.-in-C.'s ear was Charteris, the chief intelligence officer, another of Haig's young men and an incurable optimist. It was Charteris's opinion, given with all the authority he could command, that the Germans 'were falling in effective strength and deteriorating in morale', a forecast that proved unreal, because they too could concentrate against the British, the only active front for them as it was for the Allies. Again, to change the sporting metaphor, it was to be a heavy-weight slogging match between the two principal combatants. Thanks to Charteris, Gough, and the weather, the appreciation made by Haig of his prospects for the Flanders offensive was sadly unreal. Gough was no more able to carry the enemy positions at a rush than Nivelle had been; the Germans, who had also revised their minor tactics after their Somme experience, fought stubbornly; and the whole apparatus of attack was drowned in the August rains.

For us, the battle began in a city of huts and tents hidden among the oak woods of Elverdinghe. A mile or two away across the sodden fields were the ruins of Ypres, now almost abandoned; in front of us was the canal bank, pitted with dugouts, busy with traffic by foot-bridges and road bridges, the arc of the chord which was the Ypres Salient. This side of the canal you were in recognizable Flanders; across the canal you marched straight into hell; a place that offered you nothing but crater-fields and ruins and danger. To me, it always seemed like a scene from *Pilgrim's Progress* which, to their loss, people

don't read nowadays. There were always a few shells bursting somewhere in the landscape, most probably on the duckboard tracks along
which the infantry moved in single file, or on the few plank roads by
which the ammunition columns supplied the batteries with shells. I
think the gunners, always in the line, had a worse time at Passchendaele
than the infantry, and the drivers, perhaps, a worse time than the
gunners. I cannot speak for the mules, splashed to the withers in sludge,
except that dead mules were more conspicuous in the landscape even
than dead men. Once a mule went down in a mud-puddle it was down
for ever and perhaps the mules were the most unfortunate of all; at
least they could not be twitted with having volunteered for the job.

We were not to lead in the opening attack but, again, were in
reserve, behind the 51st Highland Division which then was at the
summit of its great reputation. By this stage of the war some check had
been placed upon the drain of officer-casualties. No more than twelve
of each battalion led the assault, wearing the same cut of uniform as the
other ranks, and it was my turn to stand back. Accordingly, I was under
orders to go to the Army School, which I have mentioned, when the
division should move forward from reserve. As I lay asleep in my tent
I was awakened by the ground throbbing like an earthquake beneath
me. It was the drum-fire of the attack. Lloyd George could hear the
distant mutter of the guns from his house in Surrey, more than a
hundred miles away.

The first reports that came down were of advance all along the line.
Batches of German prisoners marched back, and many tanks—still a
rare novelty to see—moved up through the woods and across the
Canal. Then it began to rain. In our camp under the dripping oak trees,
without a commanding officer since our colonel was wounded on a
reconnaissance, rather harassed by German aircraft dropping gas-
bombs around at night, the first bloom of the Flanders offensive
quickly faded for us. No talk now of general advance but of relieving
the Highland Division and of improving the newly captured position
by local action. It was the Somme over again, except that a Somme
battle fought knee-deep in a marsh was so much the worse. The entry
in my diary for Wednesday, 1st August 1917, is 'Heavy rain. Slight
alteration of plans'. It was, I think, 6th August, when infantry of the
Highland Division came marching down, muddied up to the bare
thighs, and with kilts hanging in laps and folds of clay like sculptor's

work. Highland dress—'*Bon pour l'amour*', as Foch said, '*mais pas pour la guerre*'—did not seem practical in the Ypres Salient that year. A huge husky Highlander broke out of the ranks and spoke to one of my men:

'Gie us a drink, Tommy.'

'What's it like up there, Jock?' asked my boy, handing him his water-bottle.

'Och,' said the Highlander with gutturals I cannot write down, 'thae buggers wouldna fecht.'

If the Highlanders had not yet had their bellyful of fighting there were not many like them. As I made my way to a camp at Poperinghe, and by a tediously slow train to the Army School, my own feelings were mixed. My men were going into the battle without me for the first 'battalion show' in which I had not taken part. I did not feel pleased with myself even though I was glad of another lease of life. I did not look forward into the future, since infantry subalterns had ceased to expect such a thing, and certainly I never supposed that, three and twenty years later, I should see the sons of those Highlanders, still as pugnacious, in another ill-fated battle at Abbeville. Perhaps my thirsty friend was there, for the weakness of the Highland Division in 1940 was that it had too many middle-aged officers and N.C.O.s still spoiling for a fight.

None of the news that leaked through to us from our friends in the Salient was good. With every wet day the ground grew worse and the prospects more hopeless. A series of partial attacks, as at the same stage of the Somme Battle, brought inadequate gains. Our 48th Division like many others was frittered away and my battalion, depending in three small actions on Tanks which could not navigate through the mud, lost the colonel, seven officers and three hundred men. Generals grew angrier with their troops and troops with their generals. But the blame was now to be laid definitely at the top. Charteris continued to assure Haig that the Germans were almost exhausted, and Haig noted confidently, on 28th August, that 'every day we seem to get more of the upper hand', adding that 'if the French could only support us in a moderate way, there was a chance of ending the war this autumn'. September was a drier month in which Haig, far from admitting failure, extended the front of attack, swinging the weight of his effort from Gough to Plumer, who reverted to his own style of battle, taking his time to prepare. Very late in the season, when the rains were setting in again, Plumer delivered three successive blows, on 26th September, 4th October, and 12th October, with limited objectives, the third being the approach to Passchendaele, which the soldiers have always used as a popular name for the whole Flanders campaign of 1917. As I commanded a company in the first assaulting wave on 4th October (known as the Battle of Broodseinde), I shall describe it as I saw it.[1] What surprises me is that the historians have elevated it into a tactical masterpiece like Messines. It was just all-in wrestling in the mud.

(2)

We spent September out in rest near St. Omer in rich rolling country with golden harvest weather and comfortable billets. Now, I suppose, if we had been properly instructed by the political commentators of the next generation, we should have turned against our persecutors. Nothing of the kind occurred, or was whispered about, or was guarded against by 'Higher Authority'. We spent long happy easy days luxuriating in the sun, glad to be alive, more concerned with the Divisional Football Cup than with the war, but quite concerned with incorporating our drafts of new recruits—conscripts now and just as good soldiers as the old volunteers. I had a company at last, though not yet a captaincy, and it was my company that was chosen to represent the battalion in a brigade field-firing competition.

And yet when I remember these days of riding over the stubble-fields I have to admit that I have said nothing significant. Something had happened inside my head that deprived these external activities of any meaning. Always a little schizophrenic (though the word had not been invented) and disposed to stand off and look at myself from about forty feet away, I had now withdrawn myself altogether, leaving a Zombie in command of 'B' Company, the 1/5th Royal Warwickshire Regiment. I knew that my luck had turned. I felt sure that I should not survive the next battle and, putting a cheerful face on it, like the prisoner eating a hearty breakfast in the condemned cell, I persuaded myself that it was not true. I should pretend to walk to the scaffold but should wake up from the nightmare, screaming, before I reached it. Meanwhile it was strange to me to observe that the Zombie was a quite good company commander and kept up appearances except when,

1. For a fuller account see *A Subaltern's War* by 'Charles Edmonds'.

rarely, the live man took charge in a state of high panic. Let others tell their own tales, that is how the neurosis of 1917 affected me. Neither the inner nor the outer man ever supposed that there was a political solution to his problems or thought it could all be put down to the account of those dreadful brass-hats. No one had deceived or deluded me. I was a volunteer and I knew where I was going. Yet I have not often been as unhappy and inwardly confused as when with outward calm I checked the plans, the orders, the routes, the supplies, the detail, at the brigadier's conference, giving quite intelligent answers to questions, while all I saw was the noose and the trapdoor. Were others in the same state?

Our starting line was in front of St. Julien, just where the Canadians had made their stand against the gas-attack two years earlier, and we were to advance in a square formation, 'A' Company on the right, 'B' Company on the left, followed by 'C' and 'D'. On our left was our 6th Battalion; on our right the New Zealand Division, which seemed to be at about twice our strength. My company, also, was in a square formation with two platoons led by officers in front, about two hundred yards apart, and two platoons following at the same distance. I and the sergeant-major were to take the centre of the rectangle, with four orderlies of whom one was my personal servant, and a section of signallers who were to unroll telephone wire behind us as we advanced. These were but two of the ways in which we could send messages back; there were also visual signals by flag or heliograph, 'contact' aeroplanes with which we communicated by lighting ground-flares, carrier-pigeons, dogs trained to carry messages through fire, and at battalion headquarters a formidable telegraphic gadget known as the 'power-buzzer'.

The barrage was of such weight and density as to belittle anything we had seen on the Somme. Certain vital points were neutralized by projectors which threw cylinders of gas into the air to land and deliver their contents fifteen hundred yards away. A standing barrage of heavy shells fell on our objective a thousand yards away; a creeping barrage of shrapnel moved forwards in front of us at the rate of thirty yards—was it?—a minute; and between the two a searching barrage rolled backwards and forwards, to discourage movement behind their front-line posts.

The greatest difficulty for us was to identify any place whatever on the ground, even after days spent studying large-scale maps, air photographs, and the 'Corps Model', a toy landscape that would have made that typical old soldier, 'Captain Shandy' happy. My objective was 'Winchester Farm', which proved to be a small square blockhouse of concrete—what in those days we called a 'pill-box'—and fortunately for me it was smashed by a shell before I got there, but how could one tell it from any other 'pill-box', of which there were half a dozen in front of us? We found an unsuspected one during the day and named it Warwick Castle. To mark one's objectives and boundaries on a map was easy; to know whether you were at your objective or inside your boundary was impossible, without identifying two objects and taking compass bearings, an unlikely thing to do during a hand-to-hand fight. What confronted you was a lunar landscape of shell-craters, one touching another, filled with water or with sludgy clay that could almost wrench the boots off your feet. To keep direction or to maintain the formations we had practised in battle-drill were equally impossible, as the sections straggled round the rims of the shell-holes. A party of sappers was detailed to follow the attack with signboards to be posted up on captured objectives. We questioned more than one of their identifications, and were much amused when a sapper marched out into No Man's Land and nailed up his notice on a tree-stump well inside the German front. I think everyone lost the way two or three times a day. In the assault we all edged to the left so that I took part of the 6th Battalion's objective, and the New Zealanders part of mine, though only a fraction of what they claim in their official history.

We knew, of course, that the Germans, like ourselves, would be disposed in depth so that the assault, even if one could mount it over the mud-holes, would be quite unlike the trench-to-trench attacks of the previous year. As we were marching off, a message was put into my hand to say that they had again changed their dispositions, doubling the strength of their front-line posts so that I with one company was going to attack two. As an experienced soldier I should have reflected that this was an error on their part—as in fact it proved to be—since it merely provided a richer target for our artillery. Just then, it did not strike me quite that way and, after a night of misery, waiting for zero, I was still further depressed by a bombardment that the Germans loosed on us twenty minutes before our guns began to fire.

When the barrage opened, with so shattering a noise as to erase all

N

other sensation, the Zombie took charge and I felt nothing at all. I think I should not have known if a bullet had struck me. It was six in the morning, the dawn just breaking on a damp cloudy day, and at first I could see nobody but my own group following me over the shell-holes. At once the signallers dropped behind, burdened with their gear, and I don't know what became of them. Our advance stopped when the six of us ran slap into a group of four or five Germans lying low in a shell-hole, coolly shooting. In a moment we are reduced to three, with two dead men and one man dying horribly. As we shot it out at twenty or thirty yards' range the barrage thundered away, leaving us alone in the world. Two against three, now, it might be a gangster fight on a film and, low down among the shell-holes, one can see nothing but one's own predicament. But the battle-drill had not been in vain, and soon I heard the welcome voice of Corporal Whittle from the support platoon bringing his Lewis gun into action. I shouted instructions to him and we coped with our little problem. Just then twenty or thirty Boches rose out of the ground and came running at us. Counter-attack! We all opened fire until we saw their hands above their heads. Prisoners! Then they can find their own way down the line carrying our wounded, especially Corporal Whittle, who somehow has been shot through both thighs and is spouting blood from four wounds which I can't bandage with one field dressing.[1]

How long this incident took I cannot say, perhaps twenty minutes, but long enough to bring daylight. When we emerged from our shell-holes and I could rally my handful of men, I could see what I had never seen so clearly, the panorama of a battle. There, hundreds of yards away, was the barrage, a line of continuous explosions, pausing on the first objective. On my right the New Zealanders were advancing, and one of their platoons, a little off course, was coming our way. Before me, the ground fell away to a drainage ditch called the Stroombeek, which you might have jumped across if the bombardment had not spread it out into a Slough of Despond. Straight to my front a few planks made an easy crossing place on which parties of our men were converging from right to left. Far away we could see and hear two tanks clattering into the ruins of Poelcapelle. And ahead in the distance was the spire of Passchendaele church rising, not from the mud, but from green trees, an amenity it would not enjoy much longer. We

1. I'm glad to say he survived.

moved forward and, for a few minutes, I manœuvred troops as if it had been a 'field day' at Aldershot. I picked up a strayed platoon of 'A' Company and placed them, with the one Lewis gun I had in hand, to hold the crossing of the Stroombeek which seemed to me the vital point. I then took charge of the New Zealand platoon and to my surprise discovered that its commander was a school-friend. 'Hullo, "Mossy",' 'Hullo, Charley,' we said, reverting to school nicknames, and stood there shaking hands, with a German machine-gun firing on us. I sent him off to 'strafe' the machine-gun, which shortly cease firing, and from that moment to this I have never again seen or heard of 'Mossy'.

My handful of men crossed the Stroombeek and skirmished up the other bank in the approved style to the pill-box called Winchester, where we met a platoon of the 6th on the flank of our objective. As we went forward we had passed many dead and wounded men and noted grimly that the Germans far outnumbered the British. At Winchester, where shot and shell were flying briskly in several directions, I found the body of my friend Captain Powell of the 6th (with whom I had served in the Birmingham Battalion in 1914), and the body of the German officer commanding that post. I took his automatic pistol which we thought a better weapon than our Webley revolvers.

Here we were, having reached our objective and dissipated the company in the process. Where were they? What had become of my two officers? How was I to find out? Nothing for it but to send out my handful of men to search for them. A major of the 6th Battalion, who was in charge thereabouts, wanted me to advance, as there seemed to be no enemy near us. Not I! In this battle of defined objectives, in which the Boches were so quick to counter-attack, I would cling to what I had got, especially as I had no men to advance with. When our 'C' and 'D' companies had passed through us, 'C' having lost its captain and 'D' all its officers, I withdrew to the crossing of the Stroombeek and there tried to assemble what was left of my company. Every group had been engaged in a petty struggle like mine and all had fought their way through, at a cost which put an end to my command. Both officers were gone, all four platoon sergeants, eleven out of twelve section commanders. We scrabbled together twenty-seven men (out of 109 who started) and with them the sergeant-major and I consolidated our position, as the jargon ran. Luckily we had all four Lewis guns still in action. My busy stretcher-bearers, going about the battlefield to give first aid, found two more of my sections which had reached some point they supposed to be their objective and had resolutely dug in, without orders or information. This brought our numbers up to forty-four.

The evening and the morning were like this on the first day, Thursday, 4th October 1917. Late at night a reinforcement arrived with one of my reserve officers, H. A. Spencer, to whom I willingly resigned responsibility. I went back to report at battalion headquarters, where they were surprised to see me alive. Three times during the morning's action I had sent back situation reports (marked maps with a *pro forma* list of items to be ticked off: 'I have reached my objective', 'I am held up by wire,' etc.) by runners who failed to get through, and they had no news of me. They fed me and let me sleep a few hours on the dugout floor. Next day, Friday, the rain set in with drenching persistence making a lake of the Stroombeek ditch; and with the rain came the shells. The German artillery now searched our whole area systematically with heavies at long range so that the gouts of mud and splinters of jagged metal from one burst had hardly settled before the moaning of the next shell began to swell into a roar like a hurricane. We sat about all day with nothing to do but take what was coming. On this day I came out of the anaesthesia. The Zombie withdrew to his own place, leaving behind him a tired and frightened young man, short of sleep, wet through, and very well aware that he was going to be wet through for two days and nights longer. Saturday was better for weather, and worse for shelling, and on Sunday we were drawn back into reserve at the starting line, where there was a sort of hutch for company headquarters which gave some shelter from the weather, at the cost of presenting a target to the guns. We had now got all our wounded in and even the German wounded, and began to collect arms and stores, and to identify the dead. When they found the body of my friend who had commanded 'C' Company, the salvage party observed that some keen pilferer had taken his signet ring and had cut the finger off to get it. On Sunday evening we were to be relieved by the 4th Oxfordshires and would have got away in comfort if the New Zealanders had not sent up SOS rocket signals, which let loose another bombardment by both sides. I lost some more men on the way down.[1]

1. The Battalion had taken all its objectives, 150 prisoners, an anti-tank gun, and several machine-guns, losing 4 officers and 81 other ranks killed, 6 officers and 171 other ranks wounded out of about 16 and 550 who took part in the battle.

During the last two days of this affair my mind was so numbed and my body so exhausted that I was utterly useless. Judging by their inactivity the Germans must have been in the same state. Why not? But they gave that Zombie a Military Cross for his part in the battle and the live man was inordinately proud of it.

(3)

My state of mind had been so self-centred during this autumn that I can record no comment of my own on the strategy of Passchendaele. What is clear to me is that I regarded the whole British Army as committed. It was 'we' who had got into this bog and had to fight our way out of it; it was not 'they' who had misdirected us. Hindsight teaches me that Haig is to be blamed for failing to know when he was beaten, not by the Germans but by Flanders mud. We came out of the battle confident that we could capture any thousand yards of Flanders if we paid the price, and could balance the account by killing more Boches than they killed of us, but we had begun to realize that we should never get to Berlin by that technique. As we used to sing, to the cheerful tune of an Irish jig:

> 'Oh what with the wounded and what with the dead,
> And what with the boys who are swinging the lead,
> If the war isn't over, and that bloody soon,
> There'll be nobody left in this bloody platoon.
> Tra la la. . . .'

Taking the shorter view we should not even get to the Flanders coast before winter at this rate. What, then, was the factor in the sum that had been miscalculated? My answer to this question, confirmed by experience in the Second World War, is that it lay in the nature of battles fought by infantry under cover of bombardment. At that stage in the development of weapons of war it was necessary to destroy your objective before you could occupy it. The preliminary bombardment, without which infantry could not move, obliterated the roads, and even the cross-country tracks, by which alone they could move quickly. The means precluded attainment of the end. To a large extent this factor had been present in the dry chalky uplands of the Somme; in the man-made country of Flanders destruction of the artificial drainage reduced the country to primeval marsh, in which no war of movement was possible. Plumer's well-planned lurches forward from one useless objective to another were no more valuable strategically than Gough's untidy advances; it was only in terms of the war of attrition—killing Germans—that Plumer did better. But all the generals were deluded together, Gough as much as Haig, Plumer as much as Gough, Monash the Australian (who thought 4th October a lovely battle) as much as Plumer. Attrition was still the ruling principle, and my men who died for it gave me no indication of mutiny. Perhaps we were all Zombies together.

Twenty-seven years later I was to make the same observations about the battles in Normandy and the Rhineland. In that war the equivalent factor was the employment of what were inaccurately called 'strategic' bombers to blast the way through an obstacle before an infantry advance. However successful they were in silencing enemy opposition, they actually slowed down the rate of movement of the armies by destroying road and railway junctions. Sir Arthur Harris said to me, on 22nd July 1944, after one of the bombings in the Normandy beach-head: 'I have dropped a thousand tons of bombs in front of the Army and they have gone forward one mile. At this rate it will take six hundred thousand tons of bombs to get them to Berlin. You can tell them I'm willing, but I'd rather begin at Berlin and work backwards'. But that is another story.

When we were pulled out of Passchendaele—what was left of us— we were sent at once to recuperate on the Vimy Ridge, which the Canadians had captured by a famous operation in the spring. Since then it had sunk into quiescence and here we found ourselves in cushy trenches, with wire and a continuous front line and dugouts, all admirably sited and maintained, just as if there had been no change in the nature of the war. With reliefs and sentry duty, route marches, and patrols that were exciting but not too dangerous, it was an ideal training ground for our new drafts.

At first I was so low in spirits, so nervously exhausted, that I could hardly apply myself to reconstructing the company, the first task being to write twenty-two letters to the wives and mothers of men killed under my command. We built up the cadre of the company with the help of the ten per cent who had been held back in reserve and others recalled from leave or convalescence. Everyone jumped up one or two ranks; I became acting captain, lance-corporals became sergeants, and several surviving old soldiers of an early vintage were—not always willingly—raised to the rank of full corporal. One of the genuine folk-songs of the Army was the catch with a gnomic quality, sung sadly over and over again:

> 'Old soldiers never die
> They only fade away'.

The new drafts seemed more vulnerable, coming and going, while a residue of tough old 'swaddies' among whom I could now number myself, seemed to go on for ever. We were banded together by a unity of experience that had shaken off every kind of illusion, and was utterly unpretentious. The battalion was my home and my job, the only career I knew. We re-formed our unit around this nucleus stronger and prouder than before, and again we were lucky in our transfusion of new blood. This time we got a hundred or more of dismounted Warwickshire Yeomanry, pre-war volunteers who rejuvenated our territorial character. Within a few weeks the battalion was as good as ever, putting up a good show—as we said in the slang of the period—for the American officers who were sent 'for instruction' to our trenches, as two years ago we had done for Kitchener's Army officers new to France. I have never forgotten the day when, as I marched through some village at the head of my company, all singing, the staff captain, Geoff Walker, leaned out of the window of brigade head-quarters to shout to me: 'Damned good marching, Carrington, the best in the brigade.' My heart swelled with pride, as if 1915 had come again. More than that, Geoff Walker was one of us; he had been out with us since the beginning, so that I valued his praise higher than the Corps Commander's.

From Vimy we were hauled out of the line and sent away on a secret mission which proved to be a five-day train journey to Italy. Before trying to put the breakthrough at Caporetto, and the transfer of French and British troops to that front, in its relation to the strategy of the war I shall complete my own story. The train journey was an exhilarating adventure and Italy itself a delight to me, even though I saw it first in the chaos that reigned behind a great military disaster. We did not go into the line but were held in reserve in the angle between Monte Grappa and the Piave River, where the Italian Army made their stand. That winter I came no nearer the fighting front than to watch the distant shell-bursts over Browning's Asolo on the slopes of the Grappa and to make one or two reconnaissances of the mountain front, I was prepared for Italy, having been reading Browning for months, but woefully ignorant. Since nobody told me that Vicenza was one of the most beautiful cities in the world, I chiefly noticed the beautiful women. We lived in peasants' huts where the people kept warm by sitting in the byre with their draught-oxen and lived upon *polenta* cooked in cauldrons of pure copper. This is not to my purpose and I hasten on to say that in January 1918 having been for two years continuously on active service and being still alive—indeed unhurt—I was given a month's privilege leave. While in London I submitted to a medical examination and was ordered into hospital for a few days' observation—'thoroughly run down'. My private opinion is that my aunt had squared the principal medical officer, a friend of hers. A Board of benevolent elderly doctors looked me over and despite my half-hearted protests 'struck me off the strength' and sent me to the reserve battalion. So I just faded away.

14

Soldiers and Statesmen, 1917–18

THE deadlock in which the combatants were held had reached its gloomy climax in the summer of 1917. Faint possibilities of a negotiated peace which had been in the air during the previous winter disappeared when the Germans launched their unlimited submarine campaign, bringing America into the war and so ensuring their eventual defeat. Neither that, nor the Russian Revolution of which no one could foresee the end, was to have an immediate effect upon the year's land campaign. The Germans stood on the defensive, waiting for the victory the U-boats did not bring, while the French Army dashed itself to pieces in the Nivelle offensive and the British Army fought the ill-conceived Battle of Passchendaele. In each of the great combatant countries, even in France by the end of the year, a strong government was in power committed to fighting the war to a finish, and all alike were frustrated, not least the Americans who then learned, as the British had learned before them, that two years' preparation would be needed before they could exert their decisive strength. No civil government and no general staff could find a way out of the deadlock. Haig's plan, to batter his way through, was accepted because there was no other plan. Lloyd George, having mobilized the labour force and the industry of Britain, was exasperated by the failure of the generals to produce some brilliant improvisation, and was repeatedly frustrated by discovering that wars are not conducted by such methods. If only he could have found some other general, with more imagination than Haig—he supposed—the logistic factors could be wished away. There were no such generals and there could not be. The war would be won, as all wars are won, by the general who made the most effective use of the manpower and the material at hand. Since the lost opportunity of Gallipoli, few serious students of war in any country doubted that the military decision must be taken on the Western Front and, appalling as was the cost of Haig's generalship, his record, when at last a decision was reached, stood better than Falkenhayn's,[1] better than Nivelle's, better than Foch's. There was no one in whom the soldiers had more faith, even after Passchendaele, no one who could solve the problem which, so far, Haig had not solved. If Plumer or Allenby had been in Haig's shoes, they would have acted much as he did.

In his persistent endeavours to supersede Haig, Lloyd George first put his faith in the Frenchman, Nivelle, who failed because he did not do well enough to justify his inflated reputation. When Allenby's Battle of Arras brought in a small dividend, the only advantage gained in the Nivelle offensive, Lloyd George was inclined to run Allenby as a rival to Haig. They were contemporaries, both cavalrymen, and were said to be unfriendly, though there is no sign of bad co-operation between them in the field. Allenby was the better educated man, a classical scholar, and had rather more to say for himself than the taciturn Haig. His military career was strictly conventional, and something may be learned from his nickname 'the Bull'. After commanding the cavalry in 1914 and finding no greater use for shock action than any other cavalry leader, he was given a corps, and then the Third Army. His first battle, the assault on Gommecourt Wood on 1st July 1916, was the most disastrous failure of that bloody day. At Arras, in April 1917, although he showed that he had learned the tactical lessons of the Somme, his battle like so many others lost momentum. No more than anyone else could he convert a break-in to a break-through in France. He was then sent to Palestine to save Lloyd George's reputation by doing something spectacular, which indeed he did. His two campaigns against the Turks, perhaps the best fighters in the world but in inferior numbers, are models of generalship. He did nothing in the East which he might not have done in France if he had enjoyed the same superiority, and his final success was a cavalry break-through, the ambition of all the orthodox soldiers. He initiated no new method or device.

At the end of the war one name was coming to the fore, the name of Sir John Monash, the only civilian who attained to a lieutenant-general's command in France. It has often been suggested that only he could have succeeded Haig as Commander-in-Chief if the war had dragged on a year longer. In May 1918 he was given command of the

1. Falkenhayn was beaten again by Allenby in Palestine.

Australian Corps after leading a brigade and a division. Under Monash the Australians made a contribution to the final victory out of all proportion to their numbers, and we might suppose that this brilliant interloper, commanding men renowned for their unwillingness to truckle under, would have behaved very differently from the other 'donkey' generals; but we find nothing of the sort. Though critical of detail, as any man of spirit might be, he worked very well with Haig, who thought well of him. His battles were set-pieces, mounted according to the techniques developed by Rawlinson and Plumer. He used the same methods to produce the same tactical results and the difference between Monash and the other Corps Commanders was only that he excelled them in thoroughness of preparation.

During the winter of 1917–18 Lloyd George spent much energy in manœuvres to outwit the generals whom he dared not dismiss, and his opportunity occurred over the Italian breakdown. He had for long been urging the General Staff to turn the flank of the Western Front by an Italian campaign and had been thwarted by Robertson's demonstrations that you can transfer troops to Italy more rapidly from southern Germany than from northern France, the sort of argument that merely strengthened his belief in the stupidity of all soldiers.

From the central fortress of *Festung Europa* the Germans, every autumn, had scraped up a small reserve of selected troops under a good commander to lead the assault on one of the lesser Allied powers: in 1915 Serbia, in 1916 Roumania, and in 1917 it was to be Italy. Using the strategy of inner lines they could knock away these props of the loose alliance before help in sufficient strength could be sent from Britain and France. They moved down the spokes of the wheel while we were obliged to move round the rim. Sea-power, which should have been to our advantage, was diminished at the same time by the submarine campaign. Year after year the Germans succeeded and, year after year, our problems of transportation involved us in campaigns which could contribute little to the defeat of Germany, while they added much to our obligations. At last, in 1917, Maude in Mesopotamia and Allenby in Palestine had won victories by conventional tactics skilfully applied, but without weakening the German effort in France. These campaigns consumed more man- and machine-power than they were worth. The sideshows in the Turkish war had publicity value which Lloyd George could exploit by contrasting them with the barren struggles in Flanders, and since his war-policy depended upon belittling Haig and Robertson, the defeat at Caporetto gave him an opening. Now they would be obliged to divert troops from France to Italy as he had long been urging them to do.

On 24th October 1917 an Austrian army stiffened by German troops under Von Below, our opponent on the Somme, pierced the centre of the front at Caporetto, destroying the Italian Second Army. At last this seemed to be the breakthrough which no one had previously accomplished on the Western Front. Foch was sent to report, and with great smoothness two French corps and two British corps were despatched by train to Italy; but Caporetto was not yet the complete victory. The Italian Commander-in-Chief, Cadorna, whom we used to laugh at though I now think he did very well, extricated the other Italian armies, retired eighty miles, and made a firm stand on the Piave-Grappa line before he was superseded. The Franco-British reinforcement had a political effect on the alliance and a moral effect on the Italian people, but no tactical effect on the battle, since the Italian Army had already made a stubborn recovery from what was near disaster. By 10th November the crisis was past, before the main body of British troops had arrived, though no one, of course, could be sure of this rally until much later. We can now see that the middle of October 1917, when my friends and I were recuperating in cushy trenches on the Vimy Ridge, was a crucial moment in the history of the world.

Lloyd George's intrigue against his own generals was conducted with immense adroitness. Paying no attention whatever to the unshakable array of facts and figures presented to him by Robertson, he devoted himself to manœuvring that single-minded man into a situation where he would be either deprived of his control over strategic planning or would be forced to resign in protest. While Robertson was well aware of the dilemma, he was unable to extricate himself from the toils of the Welsh Wizard, who so skilfully divided his friends and brought his enemies into combination. The Prime Minister had found a rival general in Henry Wilson, who had come unstuck in the middle period of the war. There had even been a moment when, quite unemployed, he had appealed to Haig: 'find me a job or I shall get into mischief'. On the French side, Foch too was *dégommé* in 1917, and the two friends, intellectually the ablest soldiers of Britain and France, now felt that their moment had come. Wilson, with his Irish blarney, was the one soldier capable of matching Lloyd George in the political game.

The Rapallo Conference on 7th November 1917 enabled the politicians to create a Supreme Allied War Council, a very necessary organ, though it did not solve the problem of who was to give executive orders to the generals. Robertson pointed out that it would be unconstitutional for the Allied Council to do so, while Haig and Petain notified their respective governments that it would not work. Except that Lloyd George could now play off Wilson at Versailles, the seat of the Allied Council, against Robertson at the War Office, nothing much happened because the French Government fell, and Clemenceau, the new premier, was at first almost as jealous of Foch as Lloyd George was of Haig. The only achievement of the Council was that Wilson made an appreciation of what was likely to occur in 1918 and proved to be as fantastically wrong as he had been on previous occasions.

(2)

The month of November 1917, an interval between the first and second phases of Lloyd George's plot against the generals, produced the Battle of Cambrai, a highly speculative gamble which I find inexplicable, so out-of-character is it with the rest of Haig's career, not because it was inventive but because it was haphazard, not thought through. We must now look back to the small body of enthusiasts who had been nursing the infancy of the tank. The main problems, as always with a new invention, had been mechanical and the Mark IV tanks of November 1917 were vastly different from the inefficient prototypes of September 1916. A body of tank doctrine had been developed by the enthusiasts who protested, without getting much attention, that the new weapon had not yet been given a fair chance. In the 1917 battles tanks had been used in ones and twos to save the lives of infantrymen, whereas they should have been used in masses, it was said to provide a modern substitute for that fading dream, the cavalry breakthrough. Inventors and innovators are quite commonly difficult men to deal with and no one need be surprised, when the first experiments produced such slender results, that the tank fanatics failed to revolutionize the art of war in twelve months. Until they staged a dramatic performance they could not capture the sustained attention of men who were fully occupied with fighting for their lives.

The man who devised the new tactics was a comparatively junior soldier, Colonel J. F. C. Fuller, whose character may be indicated by his army nickname, 'Boney' (for Buonaparte). He was and remained fertile in expedients, not only for Tank tactics, and while we admit that he revolutionised the art of warfare we had better be thankful that British governments did not adopt his numerous proposals for other revolutions in the national life. On tanks he was remarkably sound, and to keep the tank problem on a practical level I shall recall a story I heard Lord Alanbrooke tell in 1941. 'Boney' Fuller was then in retirement and a younger general was sent to ask him what message he would give to the men engaged in forming the new armoured divisions. 'Tell them' said "Boney", 'that when I die you will find written on my heart the words: "Spare Parts".'

Fuller's plan for the demonstration was a tank raid by three or four hundred machines supported by artillery and aircraft, who would 'Advance, hit, and retire', repeating with a modern technique the great cavalry raids of the American Civil War. A plan for such a raid had been approved in August but was shelved since the artillery was required for Passchendaele. The opponent of a tank diversion at G.H.Q. seems to have been General L. E. Kiggell, the dull conventional office soldier whom the War Office had foisted upon Haig as Chief of Staff, when he would have preferred a younger man. Kiggell was the staff officer of whom the famous tale is told that he visited the Flanders battlefield for the first time in November 1917 and burst into tears when he saw what he had been responsible for.

The decision in mid-October to switch from Passchendaele to Cambrai must have been related to the external pressures upon Haig at that time. The plan for a tank raid was pulled out of the pigeon-hole and entrusted to Byng's Third Army with quite inadequate preparation and without counting the cost. The raid, for which resources were sufficient, was allowed to grow into a full-scale battle, with the usual optimism about a possible breakthrough, although no reserves were available to exploit any gains there might be. Passchendaele, the scheme that is so difficult to defend, had been prepared with minute care and, dreadful though the course of the battle had been, it was most skilfully conducted, at least by Plumer's Army; Cambrai was a harum-scarum affair, ill-planned and feebly directed, yet in military history it stands as the most significant battle of the First World War. The total number of Tanks employed was 476, of which a quarter were specialised machines for supply and maintenance or with devices for particular tasks. There was no preliminary bombardment, so that complete surprise was attained. Not only the artillery but also the 289 aircraft—and this was perhaps the most fruitful innovation—worked to a programme co-ordinated with that of the tanks; and the tank general, Sir Hugh Elles, instead of sitting back in a château, led the advance. This was the first example of the blitz battle, which the Germans were to develop so brilliantly against us in the Second World War. As a demonstration it was overpowering; as a battle it was an almost complete failure. Eight divisions attacked and all, except one which misused its tanks, overran the Hindenburg Line and advanced three or four miles with very light losses. Ten thousand prisoners and two hundred guns were taken. So unexpected was this sudden gain, after the massacres in the mud, so new and exciting was the technique, that a wave of enthusiasm unlike anything in the previous two years swept through the armies, and through Britain where it set the church-bells ringing. (We heard the news at a wayside railway station on our way to Italy.) Sir Douglas Haig rode forward to reconnoitre the front on horseback, a thing he had not done since that day in 1914 when he rode through the Menin Gate.

The 1st Cavalry Division advanced hopefully and was quite unable to force its way through. Once the effort of the tank assault was expended, with a loss of 179 machines, the battle took the form that other Western Front battles had taken. The advancing troops had not broken the front but had put their heads into a bag with a narrow neck. For two or three days they fought on, failing to take some vital points, and the battle then died away, leaving our men in an exposed salient. On 30th November, the Germans, whose strength was rapidly being increased by troops withdrawn from Russia, struck back at the southern flank of the salient, recovering half of the lost ground and many of the captured guns, together with part of our original front. Instead of ringing their bells, the British people wrung their hands; it seemed that nothing could go right on the Western Front. A greater disaster was avoided by the initiative of the Guards Division, which was marching out to rest with bands playing when the counter-attack burst on them. The Guards turned about, went straight into action, and drove the Germans back pell-mell. Not many other troops on either side were capable of doing such a deed.

The stroke and counter-stroke at Cambrai gave just that jolt that was necessary to shake the armies out of their conventional frame of mind. The trench-warfare notions that had prevailed since Neuve Chapelle were now blown away and mechanized war took a great step forward. Later generations have been disposed to blame the generals for their tardy recognition of the change. It seems to me to have come rather quickly, if we compare it, for example, with the five years of complete scepticism and neglect that the Wright Brothers suffered in America after their discovery of the art of flight in 1903. Instead of abusing the men of 1916, critics today would be better employed in examining what inventions (monorail, hovercraft, bathyscaphe?) we shall be blamed for having neglected, twenty years hence. Nor, on the other hand, should we overlook the millions spent, since 1945, on new weapons which became obsolete before they were in production.

Cambrai has been advertised in the war-histories as the Tank Day to the disadvantage of other improvements in the technique of making war, not only because the tanks made this sudden emergence into the limelight but because of the neglect into which they were afterwards allowed to lapse during the bad days between the wars. It must not be supposed that they were the only innovations or that the choice for Haig lay between tanks which belonged to the future and cavalry which belonged to the past. There were other inventors plucking at his elbow, for example Captain W. H. Livens, whose batteries of mortars, electrically controlled, fired volleys of cans containing phosgene gas into the German lines—an enthusiast who would not be gainsaid. His was a minor invention, useful then and there, not revolutionary like the tank, or like the aircraft which at the same period of the war, differentiated into their two main classes, fighters for defence and bombers for attack. 'Boom' Trenchard, a wiser man than 'Boney' Fuller, did for the R.F.C., what Fuller did for the tanks and, with fewer set-backs, carried out a more fundamental change.

But new weapons are not enough for winning battles. The insuperable problems of 1917 were in the field of communications, and the signalling system at Cambrai was as important a matter as the new use of tanks and aircraft. In the rear, the Commander-in-Chief was more concerned with railway- and road-making than with minor tactics. His limiting factor was the physical problem of conveying men, guns, ammunition, and stores to the place where they could be used. Even more than he needed aeroplanes and tanks, he needed locomotives, sidings, plank roads, hutments, and timber.

(3)

The astonishing Cambrai interlude came and went in a few days, leaving Haig to face the fact that his strength was down by 20 or 30 per cent and the German strength up by 50 per cent. All the advantage he believed himself to have gained by his battles of attrition, taking the view of them that Charteris (now replaced) had presented to him, had vanished in a few days with the emergence of a new factor. The withdrawal of Russia from the war enabled the Germans to increase their strength on the Western Front from 124 to 194 divisions. By February 1918 they had an actual superiority over British (65) and French (100) together. The Americans as yet had no formations ready for fighting, but hoped to have eight divisions by March and thirty-five by mid-summer. On 3rd December Haig warned his Army Commanders to expect a heavy offensive by superior numbers of Germans. At this moment he was ordered to take over twenty-five miles of frontage from the French. Gough was brought from Flanders with twelve divisions and some cavalry to hold a front of forty-two miles, on which there were no prepared defences, and, since the relief was completed only on 30th January 1918, with little time to prepare them. All the British divisions were well below strength, so that manpower for digging was scarce.[1]

There now ensued in January and February 1918, a political struggle between Lloyd George and Haig which has few parallels in military history.[2] The Prime Minister was well aware that a German attack of

1. The British, in January 1918, held 126 miles of front with 59 Divisions which were opposed by 81 German Divisions; the French held 324 miles, mostly dormant, with 100 Division sand were opposed by only 71 German Divisions. The Germans also had a strategic reserve of 25 Divisions.

2. But compare *Henry VI*, Part I, Act i, scene i.
> 'No treachery; but want of men and money,
> Among the soldiers it is mutter'ed,
> That here you maintain several factions,
> And whilst a field should be despatched and fought,
> You are disputing of your generals;
> One would have lingering wars with little cost;
> Another would fly swift but wanteth wings.'

O

unprecedented strength must shortly fall on the British Army. So vindictive was he against Haig, whom he still dared not dismiss, that while Haig prepared to fight the decisive battle of the war, the Prime Minister devoted his time to whittling away Haig's authority and reducing the forces at his disposal. To Haig's requests for men to make up his strength Lloyd George replied, through the medium of those newspapers which his friends controlled, that Haig must be kept short so that he could not fight another Passchendaele. In January the establishment of Haig's infantry was cut down by a quarter, by reducing the number of battalions in a division from thirteen to ten.

The next step was to deprive Haig of as large a slice of his command as could be amputated, by creating a general reserve to be placed under the Council at Versailles, which perhaps pleased Foch as it meant putting part of the British Army effectually under his command. But to fight a battle with one general commanding the front line and another general the reserves is a method which can only be quoted as evidence of Lloyd George's inability to understand the nature of strategy. It scored for him the tactical point that Robertson at last resigned, and Haig, who wasn't the resigning sort, thought the worse of him for giving way. Wilson now achieved his ambition by becoming Chief of the Imperial General Staff which Lloyd George supposed to be to his advantage, and was right to the extent that the country was better served when the Prime Minister and the C.I.G.S. were on speaking terms; but wrong if he supposed that Wilson would be subservient. In office Wilson was far less of a dangerous troublemaker than in opposition. His contempt for the 'frocks', as he described civilian politicians, was real, if humorously expressed; and by his dialectical skill he was able to support the cause of the armies more effectively than the inarticulate Robertson. With Wilson at the War Office, Haig had less to fear from Lloyd George's stabs in the back. He said quite flatly that he had no spare troops to contribute to the allied general reserve and, as Petain said exactly the same, that absurd proposal merely lapsed. When the crisis came on 21st March 1918, Haig was firmly in the saddle. All that Lloyd George had achieved was to reduce the strength of the British Armies to a minimum, before their greatest battle.

Nevertheless Haig held firm, his only error of judgment being his mistaken confidence in Pétain whom, on his reputation at Verdun, he had supposed to be a loyal soldier. This fair-weather friend had indeed placed troops in rear of the British at the moment when, like everyone else, he had supposed Cambrai to be a victory. When the hurricane blew he quickly showed his true character. The alliance was nothing to him if it did not sustain the strength of the French Army.

Haig had correctly formed his front upon the strongly defended lines of the Third Army covering Arras, with the provision that he could afford to give ground in the open downland country of Picardy, The place and date of the German attack had been accurately forecast by his intelligence, and Gough was ready, so far as twelve divisions could be ready, to resist the shock of forty-three. But the Germans with their experience on the Eastern Front, and at Caporetto, had become experts in the tactics of the breakthrough (or the near-breakthrough) and, it is important to notice, had found a way of piercing the line without using tanks. The method of infiltration, helped adventitiously by morning mist, and the training of special bodies of storm-troops, enabled them to break Gough's line of resistance as well as his line of observation. This did not much matter as long as the Germans were made to pay the price. The crunch came when on 24th March they bounced Gough's armies off the crossings of the Somme. Pétain visited Haig that night to warn him that he proposed to withdraw southwards uncovering Haig's flank,

This was the reversal of what French had said to Joffre in 1914, and again it was the British Cabinet that intervened to hold the armies of the alliance together. Lloyd George, who was no defeatist, sent his strongest colleague, Milner, to the conference at Doullens—so near the threatened battle-front that the entrances to the town were guarded by Tanks. Pétain, in a state of gloom, pointed at Haig and said, 'There goes a general who is about to capitulate in the field,' not the last time he was to make this miscalculation about the British. Haig and Milner, not very sympathetic with one another but in agreement upon the necessities of the hour, proposed that Foch should 'co-ordinate the action of the allied powers'. This was accepted, and the High Command was back where it had been when Foch had co-ordinated British and French action during the First Battle of Ypres. Haig had no doubts that Foch would fight.

On 3rd April Foch's authority was further extended to cover the 'strategic direction of military operations', while each C -in-C. had 'full control of tactical action'. The wording no longer mattered much since the soldiers understood one another. The strategic reserve at Versailles was heard of no more and Haig (who did three-quarters of the fighting) could devote himself to opposing the Germans when, at last, Lloyd George's meddling was stalled off. Having defeated Lloyd George, Haig could give his full attention to defeating Ludendorff.

The 'Michael' offensive, the great German attack of 21st March, destroyed Gough's Fifth Army, which went down fighting. 'Michael' punched a hole in the British front just as the Caporetto offensive had punched a hole in the Italian front, and again the defenders recovered from the blow before the attackers could reorganize. Only the driving of a wedge between the British and the French could have been decisive and this, in spite of Pétain's defeatism, had been prevented by the Doullens agreement. The gap was closed; the line was restored; and the attack exhausted its force in front of Amiens on 28th March. An extension of the battle northwards against the Arras front was completely smashed against the strong British defences. By 4th April this second battle had ended in the familiar way. The attackers had lost more men than the defenders without gaining any strategic objective.

Haig now reported that a third attack threatened on the Artois front but could not persuade Foch to give any aid. On 7th April the 'George'[1] offensive was begun in the Armentieres sector. The apex of the attack was the front held by two Portuguese divisions which represented their country in the old alliance. Not deeply involved in the war, not well officered, the Portuguese, who had been long in the line without relief, broke and fled. In those days we sneered at them as troops of poor quality, but we may well ask why these conscripts should give their lives for an alliance based upon an historic treaty. A little more knowledge might have assured us that, in a worthwhile cause, the Portuguese have been among the stoutest fighters in the world, and if we could have foreseen the future we might not have found much to boast about in the part we should play when they needed our reciprocal help under the terms of the same old treaty.

The offensive in Artois was pressed by Ludendorff throughout the whole of April. The crisis came on the 11th when the taciturn Sir Douglas Haig issued his 'Back-to-the-Wall' message, the only appeal

1. The German staff called it 'Georgette'. So severely had they been punished by Haig and Gough that the original 'George' had to be reduced in size.

of that kind he ever made, and by that the more effective.[1] Unlike Gough's Army, which could make a fighting retreat through the devastated area, there was no ground in Artois that the British could afford to lose. If the railway junction at Hazebrouck were taken the whole front might collapse. The British Army then fought a defensive battle comparable with the First Battle of Ypres on a greater scale. Again, it was comforting to know that Foch was there but, according to his principle, he put no new troops into the battle until those already engaged were exhausted. 18th April was the first day since the German Offensive began on 21st March when French troops were actively engaged to relieve the British, and Foch insisted that when they were put into the line the tired British troops should be sent to replace the French in a quiet sector. The British were not pleased when the French lost the important height of Kemmel Hill at the end of the month. The Germans, however, had had enough and called off the battle, having again failed to reach their objectives.

By the end of April Ludendorff had lost the war as we can now see, looking back, though it was not evident at the time. If at the moment of his greatest strength Ludendorff had three times failed to defeat Haig at his weakest, the chance of a victory grew less with every month that passed. The reinforcements that might have saved Gough's Army in March were at last being hurried to France, and, in May, the turning of the tide came when the first American division went into action.[2] There could be no such assurance at the time since Ludendorff still had large reserves in hand and might, by a supreme effort, force the British back upon the Channel coast, a danger that was not removed until July. As the battle developed, the allied success could be attributed to a new cause. In front of Amiens on 28th March, and again in the Lys Valley on 11th April, it had been a fight to a finish and the better men had won. As at the Marne in 1914, the German Command had flinched from the supreme test. Ludendorff had feared that another effort was

1. It should not be thought that the War Office failed to rise to the occasion. In April 1918 they turned over in their sleep and they too issued an Army Order (AO/246). It abolished the practice of saluting with the left hand.

2. Thirteen months after the U.S.A. entered the war. In September 1915, when the British had been at war for thirteen months, their forces on active service amounted to eleven divisions of regulars, fourteen of Territorials, and the first fifteen divisions of Kitchener's Army, not counting 'Empire' troops from overseas. This was what we owed to Haldane and Kitchener.

beyond the power of his troops and his courage had failed. It was Haig's iron nerve, his confidence in the British soldier, that had won the battles. Haig was now master of the field. During the next phase, in May and June, it was the bad judgment and weakening morale of the German Command that was responsible for their lack of success. Ludendorff lost direction, failed to maintain the aim—as the strategic jargon goes—and struck out wildly instead of pursuing a systematic plan. Not only did the German High Command show a lessening grasp of the situation, the German soldiery also lost their fighting quality. The breakthrough tactics had been achieved by the short-sighted policy of creaming the regiments for their best men who were trained as 'storm-troops', with the obvious consequence that the skim-milk left behind steadily decreased in value. All German observers agree that straggling in search of loot largely accounted for the loss of momentum which brought each of the offensives to a halt. The storm-troopers fought well and continued to do so when the German cause was hopeless, as their successors did again in 1945.

At the end of May Ludendorff launched a diversionary attack against the French on the Aisne, with the intention of drawing reserves away from Flanders where he still hoped to strike the decisive blow. Most of the French Army had done no serious fighting for twelve months and the generals were confident that they would never be overrun as the Italians had been at Caporetto and the British on 21st March. It was their turn and the French Sixth Army was broken, the best fight being put up by the four British Divisions which had been sent there for a rest. In a few days the Germans were back on the Marne, even across the Marne, and were again at Noyon within forty miles of Paris. This new bulge proved to be not so dangerous as it seemed, because it brought the American Army into the field at Château Thierry where they did very well, and because Pétain skilfully launched counter-attacks into the German flank, under a swashbuckling general called Mangin, who had come to grief in the Nivelle battles of 1917 and was now given a new chance. Ludendorff fell into the error of throwing good money after bad by committing himself to further battles on this front, each less successful than the former. On 15th July his last offensive, the Battle of Rheims, was a total failure, and was followed by Mangin's counter-attack into the German flank, almost a repetition of Gallieni's counter-attack in September 1914, except that it was supported by light tanks. This was the turning-point. From that moment the pressure on Haig's armies was released; the Allies began to go forward and the Germans began to go back.

Lloyd George now came under fire from the many politicians who mistrusted him and who realized that the army leaders had been badly treated. As a liberal at the head of a coalition government that depended chiefly on conservative votes, he had no organized party behind him. This was not the only respect in which his position was weaker than that of Churchill's in the Second World War. There was no broadcasting, which which he could make a direct appeal to the nation, so that he was dependent on the whims of the newspaper proprietors among whom he manœuvred as adroitly as among the generals or among the conservative leaders, playing off one group against another. There was no Ministry of Defence by which he could co-ordinate the policies of the Admiralty and the War Office (the third service, the R.A.F., was brought into existence at this point of time, April 1918). All had to be done by those arts of political management in which he excelled, and the manifest success of Haig whose position he had tried to undermine—as everyone in the political world knew—told hard against him.

He dared not touch Haig and could do no more than vent his spite by dismissing Gough ignominiously from his command. Gough and the Fifth Army had resisted enemies three times as numerous, had made a fighting retreat to the last ditch and had there stood and expended their strength, until the few survivors were relieved, and it is difficult to say what more they could have done. Gough, however, not yet forgiven for his part in the Curragh Incident, was made the scapegoat. In the course of time, informed opinion came round to his side and, nearly twenty years later, he was awarded a decoration as a belated consolation prize. The youngest among the high commanders of the First World War, he proved to be the longest lived. When he died in 1963, at the age of ninety-two, his obituary notices seemed to recall a distant past.

(4)

In May the Director of Military Operations at the War Office, Sir Frederick Maurice, coolly decided to risk his career by denouncing the conduct of the Prime Minister. He wrote to *The Times* giving some figures to demonstrate that the Government was responsible for the disaster to the Fifth Army, having failed to supply reinforcements which were available at depots. The Prime Minister had no difficulty in crushing a mere major-general but he also had to face a resolution moved by Mr. Asquith as Leader of the Opposition, and chose to take it as a challenge to the Government.

On 9th May 1918, I happened to be on leave in London (as I shall narrate in a later chapter) and had the great pleasure of meeting my brother, Hugh, on leave from France. Merely as sightseers we went to look at the House of Commons where a friendly Member picked us up in the lobby and found us seats in the Gallery for what proved to be one of the parliamentary triumphs of Lloyd George's career, the Frederick Maurice debate. 'Old men forget . . .' and, alas, my intermittent First War diary has no entry for that day. What I remember is visual, like a silent film. On the Opposition Bench the only face we recognized was that of Asquith, 'old Squiff', past his best days, dull and hesitant, we thought. Balfour came into the House, tall and thin and stooping; and after him Churchill, a plump young man with reddish hair, thin on the top, to sit on the Treasury Bench. Then a tall grey-haired man with a heavy moustache said something (which I can't now find in *Hansard*) in a strong Scottish accent. 'Why, that,' we thought, 'must be that dangerous Bolshevik, Ramsay MacDonald.' After Asquith's speech, which we found inadequate, the Prime Minister rose. There he was at the Despatch Box with his mane of white hair, his mobile features, his eyes gleaming, first with fun and then with fury, his eloquent gestures and his words that carried us away. Asquith's case was demolished, General Maurice was made to look a fool, and the House gave Lloyd George a vote of confidence with a huge majority.

I have now to admit that I do not recall a single word or phrase that he used or even the sound of his voice. He dominated the House and he hypnotized my brother and me—both very young—by sheer force of personality. It was enchantment, utterly unlike the outflowing humanity, the homely phrases, the comfortable words and easy tones with which Churchill was to console and inspire us twenty years later, tones and words that we shall never forget. Lloyd George made his effect. The magic worked and years passed before I discovered, by reading *Hansard* and checking the figures, that his speech had been a pack of lies, defending a policy which brought death to many of my friends.

I observe that my personal detestation of Lloyd George as a human being, though I could not overestimate his gifts as a politician, are carrying me outside my subject. I shall conclude the chapter with a considered opinion by a better qualified contemporary, Lord Hankey:

. . . 'Perhaps the greatest work he accomplished was in the sphere of organization. Co-ordination . . . in one great field of war effort after another, first, in that of home administration by the creation of the War Cabinet and its Secretariat; then in that of the Empire by calling into existence the Imperial War Cabinet; and finally in the vast arena of inter-allied war effort by the establishment of the Supreme War Council. In neither case did he act on a mere impulse or brainwave. In all these matters he had matured his plans long before. Day and night, month in and month out he was looking ahead and planning his schemes of organization. But when the psychological moment came he invariably acted with lightning rapidity. . . . His political courage was tremendous and inspired by the public interest'.[1]

1. Lord Hankey, *The Supreme Command, 1914–1918* (Allen & Unwin, 1961), p. 868.

15

England in 1918

WHEN the storm broke on 21st March I was still on leave in London and rather ashamed to be there. Sick leave, which I hadn't earned, as I did not admit to myself that I had been sick, was less of a pleasure in a country at last committed to total war. Food rationing and food cards were introduced at this time, not that they bothered me, since soldiers drew double rations or near it, and I came to learn that the old family friend on whom I took the liberty of billeting myself when I arrived at Victoria by the leave-train, now valued my visits because a soldier's meat ration helped to feed her children. There were nightly bombing-raids in the full-moon periods by Zeppelins which managed to score a number of direct hits with their piddling little bombs. Five-and-twenty years later, in 1943, the hit-and-run raids on London by single aircraft rather resembled them. On my first night at home I was with a girl-friend in the Coliseum, then a high-class variety theatre (showing George Graves, Mark Hambourg at the piano, Lillah McCarthy in a slight sketch by Bernard Shaw, and Vesta Tilley as a soldier, singing: 'I take the air, in Leicester Square, and I stroll down Piccadilly . . .') on the night when a bomb fell on Odham's Press, killing thirty-eight people two hundred yards away. Londoners seemed nervy and queru-lous, and the carping at the Generals, or at those who criticized the Generals, in newspapers of every complexion, was a sympton of national discontent. It was a year of strikes in the munition factories, and, I may say, I never heard a word in the trenches to suggest any solidarity between 'workers' and soldiers, such as there seemed to be in Russia.

It did not take me long to learn that the companionship of the trenches, about which sentimentalists spouted, was in some un-explained sense a reality. It was something, and one must remember that even the phrase did not seem so banal when it was new-minted. Why else should I write to my mother to say that, in spite of everything, my two years in France had been 'the happiest of my life'? I did not then, and I do not now, quite know what I was trying to say, unless to imply that I liked army life better than school life. In those days only the highly educated had been introduced to the notion of the subconscious, and perhaps if I had been writing in a more recent idiom I should have hinted that the soldier's life satisfied hidden desires at a deep level of the mind. Some emotional need was met by the necessity to exert the whole of one's nervous strength in generous rivalry with one's friends. As men used to say in the Second World War, 'if they can take it, then I can take it'. I could not bear to think that 'the lads', my regiment, had been put to any test at which I had not qualified and, if there were to be more burdens to bear, I wanted to share them. Since the future could hardly exist for an infantry subaltern, I thought wholly about the present and was a 100 per cent regimental soldier, who would have resisted a staff appointment if he had been offered it. In London, at the War Office, or at a high headquarters, one seemed to hear nothing but snarling and back-biting, and—believe it or not—a front-line fighting regiment was the only place where you could be gay and reckless, in 1917, between battles. I had not forgotten that Zombie who saw me through Passchendaele and yet I wrote in my weekly letter, almost apologizing for my long holiday: 'I should like to have another smack at the Boches before the war is over.' With the lads, of course! I did not particularly enjoy the prospect of a new initiation into another savage tribe.

My mother, naturally enough, thought that I had done my bit, as we used to say, and that it was someone else's turn for the trenches, a consideration that I did not exclude. Some of my friends had seen more fighting than I had seen, had been 'over the top' more often, but few— and no officers in my battalion—could boast of a longer unbroken spell of trench duty. Yes, I was entitled to a job in 'Blighty', provided that I did not sever my ties with the battalion, provided that I could get back to the only company I cared for, to be 'with the lads' some time or other.

So obsessed was I with the sense of unity among front-line soldiers that I resented the barrier between officer and man. It seemed to me that the small privileges we enjoyed, though offset by the greater chance of being killed, deprived us of the complete experience. As an officer I could never quite penetrate the innermost core of the soldier's life, since there were some physical hardships which I was spared. The most satisfying moments of trench-life were those when my men and I were isolated as a unit in conditions where rank could claim no privilege, where the primacy I exhibited was due only to my superior knowledge. I did not want to belong to a distinct caste, though I accepted the social necessity of the military hierarchy; I wanted to identify myself 'with the lads'.

Whether this mental aberration was rare or common, I do not know, but to present my case-study of a young soldier I must relate an episode in my life which was unknown to my family or to my friends. During this leave, in London, in the early weeks of 1918, I grew tired of upper-middle-class society, and secretly longed to escape from the world of subalterns and 'flappers' into the life of cockney London, where I could associate with my true friends, 'Old Bill' and 'Young Bert', as equals. In my kit I had a smart, well-cut, private soldier's uniform which I wore in the trenches, since we had abandoned the habit of making targets of ourselves by exposing the distinctive silhouette of an officer's tunic and breeches to the German snipers. It was easy to remove the rank-badges from my shoulder-straps, and to convert myself into a private soldier, but difficult to organize the change of life. I knew a girl who worked in the almoner's office of a military hospital and per-suaded her, 'for a rag', to provide me with a new personality by stealing a hospital-discharge form, with which I became a private soldier on leave, sufficiently documented under a fictitious name to pass the scrutiny of any 'redcap'. Next I took a room at a West-end hotel and shed my captain's uniform, changing into the only suit of 'civvies' I possessed. (By the way, it was unusual in the First World War for soldiers on leave to change into plain clothes, and quite common in the Second War.) In my suit of 'civvies' I took a room at a cheap little hotel down in the city and emerged from it as a private soldier, on my way back from leave, as I told the landlord. I was now uninhibited, safe, and happy.

Removing myself to one of the many soldiers' clubs run by welfare organizations, I had no difficulty in making friends, and spent the next part of my leave in fish-and-chip shops, public bars, and music-hall galleries, keeping the company that I delighted in, more innocently, perhaps, in the East End, than if I had been making the round of the Piccadilly night-clubs. My only misadventure was when I met a man of my own company—fortunately a new recruit—face to face in the Holloway Road. I believe he thought he had seen a ghost. Is this an interesting story? What does it signify? I can't say, but it is essential to my secret history. I played this game three times during the War with variations of style.

(2)

Everyone was talking a great deal about war aims in the early months of 1918. We soldiers never had the slightest doubt about our war aims, which were to drive the German Armies out of France and Belgium and to give them such a pasting in the process that they would not again make unprovoked assaults on us or on our neighbours. There was difference of opinion about the 'peace-feelers' which the Germans put out in 1916 and 1917, and I am now disposed to regard them more favourably than I did at the time. Any chance of a negotiated peace vanished when the German General Staff imposed a punitive dictated settlement upon Russia in March 1918, treating Trotsky's new slogan, 'self-determination', with cynical contempt (which was not, however, more cynical than Trotsky's advocacy of it.) We should regard President Wilson's interventions in the European scene in the light of this revelation of German war aims. Wilson's Fourteen Points, delivered to an attentive world in January, were propositions that an unschooled boy of twenty, not far from a nervous breakdown, might be forgiven for taking seriously. They at least presented wide horizons and introduced new conceptions to those who considered world affairs for the first time. Since this incoherent jumble had been sponsored by a President who was also a Professor of Political Science, the boy of twenty may be forgiven for accepting Wilson as a major prophet. A great deal of leftish theory was in the air and I remember walking up and down Hyde Park on a Sunday morning, at the social function known as 'Church Parade', agreeing with the most blimpish colonel you can imagine that nothing would put the country right except a revolution. I talked a little socialism, defended Bernard Shaw's most extravagant views, and quoted the *New Statesman*. Never for one moment did it occur to me that the revolution might begin within the Army. We were a band of brothers pledged to destroy German militarism, to extend the comradeship of the trenches into the life of the nation, and then, perhaps, to set the world to rights by way of the Fourteen Points.

You could not, however, ignore the growth of pacifist sentiment. There were diplomats who worked for a negotiated peace; there were radicals who questioned the sincerity of our war aims; there were soft-hearted persons of such sensibility that the horrors of battle blinded their judgment, and who could blame them; and there were non-resisters who accepted the doctrines of Jesus Christ and Mahatma Gandhi. I could find little sympathy for any of these classes except the last. Of the justice of our cause I had no doubts, so that utilitarian considerations guided my actions and my opinions. What was I to do in the predicament in which I found myself? The answer I gave as a boy, and from which I have not since dissented, was that there were two reasonable courses and two only, to fight my way out, or to submit and to rely on the power of soul-force. I fought my way through.

There were few genuine non-resisters, many of the conscientious objectors being persons who objected to fighting in that war, not to fighting in any war; and these got no more support from me than did my other political opponents, the Germans. I respected true pacifists as, I believe, did many soldiers. When my Cambridge brother developed pacifist principles, moving rationally from a Christian standpoint, I saw no reason to quarrel with him even though I disagreed. Some of our elderly civilian relatives were more bellicose on principle and I think his happiest times were when one of his three soldier brothers was on leave from France. Through him I met other pacifists, notably a clergyman who went about defending conscientious objectors when they fell foul of the law. He volunteered the information that those who came under military law were lucky because courts martial were more unprejudiced than civil tribunals, and were more inclined to give humane verdicts.

The old acceptance of the war as if it were a natural disaster like an earthquake had been replaced, everywhere, by a new scepticism which affected me as it did my betters, though without indicating any other course of action than that to which I was committed. The first of the war-books, so celebrated ten years later as the school of 'disillusion', came out that winter, and gave me nightmares by the realism of its trench-scenes, without teaching me anything that I did not know. This was *Le Feu* by Henri Barbusse (*Under Fire* in the English translation), and though it does not now stand up to critical analysis it was important in its day. It demonstrated the gulf that lay between civilians and soldiers who now lived in different worlds. Such rays of lurid light directed into the gulf widened the gap. It was the civilians, not the soldiers, who had indulged their fancies in the romance of war; the civilians, not the soldiers, were disillusioned by such expositions as this.

(3)

The first of Ludendorff's attacks had already reached its crisis when I joined the Reserve Battalion, at a bleak camp of wooden huts set between two collieries on the flat coast of Northumberland, where the east wind never stopped blowing. At least, it was pleasant to meet many friends. My regiment, the old Volunteer Battalion of the Warwick-shires, had established itself, back in Victorian times, at a headquarters in Thorp Street, Birmingham, where there was a drill hall, an officers' mess, a sergeants' mess, and a social and athletic club. At the Haldane reorganization, the Volunteers had been re-formed as two Territorial units, the 5th and 6th Royal Warwickshires, which continued to share social amenities. In the great recruiting days of 1914 and 1915, each battalion had doubled in size, as a first-line for service overseas and a second-line for home defence. Then as the armies grew, the second-lines, in their turn, had gone on active service, and a third line had been formed as a reserve. After various adjustments, the 5th (Reserve) Battalion, which we generally called the 'Third-Fifth' acted as a depot for the 1/5th, 2/5, 1/6th and 2/6th; and the senior officers and N.C.O.s of all four service battalions, who knew one another from the old days at Thorp Street, regarded the Third-Fifth as a rendezvous. Sooner or later, sick or wounded, everyone who was still alive turned up at Cramlington.

Life at the Third-Fifth was very unlike the haphazard goings-on at that misbegotten unit on Cannock Chase where I had been so unhappy in 1915. This was a forcing-machine for recruits where, in the fourth year of the war, all the wheels turned with the least possible friction. When I arrived, the depot was busily emptying itself of a batch urgently required in France, and it was indicated that I need not expect to stay for longer than was necessary to pass my papers through the proper channels. Meanwhile, as there was nothing much for me to do, according to custom I had better go on a course. Someone was wanted to attend a session at a gas and anti-gas establishment seven miles away. I was provided with a clumsy service bicycle, and instructions to ride over to my Gas School every day. My conviction, as usually when I was sent on a course, was that I probably knew more about giving and taking war-gases than these stay-at-homes and, more than that, I found the subject distasteful. On the first morning, having signed the book, I stayed long enough to discover that no roll-call was taken, and thereafter played truant, setting off from camp every morning on my bicycle to ride about and enjoy the pleasant countryside behind the coastal plain. No one knew, and perhaps no one cared, and in the mornings and evenings I took stock of my colleagues in camp.

Though it had always been customary in the Old Army to affect a certain cynicism about such matters as honour, glory, and patriotism, a habit of mind which sharply distinguished British from French soldiers, this derogation of the martial spirit did not apply to matters of plain duty. A soldier of any rank was expected to 'do his bit' and to take pride in doing it thoroughly. It was one thing to make jokes about 'swinging the lead' (shirking duty), or 'working your ticket' (getting your discharge papers), and quite another thing to avoid a dangerous task which someone else must do if you did not. Officers or men whose dislike of doing what everyone disliked was so strong that they 'dodged the column' (found an excuse for not marching up the line) very soon acquired a reputation that nothing but an act of outstanding courage could repair. Just that raised eyebrow or wry smile, when Sergeant So-and-so's name, or Captain What's-it's name was mentioned, damned him; and no one was surprised when he was posted to the salvage unit, in which everyone else had a low medical category, to be discreetly forgotten by his former friends. The assumption in a service battalion was that every man could be trusted to behave like a soldier on the day.

In a reserve battalion, a subtle difference of atmosphere could be detected at the first encounter. Do not misunderstand me; I begin by declaring that the Third-Fifth was a highly efficient unit, that officers and N.C.O.s were able, hard-working men, most of whom had served in France before finding their way to Cramlington. I recall no case of corruption or oppression, but, on the other hand, many instances of forethought and kindness, as we prepared our new recruits for the slaughterhouse. The dominant note in conversation at a reserve battalion was determination to stay there. You could hear good men almost boasting that they were still in Category 'B' (unfit for active service) and admitting concern that the next medical board might pass them as fit. Perhaps the comment of some readers will be: 'very sensible, too'.

There were officers and sergeants whom I had known in France, perhaps wounded once or even twice after much hard service, who received me with pleasure and made no pretence about their intention to hold down the good jobs they had got—useful jobs which they were doing very well. There were also, I'm bound to say, some seniors ('No names, no packdrill') who had taken a quick look at trench-life and had decided it was not to their taste, in the early days when the Third Lines were being formed and needed officers. The French called soldiers of this kind *embusqués*, a good word for which there is no adequate equivalent in English. They formed a closed establishment of which the unspoken rule was, admit no newcomer lest he should take your job.

As I shall explain presently, the principal occupation of this establishment was to pass recruits through a course of military training by what would nowadays be called a crash programme, and, at this stage of the war, the Third-Fifth was not much concerned with old soldiers. I found myself one of a transient group, a mere procession of casualties, discharged from hospital, who reported at Cramlington to be posted back to the First or Second Line as soon as they were in Category 'A', fit for active service. There was no suggestion that we belonged here. I was ready, and in three weeks my orders came through for France. My first embarkation had been on Christmas Day; for my second 'they' unwittingly chose my twenty-first birthday; but I was not so green now and was not going to submit to that. I went to see a man I knew in the A.G. branch at the War Office, with two objects in view. I could sneak a day or two for my birthday by starting an argument in London, and I could, perhaps, ensure that I was sent to my own battalion, the First-Fifth, not to a new life in the Second-Fifth where I should be half a stranger, and—above all—not be posted to some other regiment, a fate that was not unlikely when so many units had been

P

wiped out in the March Retreat. As there was a crisis in France, the British and French troops were being withdrawn from Italy where all was quiet, and we thought that the 48th Division was on its way back. I persuaded the man in A.G. that it would be absurd to send me hunting round Europe for my unit and that my posting should be held up until they settled somewhere. The trick worked and back I went to await further instructions at Cramlington and to be congratulated on having invented a new and ingenious way of 'dodging the column', a view of my conduct that was so near the truth as to make me very uneasy. It would be only for a few days, I thought, and I had secured my chief object by getting my name down on the list as destined for the First-Fifth, wherever they should be. Days passed, weeks passed, no officer replacements were sent to the First-Fifth and, since the Italian front was livening up, three British divisions, among them the 48th, were—after all—retained in Italy. When I was allowed some leave in the summer I went to the War Office again to enquire what had become of my posting, but all I got now was a pretty sharp notice to shut up and stop bothering them. By this means I became one of the establishment at Cramlington with a reputation as a clever fellow at wangling my way round the War Office; and since no one believed me then when I said that my only interest in life was to get back to my beloved First-Fifth, I suppose no one will believe me now. I was always ready to go at a few hours' notice, expecting every day the order that never came, and was far from pleased with my situation. When in June the 48th Division fought a good battle[1] in the Alps and my battalion lost some officers I was miserable with frustration, and even planned an escapade with the connivance of my colonel. I thought of bluffing my way through France with a used pass and railway ticket, posted to me from Italy by a friend who had returned from leave. The chance would come if I were sent to conduct a draft of our young soldiers across the Channel. It did not come, and it was not until late October, when the war was nearly over, that I was posted overseas.

1. I wrote an account of this battle, Asiago, 15th June 1918, for the *Army Quarterly*, July 1927. It was a brilliant example of flexibility in defence by General Fanshawe, who was most unjustly sent home by Lord Cavan, the Corps Commander, an exponent of rigid defence and of cramming the front line with troops. Cavan was a tough fighting soldier, and a charming man, but as the official historian wrote to me, 'bone from the neck up'.

(4)

We were isolated at Cramlington, as there seemed to be no neighbours except the miners who were as clannish as we were. I went down
a coal-pit and came up convinced that miners were entitled to wages as
high as they could get, my only contact with the Northumbrians. We
lived our life in the mess, endlessly talking about our war experiences,
with a round of jokes and anecdotes, shared by the *pukka* fighting
soldiers from France who thus excluded the *embusqués* from their company. These conversations were governed by a strict convention that
no one should claim to have been brave. The *coda* with which you
ended your recitative had to be: 'Did I get the wind-up, Old Man?
You bet I did. Did I run for it? I put my skates on'. I read all the
military commentators, especially Hilaire Belloc with whom I even
exchanged some letters; I was the one who stuck pins in the war-map
in the ante-room, knew the names of the French generals, and was the
expert on strategy. My first appearance in print was when I wrote a
letter to *The Times* (the first of many, I'm sorry to say, for the habit has
grown on me) about the man-power question. With no one to guide
me I began to widen my range of reading in a desultory way—*Don
Juan*, Florio's *Montaigne*, *Tristram Shandy*, and a great deal of trash.
I even tried to rub up my schoolboy Latin so that I could read Horace.
A reaction against the philistinism around me turned my attention to
the decadents of the nineties by way of Oscar Wilde. Who remembers
now the Pemberton Billing scandal which stirred up as much mud in
1918 as the Profumo scandal in 1963? Pemberton Billing claimed to
have uncovered a ring of perverts in the highest society who were liable
to blackmail by the German Secret Service, a tale which was inflated by
rumour with new names every day, until his supreme moment when, in
the witness-box, he implicated the name of the judge then sitting on the
Bench. I had been so innocent as not to know that sexual aberrations
existed in Society and can describe my experience only as being corrupted by what I read in the newspapers. Some morbid streak in me
was strangely stimulated by these new suggestions at a time when my
mind was off-balance. An older man named Henry Sanders,[1] a

---

1. Second-Lieutenant H. S. Sanders, killed 21st August 1918, when serving
with the 14th Royal Warwickshire Regiment. He was moving towards pacifism
and had reached a stage where he was willing to die as a soldier but not to kill.

musician in civil life, steered my intellectual course towards sanity, until he was posted abroad and almost immediately killed. We shared a room which we decorated with colour-prints from the art monthlies, my introduction to contemporary painting, and we talked at length about books. When he was gone there was nobody to confide in but my honest trench-fellows, nothing to talk about except the war.

As I write these words I am struck by the frequency with which singing dominates my theme. No broadcast music in those days, no hi-fi, no cheap long-playing records. If we had a gramophone it was tinny and hand-operated with a few brittle discs that soon wore into scratches. But every civilized house or mess-room had a piano and in any group of friends there would be one or two who could at least play the accompaniment to chorus singing. Songs at the piano have become almost a forgotten pleasure, not that I decry the new music of the present generation by saying so. The folk-art of the late Victorians was the popular song with a strong melody, a simple rhythm, and a chorus, and it is now almost extinct. Everyone joined in, and everyone knew some dozens of traditional songs, the most celebrated collection being the *Scottish Students' Song Book*. This, assisted by innocuous beer-drinking, was our solace, and our aesthetic outlet in the officers' mess at Cramlington. Singing preserved our intellectual self-respect and if there was someone, like Henry Sanders, who sang well he got a respectful audience that, five minutes later, broke into some ribald chorus without embarrassment. I relished the bawdy Army folk-songs which had existed in many versions for generations if not centuries:

> 'A German officer crossing the Rhine, *parlez-vous*,
> Called for a bed and a bottle of wine.
>
> Oh Landlord, have you a bottle of wine, *parlez-vous*,
> Fit for an officer of the line.
>
> Oh Landlord, have you a daughter fair, *parlez-vous*,
> With bonny blue eyes and golden hair . . .?

But on Sunday evenings we just as easily turned to *Hymns Ancient and Modern*, as genuine a part of our folklore.

I remember that someone produced a score of *Patience* and we all sang with gusto:

> 'Conceive me if you can,
> A matter-of-fact young man,
> A commonplace type, with a stick and a pipe,
> And a half-bred black-and-tan,
> Who thinks suburban hops
> More fun than Monday Pops . . .'

Yes, that's exactly what we were, and I wasn't a *je-ne-sais-quoi* young man for long at a time.

(5)

Commanding a company in a reserve battalion was a dull business. By this stage of the war the routine was so perfected that we all worked to a programme dictated to us in detail by the War Office. The curriculum was formalized and the instruction was given by experts in musketry, bayonet-fighting, and the other military arts. I should have enjoyed training my company in my own way, whereas all I did was to parade them and hand them over to a sergeant-instructor before settling down in the company office to what the Army called 'interior economy', lists and schedules of pay and rations and clothing with very strict accounting to the last penny. I was bored and under-worked, with plenty of time for thinking about the War and wishing I was overseas with the lads I really cared for, which is not to say that we were uninterested in the lads we had in front of us. Every six months, the Third-Fifth received seven or eight hundred boys of eighteen and a half, to be converted into soldiers and sent to France as soon as they reached their nineteenth birthday; sooner, sometimes, in the dark days of 1918. They arrived quite raw having been called up, medically examined, and given a uniform which they did not know how to wear. By this time the Territorial system had lapsed with the result that they might come from anywhere, the batch I had most to do with being Yorkshiremen. Untrained and under age, but medically fit, they were classified 'A4'. As soon as they were trained and aged nineteen they became 'A1', when we should see the last of them. I have forgotten who was classified 'A2' and 'A3'.

The skinny, sallow, shambling, frightened victims of our industrial system, suffering from the effect of wartime shortages, who were given into our hands, were unrecognisable after six months of good food, fresh air, and physical training. They looked twice the size and, as we weighed and measured them, I am able to say that they put on an average of one inch in height and one stone in weight during their time with us. One boy's mother wrote to me complaining that her Johnny was half-starved in the Army and what was I going to do about it. I was able to convince her that Johnny had put on two stone of weight and two inches of height, and had never had so good an appetite before. Beyond statistical measurement was their change in character, to ruddy, handsome, clear-eyed young men with square shoulders who stood up straight and were afraid of no one, not even the sergeant-major. 'The effect on me', I wrote in a letter, 'is to make me a violent socialist when I see how underdeveloped industrialism has kept them, and a Prussian militarist when I see what soldiering makes of them.' Then I added, rather inconsequently, in a phrase that dates: 'I shall never think of the lower classes again in the same way after the war'. An odd forecast but true; I never have.

My best time in Northumberland was the month of August, when I ran a musketry camp at Ponteland, which in those days was not as it is now, a row of petrol pumps beside a speedway, but was a pretty rural village where I made friends with the landlady of the Seven Stars and her daughter. As adjutant of the camp I received companies which came over in turn from Cramlington for a few days of field-firing on the rifle range. It was enjoyable because we escaped from the schedules to do as we thought best, and because there was a smack of active service about it. We smelt powder. To back me up I had Sergeant Miller,[1] with whom I had been out on many a patrol in France, and when we directed field-firing practices together I noticed a common characteristic which sometimes annoyed the other officers. Miller and I, though we never spoke of it, consistently took liberties with the safety precautions that we imposed so rigorously on our 'A4' boys. We

1. Here I ought also to mention my friend from the First-Fifth, F. H. D. Allenby, with whom I shared the mixed feelings I have tried to describe in this chapter. We enjoyed Ponteland together. He was posted abroad before me, was sent to a strange battalion, and told me—not long ago—that he was none the worse for it.

took short cuts across the danger zone where there was one chance in a million of a bullet flying wide, and always stood forward of the firing-point where we would let no one else stand. It did me good to show off a little, especially as I was never much afraid of unaimed rifle-fire. If it had been the bombing-range I should have let someone else show off by handling the unexploded bombs. One had to do the manly thing at times, like unarmed combat against a bayonet-man, and, to my surprise, for I'm not that sort of person, I find from my diary that twice that year I won a black eye at boxing.

When term ended we packed the lads off, rather excited like school-boys for the holidays, washed our hands of them, never heard of them again, and got ready for the next draft. They might have been so many battery-fed chickens. In my time at Cramlington I saw the end of one batch, a second batch put through the works, and a third batch started on its course. The departure was painful; I knew well that under their forced cheerfulness there were mixed sentiments and I did not much like the headmaster's—I mean the colonel's—set speech of valediction. The boys suddenly looked much younger, loaded down with their marching order, their new steel helmets and gas-masks, their pouches stocked with live ammunition, and with their iron rations tied to their packs at the last moment in white linen bags—the unmistakable sign by which you recognized a new draft in France. I wished I could have gone with them and led them into action as a team. Though the war was drawing to a close, there was still time for many of them to die at the breaking of the Hindenburg Line, and I got no satisfaction out of sending other men to die for me, when I too was young and classified 'A.1'.

In the last days of the war, death came to us in Northumberland. The great pestilence called Spanish Influenza hit us first in June as just a typical epidemic of 'flu. In October it came more virulently when we had taken in a new draft of boys and had not begun to harden them. They fell down in scores on parade; half the camp became a hospital; and of 300 cases eighteen died. It didn't kill the old soldiers. We just had another touch of 'flu.

16

How the war ended

Now that I have reached the last phase the question that I must answer is when, and how, did we know that the war was won. Even in March, though it had never seemed farther off, we had no doubts of final victory and, as in other crises of war, the despondency grew greater the farther you got from the fighting line. In April my letters, despatched on a six weeks' voyage to New Zealand, predicted that, bad though the news was, it would be better before the mail arrived, a guess that was rather too optimistic. By July the war had come back to an equilibrium when the old soldiers, if no one else, were confident that the Boches would not now break through. Mangin's counter-attack restored our faith in the French Army while, at the same time, the French retreat of twenty kilometres in a day, a record for retreating, put them on a level with the British. If they could run so far and make so good a recovery they need not regard our March retreat as a disaster. The balance tipped at the end of the month. On 24th July Foch held a conference at which he announced the resumption of the offensive, a decision which cannot have surprised Pétain, Haig, or Pershing since he had recommended nothing but the offensive in every situation for the previous four years. His plan was to clear the lateral railways behind the allied front; by the Mangin counter-attack which was still in progress; by a British attack to disengage the railways through Amiens; and by an American attack at St. Mihiel, a sharp salient which broke the French communications in the sector between Verdun and Metz. Though the conference was secret the effects of it soon became public knowledge.

Haig was already deep in plans for his contribution which is notable as the most perfect exemplar of surprise in the First World War. He completely deceived the enemy who had no inkling of what was coming, as we know now from the reports of Ludendorff's conference which, about the same time, made a forecast of allied intentions and was wrong in every particular. The battle was entrusted to Rawlinson's Fourth Army which, two years earlier, had distinguished itself on the 14th July 1916 by a successful surprise attack; and since then, Cambrai had afforded a new method. The great Tank attack of the Fourth Army on 8th August 1918 was at last the battle of a dream, the combination that we had all longed for of modern techniques with fighting experience. The German front collapsed and the assaulting troops went forward six or seven miles, taking 30,000 prisoners and 400 guns, for casualties much less than they inflicted, though half of the tanks were expended in battle. On the right, the French, without tanks and therefore with a bombardment, conformed and brought their line forward as auxiliaries, the part they were chiefly to play for the rest of the war. As always, when in action, their officers showed skill to match the men's courage, but it was not their day. Honours went to the Australians who advanced farthest, to the Canadians who had the most casualties, and to the British 3rd Corps which ran into the heaviest opposition.

At this moment, the ten divisions from the Dominions (four Canadian, five Australian, one New Zealand) assumed a place which cannot be denied them as the best fighting troops in any army. For the last few weeks of the war the achievement of these divisions was greater in relation to their strength than that of any other formations and they must be given credit for it. In the autumn of 1918 these ten divisions constituted about one fifth of the fighting strength of the B.E.F. and suffered about one third of the casualties. Just as the French Army which had fought the first two campaigns now played second fiddle to the British, so the strain on British manpower made it inevitable that the units from Britain should be losing some of their fighting quality. My 'A4 boys', supported by sedentary middle-aged men, were not quite the calibre of the young men from the Dominions, almost all between twenty and thirty; the Canadians with their selective call-up; the Australians—still an army of volunteers; the New Zealanders whose physique may be ascribed to the fact that in those long-past days theirs was the only Welfare State in the world. For the Battle of 8th August this comment needs some qualification, for it was the day of the tanks, and the tanks were manned by men from Britain. How fortunate it was that two full years had been spent in remedying mechanical defects and in training crews after the early experimental battles, so that Haig's armies were far ahead of Germans, French, or Americans in Tank design and tactics.

Ludendorff wrote in his memoirs that 8th August was the 'black day of the German Army' but he did not tell us so at the time. To us it was a red-letter day for the British Army, not quite the same thing, and we did not give it more significance than it merited. Like every other attack it bogged down, but after a longer run, and with a balance of profit and loss strongly in our favour. This was what we had been trying to do for years, and it brought victory at last in sight. No more than that. If anyone, except Haig who did not publicize his views, thought that the War could be ended in a few weeks, he did not come my way. It was plain now that we could hold out till the American armies appeared in force and that we could give a good account of ourselves in the final campaign. Every year we had talked of victory next spring, and that is what we talked of in the autumn of 1918. Everyone, that is to say, except Haig, who had the ball at his feet and meant to kick it.

At the War Office, Sir Henry Wilson, plausible, convincing, and wrong as usual, was planning for 1919. Worst of all, General Pershing, with a wooden singleness of aim, struggled to keep his men out of the battle so that they could win the war next year under his sole authority. Haig remarked with more than his accustomed acidity that Pershing's withdrawal of three divisions from the British sector to go into training somewhere else, just at the moment when they might have been thrown in to exploit the breakthrough, was a new precedent in strategy. Haig seems to have liked no one much on Pershing's staff except a young A.D.C. called George Patton, who was full of fight. Before August was over, Haig was urging the War Office and the Allied commanders to press on and finish the war before winter. Though we supposed that the change in our fortunes was due to unified command under Foch, we have learned to modify that opinion. Haig was so far the predominant partner in the alliance and his judgment so sure on this decisive issue, that he imposed his will upon Foch, though there was nothing in Foch's character to make him disinclined to press the advantage home. Haig overruled Foch about the frontage of the next assault and proved to be right by forcing a general German retirement. He persuaded Foch to direct the Americans northwards from the Argonne towards Mezières, instead of eastwards towards Metz, thus bringing the allied attacks into a converging pattern, and he did his best to limit the weight of troops behind the Belgian advance which Foch promoted for political not strategic reasons. Haig and Foch quarrelled pretty sharply about the employment of Plumer's Second Army in this action, Haig's drive, with the strongest armies of the alliance behind him, was towards the railway system of the Sambre and Meuse valleys which as in 1914 (and again in 1940) dictated German strategy. It was Haig who saw how the War could be won in 1918 and Haig's armies alone that were then capable of winning it. Haig saved us all from another winter campaign, as Montgomery wanted to do in 1944.

On 14th August while Paris, London, and Washington were thinking of next year's battles, the Kaiser called a conference to discuss what might be saved of Germany's ill-gotten gains now she had lost the war. There was much hunting for scapegoats and many German generals were deprived of their commands. It was too late, and in the second half of the month the British harried the Kaiser's armies, with much hard fighting, across the Somme country and the devastated area. On 31st August the Australians, by one of the most accomplished actions of the war, crossed the Somme and again seized Mont St. Quentin, which had fallen into our hands so easily in 1917. By 2nd September the Canadians were battering at the Wotan Line south of Arras. Three weeks later the British were again attacking the outposts of the Hindenburg Line, with very hard fighting at Epehy which my battalion knew so well. Interested as we were in England to see these old names coming back into the War news, we were even more exhilarated by the events on the French and American front. The sore thumb of the St. Mihiel Salient was neatly bitten off by two American Corps on 12th September, the first big battle they fought for themselves, at which we were delighted. We were not told that every gun, tank and aeroplane that took part had been supplied by the British or the French, or that Pershing even had to borrow horses from Haig who could ill spare them.

September was a wet month in 1918, allowing less progress in France. In mid-month all the other battle fronts blew wide open. On the 18th the dreary Macedonian campaign in which so many good men had been side-tracked for years, began to pay a dividend. The Salonica

Army knocked Bulgaria out of the war in ten days. At the same time Allenby's blitz overwhelmed the Turkish armies in Palestine, and the British in Mesopotamia began to move up the Tigris towards Mosul. Before the end of October the Turkish Empire had disintegrated and the Austro-Hungarian Empire was cracking. It was the Italian Army that toppled the Hapsburg dynasty over and, as my regiment had some share in that, I shall refer to it again.

Foch's co-ordinated advance against the whole German position, by Americans and French on the right, British in the centre, and British and Belgians on the left, was begun on 26th September, and by 4th October the German armies were crumbling. On the right, the Americans, who insisted on acquiring their experience the hard way, repeated most of the errors the French had made in 1914 and the British in 1916. The decisive blow was struck by the British Fourth Army which broke the main defences of the Hindenburg Line where they were strengthened by the deep St. Quentin Canal—seven feet of mud and water in a cutting thirty-five feet wide—an operation of war as tough and complex as any that military history records. Again the Australians did well, as did two American Divisions who fought beside them; but the honours of the battle went to the British 46th Division (North Midland Territorials) whom we formerly met in the disaster at Gommecourt Wood on 1st July 1916. The Germans fought hard for this final position which they had been entrenching in great depth for two years, and the whole operation cost the 46th Division three weeks of attacking and 4,000 casualties. To offset this loss they captured 4,000 prisoners and won four V.C.s. On the decisive day, 29th September 1918, the 137th Brigade (North and South Staffordshires) commanded by Brigadier-General J. V. Campbell, v.c., forced the crossing of the main obstacle, led by assault parties who swam the canal under fire, an operation skilfully managed without heavy loss.[1] This great feat of arms was followed by bitter fighting in which many counter-attacks were beaten off. It was victory at last, and the High Command was left with no policy but to retreat while their diplomats begged for terms.

1. The best account of this famous exploit, perhaps the supreme achievement of the B.E.F. in France, is to be found in *Breaking the Hindenburg Line* by Sir Raymond Priestley (Fisher Unwin, 1919).

(2)

It began to dawn on us in England that the war was over. Yet, as late as 1st September I had been sent to reconnoitre the crossings of the Tyne as part of a plan for moving reinforcements in case of a German invasion of the North-East Coast. During the summer we had held anti-invasion exercises and the necessity of home defence had been given as a reason for retaining troops in England who might have fought in France. I cannot say that I had myself been much alarmed at the prospect. Neither had I foreseen that I should soon be unemployed. In September I wrote home: 'The war is looking very good in France but I don't like the labour troubles in England.' There was even a strike of the London police. My letters began to refer to what I should do after the war, a prospect which was alarming. 'I shall feel lost,' I said, 'when we all drift away from one another.' Not till 13th October did I strike a new note: 'These are great days, almost as stirring as August 1914. The place is full of rumours that the Germans have capitulated.'

The breaking of the Hindenburg Line had brought it about. On 1st October Hindenburg, who rarely intervened over the head of Ludendorff, insisted on negotiating for a cessation of hostilities, and on the 4th the first of the notes asking for terms was despatched to President Wilson. For some days more, Ludendorff clung to a belief that his armies might still stand on the Meuse and that Germany might yet get terms better than surrender; and during those days the fighting continued. While the German Army as a whole disintegrated and the common infantry units simply vanished, desperate bands of artillerymen and machine-gunners held their ground, disputing every step of the allied advance. Under the conditions of the First World War such pockets of stubborn defence could make advancing troops pay a heavy price.

Difficult and dangerous as these petty operations were, it was not fighting that delayed the allies. Their gigantic forces, advancing side by side on a front of two hundred miles, into battle-scarred country, away from their railway communications, over roads progressively worse, in late autumn when the rains were setting in, had almost come to a standstill before the armistice line was fixed. Only the most active formations, urged on by their commanders, made much progress and no one wanted to be killed on the last day of the war. The Americans approached Sedan but chivalrously allowed the *entrée* to the French, the Guards occupied Maubeuge, and on Armistice Day the Canadians entered Mons. On the night of 7th November the German armistice commissioners crossed the line to receive the rigorous terms which Foch and Admiral Wemyss dictated to them. They agreed to sign, at five in the morning of the 11th, and a period of six hours only was allowed for stopping the war. Since everyone knew that the end was coming, there was some ill-feeling against officers who pushed their men into danger between the 8th and the 11th.

By this time I had left Northumberland and had got as far as the base camp at Le Havre where I was waiting for a reinforcement train to Italy. Every day we had a new rumour that an armistice had been signed, and no clairvoyant warned me of any significance in the dating of the order I received, two or three days in advance, to parade a thousand men and entrain them for Italy on Monday, 11th November 1918, at 11 a.m.

17

In Italy after the Armistice

A MERE crowd, of five officers and 1,100 other ranks from half a dozen regiments, not organized in groups under their own N.C.O.s, were to be conveyed by slow goods train across France and Italy, a five days' journey with frequent stops. Though I was the senior I was not in command, but was assistant to a train-conducting officer, a captain whose task it was to manage parties of this sort. As we paraded them, meeting one another for the first time, the signal was given dissolving the whole Western world into a carnival that did not slacken for forty-eight hours, and kept breaking out, day after day, for several weeks.

On the first morning we were too dazed, by the news that we had received only at breakfast-time, to feel the effect. Our 1,100 set off in a state of mild hysteria, to march from Harfleur Camp to the goods entrance of Le Havre railway station, arriving at midday among crowds gathering in the streets, who sang and waved flags, or offered our men drinks from sidewalk cafés, while girls broke into the ranks and marched with them, arms enlaced. It was four o'clock before our train started, since the French engine-driver and the station staff were joining in the fun. We spent the afternoon plunging into *estaminets* and dragging our men out by the scruff of the neck, while others slipped away behind our backs. Laughing and joking, we were determined that the draft should leave, so fixed were we in our military notions. The engine hooted. We left, among cheering crowds, my last piece of trouble being with a drunken American sergeant who insisted that he was coming to Italy too, until I threw him off the footboard as the train gathered speed, and left him lying on the track.

The largest contingent was a batch of two or three hundred 'A4' boys of the Durham Light Infantry, wild with excitement and indifferent where they were going. We had bundled them into cattle

239

trucks, marked '*hommes* 40, *chevaux* 8', where they sat dangling their legs out of the sliding doors and whistling at the girls in every town. We dawdled along at ten or twelve miles an hour, stopping at sidings where a queue would form to borrow hot water from the engine-driver for making tea, or more rarely at stations where pretty ladies dispensed refreshments from Y.M.C.A. canteens. Otherwise, the fare was bully and biscuits and the bed a blanket on the wagon floor. We officers had one compartment next to the guard's van (but no guard) and lay along the seats or in the luggage-racks. As we coasted beside the Marne, the boys realized that they would now have no use for their live ammuni-tion and began a little target-shooting at interesting objects seen from the train. What could we officers do? There was no corridor, no communication cord, and no N.C.O.s to be made responsible for each truck. Hours later, when the train stopped, the culprits couldn't be found. 'No, sir,' with a bright smile. 'Not me, sir. Perhaps one of them Gordons in the next truck.' At a ten minutes' halt you couldn't inspect a thousand rifles and count a hundred thousand rounds of ammunition. Luckily the 'A4 boys' grew tired of shooting as we sagged south into the Midi, and gave their attention rather to raiding refreshment stalls at stations. A hundred Gordon Highlanders were a different proposition, all old soldiers and some of them sergeants or corporals, but utterly unconcerned with those boys of the Durhams. They were impeccably correct and regimental with us officers, and dumbly unco-operative. Down in the Rhone Valley we were on the P.L.M. main line which gave the old soldiers their opening. By ones and twos they slipped into the cheering crowds on station platforms, where a Gordon Highlander in a kilt was a welcome sight, and vanished, to catch up later by the mail-train which travelled four times as fast as we did. Somewhere in Provence we started telegraphing ahead to warn military officers in charge of stations (R.T.O.s) that our trainload was somewhat unruly, and at Marseilles, in the middle of the night, I was awoken by an elderly major in a steel helmet, shaking a revolver and asking me whether my life was safe. Was it true that the Bolsheviks had seized the train? 'The boys are fast asleep,' I said, 'and as good as gold. Don't wake them.' We passed on and round the Riviera, which none of us had seen before. The landscape—more beautiful then than now—and the carnival of flowers through which we moved, kept everyone good and happy on the last day. I think, now, it was rather mean of me to consent to an identification parade at Arquata in the Appennines, where we handed our 1,100 over to the Base Commandant. We picked out some of the ringleaders in the mischief, who looked at us so reproachfully that I'm glad to think nothing worse happened to them than a few days' confinement to camp.

Never had I known the First-Fifth more sure of itself, more proud of its tradition than when I rejoined at Valdagno near Vicenza. Its war record had finished with such a blaze of success in battle that from that day to this I have regretted not being there. If only I could have escaped from Cramlington one month sooner.

After the failure of the last Austrian offensive (in which the First-Fifth had lost heavily while taking the shock), the Hapsburg Empire had revealed cracks on every side. Foch had urged the Italians to push the crazy structure down, but had not brought them to the pitch of doing so until the end of October. On the 27th the British 7th Division, so celebrated at Ypres in 1914, together with my old friends the 23rd Division, made an assault crossing of the Piave as the first stage in the Italian advance, to which the name of the battle of Vittorio Veneto has been given, though it hardly amounted to a battle. At the same time an advance from the Asiago Plateau through the Alps was led by the British 48th Division. On 1st November the Austrian front collapsed, and the Warwickshire Brigade marched into the Val d'Assa as an advance-guard. They were the only body of allied troops on the Western Front to fight their way into enemy territory during the great battles of 1918. Brushing aside the last few Austrian rearguards, they advanced forty miles in three winter days over mountains running up to 6,000 feet. On 3rd November, when the 5th Battalion was leading, they broke through into the Val Sugana to intercept the retreat of a whole Austrian Corps. Battalion after battalion was bluffed into surrendering by my colonel and a handful of men who had pushed forward on captured Austrian gun-horses. The last words of the last British communiqué from Italy were to say that the 48th Division had taken 20,000 prisoners, including four Corps or Divisional Commanders and several hundred guns. The 48th Division received the surrender of Trento but allowed the privilege of a triumphal entry to the Italians.

The tales told by my friends were of experiences you would not expect in Flanders: one of my corporals captured an Austrian field cashier, with his cash-box; the company scapegrace, wandering—I fear

Q

—in search of loot, received the surrender of four Austrian staff officers whom he found in bed, and was puzzled over what to do with them; we re-equipped our transport with thoroughbred horses that had formerly been cavalry officers' chargers. 'We,' I find myself saying, though I had not been there. As I came into Valdagno on a winter evening and recognized the strong resonant assured voices of my company singing as they marched to their billets, I knew I was home at last, where I should be known and recognized as 'one of us', and not 'one of them'.

(2)

We spent the winter in Valdagno, a picturesque small town set among pastures and vineyards on a tongue of land running up into the high Alps. At the head of the valley was Monte Pasubio, where Italian Alpine troops had been in action above the snow-line, and below, where the valley debouched on to the plain, the highest point was crowned by the ruined tower of the Montecchi, which we called (inaccurately) Juliet's Castle. The place was shabby and impoverished, and raging with Spanish 'Flu so that one never went out without seeing a funeral. At the end of the street, beyond the grand house where our general lived, was a small textile factory which employed the village girls (like 'Pippa' in the silk-mill at Asolo) except when there was a strike as more than once that winter. All is changed now since Marzotto's little factory has grown into a great industrial combine (which owns the 'Jolly' Hotels so well known to tourists). The whole valley is filled with suburbs, ferro-concrete, and neon lighting.

The 5th were fortunate in being billeted in the town of Valdagno, with divisional and brigade headquarters, while the other battalions were quartered out in neighbouring villages. My company mess was in a large upper room over a shop, in sight of the piazza where the band played for our daily guard-mounting. As well as a canteen, an officers' club, a nightly cinema, a pantomime staged by the divisional concert-party, we had an education officer who improvised technical courses (I took some classes in reading and writing for our few semi-literates). There were improving lectures, and well-attended voluntary church services. All kinds of sport flourished, with football competitions, boxing championships, athletics, horse-racing. There were week-end trips to Venice.

Military form was preserved; spit-and-polish prevailed; and I'm not aware that anyone resented it. We were in a mood at first for parades and displays, and I was proud at being selected to command the guard of honour of a hundred picked men when some top Italian general visited us, regretting only that I couldn't manage my thoroughbred Austrian charger on parade. We kept up our military training rather scrupulously but relaxed to a peacetime degree of urgency with work in the mornings and organized games in the afternoons.

In December we were encouraged to assert our views in the General Election by the new device of a postal vote, since Lloyd George rightly assumed that he could count upon the support of the soldiers. The age-limit for the franchise was lowered to include men on active service even if under twenty-one, but I had no residence qualification in the United Kingdom and therefore no vote, which I did not resent as there seemed to be little interest in the election at Valdagno. We were not affected by the outcries in the popular Press about 'hanging the Kaiser' and 'squeezing Germany till you could hear the pips squeak' as these suggestions reached us many days late. Ignorant as I was, I rather favoured the first if not the second of these proposals. The Army, which lived among the victims of war, never approved of starving them.[1] By contrast, the election manifesto issued by the Coalition was a work of studied moderation, concerned only with proposals, indicated in the vaguest terms, for housing, education, labour relations, and resettling the soldiers.

As political life reappeared, the older and more responsible men resumed a civilian habit of mind which was impossible for the young majority, who had known no trade but war and who had no civilian jobs to which they longed to return. What was 'de-mobilization', the new vogue-word, to the likes of me? I was a little scared of it and was in no hurry to be thrown out of the nest. I clung to what was left of the battalion and only after I found myself in a spot of trouble did I make up my mind to go. Wiser heads than mine had for months been busy with plans for a systematic release of essential men from the Army, in priorities decided by the needs of the economy. We were all arranged in categories with code-numbers, mine being Class 38, 'student', since I could think of no other way to describe myself.

1. It did not fall to us but to the 2nd Royal Warwickshire in the 7th Division to convoy a trainload of food to the starving people of Vienna.

Demobilization began for us on 23rd December, when the first party of technicians—I forget in what trades—entrained for England and civil life. From this date onwards, the strength of the Battalion was gradually run down, and discontent slowly grew among those who were avid to go home but were not in a high category. In a good regiment where it was understood that all of us were in the same boat, that the colonel had his code-number just like the company cook, this mounting wave of urgency to be off did not take the form of internal sedition. Clearly the blame lay on Whitehall, not on the regimental officers, nor even on that universal scapegoat, the staff. In the big base camps where large numbers of men (like my Bolshevik trainload) were herded together without the integrating force of regimental discipline, there was dangerous unrest. As far as I am aware, no study has ever been made of the undercurrent of mutiny that ran through the British armies in the months after the armistice. What occurred overseas was not reported in the Press, and what occurred in England must be sought out in the news-columns of local papers. The few observations I can make relate to incidents that happened to come to my notice.

(3)

High-spirited young men, inured to acts of violence, with weapons always in their hands, are never easy to control, and the moderation of British troops should be thought more surprising than their occasional ferocity. There had been many soldiers' riots during the war, as in every war, though they were not publicized in the newspapers, most of them ebullitions of hot temper by men exasperated at some abuse. Not often did a 'rag' become a riot, and still less often did a riot become a mutiny. The Australians and New Zealanders had a name for solving their social problems in their own way, on two occasions at least, by reprisals on civilians who exploited or harassed friendly troops. On Good Friday 1915 they wrecked and looted the red-light district of Cairo, and in December 1918 they raided the Arab village of Surafend where guerillas had fired on them. Allenby, no weak commander, was quite unable to prevent or to punish this latter outrage. The base camps in France were always unruly and I can vouch for the Etaples mutiny of September 1917, which is not mentioned in the war histories. For twenty-four hours, until two battalions of front-line troops were plucked out of Passchendaele in fighting order to restore discipline, the town and the base were in the hands of a mob of soldiers who had thrown the commandant into the river, or so I was told. This was a reaction against acts of petty tyranny by tactless officers. The proper comment to make is that the local outbreak showed no sign of spreading. The battalion of the Manchesters whom I saw patrolling the streets of Etaples in fighting order, on 17th September, were most cheerfully engaged in restoring order. While not grudging the rioters their bit of fun, the joke had gone far enough and it was time to get on with the war. None of these outbreaks had any political undertone but who could say, considering what had happened in Russia and what was happening in Germany, whether a soldiers' riot might be the first move in a revolution. It was always behind the line that serious trouble began, in the mixed camps where men of all units exchanged complaints and did not know the officers in charge. Unrest in a regiment was of another kind or so it seemed from my experience.

One afternoon we heard of trouble in a neighbouring unit, where an officer with a bad name for hazing his men demanded too much of them. They struck work, civilly refusing to parade for a duty they thought (and I thought) unnecessary. Brigade called on the 5th to restore order and the colonel assigned the job to me. 'Parade an armed picket of fifty men and stand by for further instructions.' Thinking no more of this than that it would be like my high jinks with the Bolshevik train, I sent for the orderly sergeant and gave him his orders. Five minutes later he was back from the company billets, looking rather pale. 'The company won't go on parade, sir.' 'What bloody nonsense is this?' I said. 'I'll go and see to it.' The billets were a row of store-rooms in a courtyard behind a shop, three or four doors away from my mess. It was five in the evening, after teas, when half the company should have been lounging about the courtyard, reading and writing their home letters, or polishing their buttons before walking out to whatever entertainment Valdagno could offer.

The courtyard was empty; no one in the sergeant-major's cubicle; not a soldier in sight except one corporal who ran when he saw me coming, pretending that he did not hear my shout. In an inner room I found eight men who had not succeeded in evading me. 'What's this nonsense?' I said. 'Get out on parade.' They stood to attention, as was right when an officer addressed them, and not a man moved. I walked up to one man I knew well. 'You, Thomas Atkins,' I said, addressing him by name, 'I'm ordering you to go on parade.' He stood still, looking through me as if I wasn't there. What more could I do? No one man can make eight men obey him if they are resolved to disobey.

I put the orderly sergeant on duty at the gate to let no one go out and went to report to the colonel. We were finished. If my company refused duty there was no one he could find to impose discipline. The colonel sent for all his officers, about twenty-four in number, and instructed us to walk about the town in pairs, doing what we could to maintain order, which proved easy. The streets were now full of our men, and men of other regiments, properly dressed in their 'walking-out' clothes, with side-arms which we always carried in Italy, strolling in and out of the shops and cafés, lining up for the divisional cinema show, perfectly orderly, and saluting us scrupulously as we patrolled the town, wondering what would happen next day.

But nothing happened. Next day was normal and all the companies paraded as if no mutiny had taken place. While these men were soldiers, and good for any military duty, many of them were also trade unionists, with a strong tradition of solidarity, even if it meant a sympathetic strike. The war was over and they were soldiers now on sufferance, within limits. My outstanding problem was what to do with the corporal and the eight men who had openly disobeyed my direct order; they were good men and my friends. I had them 'put on a charge' and brought before me at company orders for 'neglect of duty'. 'Refusing to obey an order' was a serious charge which would have obliged me to send them to court martial. I reprimanded them and said: 'Today the battalion is having a half-holiday for the final of the Football Cup. There is a picket required for duty this afternoon. You will not go to the football match but will find this picket instead of the duty you shirked last night.' It was a risk and might have set off another strike, against victimization; but they took my point. The duty was done, everyone's face was saved, and discipline was superficially restored with no hard feelings. I believe that there were scores of episodes like this during the armistice winter.

I have a third failure of military discipline to record, and it differs from the others in describing how that would-be martinet, Captain Carrington, fell from grace. At Christmas we decided to finance a series of dinner-parties by drawing on regimental funds accumulated from the profits of the canteen. Each of the companies had a Christmas dinner at which all ranks sat down together in the village inn. Rather more elaborately the officers entertained the sergeants' mess, and much more elaborately the sergeants entertained the officers' mess. I was not now quite so young, and having a good head for liquor I found myself one of the last few survivors at each of these old-fashioned orgies. Two or three times that winter I was one of an after-party that would not go home till morning, the stalwarts always including with me one other officer and two sergeants who had been through much together in the war years. We four evaporated our inhibitions about rank in an alcoholic haze during the small hours. Cautiously, and perhaps imprudently, we admitted two or three guests from either side to our convivial meetings; but the Valdagno Binge Club kept up a pace that could not last. A sort of bump supper, time after time, was not easily kept private, nor were we helped in secrecy by knowing every girl in the village. (Though not so well as I thought. When I went back to Valdagno, ten years later, Mafalda at the village inn was hospitable but had forgotten me. She enquired only after the 'Tamborino', the drummer-boy. You never know with women.)

Nevertheless the club had one rule—its only rule—other than '*fay ce que voudras*'; and this I enforced as the senior. From reveille to lights out we were the two best officers and the two best sergeants in the battalion; after dark we were just ourselves. It gave me peculiar pleasure to inspect their platoons on parade at 8.30 with minute attention to military pedantry while recalling the terms on which I had parted from them eight hours previously. Not many weeks passed before someone complained of the noise on club-nights, with inevitable consequences. I was held responsible for a breach of discipline that alarmed higher authority at a time when it was exceedingly nervous about revolutionary notions, and I ceased to be regarded as the model young officer. I can't say that I feel shamefaced when I drag the Valdagno Binge Club out of the recesses of my memory now.

While adjustments were being made for demobilization and re-mobilization, discipline in the armies was inconstant. Until the armistice, we had been 'with it', willing to accept discipline, indeed welcoming it. Army life, in spite of its harshness, enabled us to extract an essence, an elixir from every experience if only it was social, not individual. Together we could face any test, even the death-pact, if discipline had its counterpart in *esprit de corps*. What else have I been trying to demonstrate in these pages except this key to our extraordinary conduct? Why did we behave in this way for four long years? What is the tropism that makes men think the worse of themselves if they have not been soldiers? Where in my tale of woe can I find the something that sustained our pride? Discipline without *esprit de corps* is a damnable thing for which no humane person is likely to offer a defence; discipline based on *esprit de corps* is the dynamic of human progress towards any goal. It must rest upon a willingness to serve. I do not offer these commonplace observations by way of apology but as an explanation. On armistice morning the surface tension broke. Whatever cohesion had held the army together, 'like a great machine', worked no longer. My five hundred or six hundred comrades at Valdagno were mine no more but living their own lives, and my delight in being with them was romantic. I was savouring an unreal atmosphere that had vanished into the past.

18

'News, Lads, our Wars are done'

MANY accounts have been written of the sudden release of tension in the belligerent countries when the signing of the Armistice was announced. The news came through early in the morning, after the appearance of the newspapers, and spread by rumour. In London the firing of 'maroons', that is rockets which burst with a dull booming explosion, relieved the anxiety of the last few days. The news was genuine, the bloodshed, which had been copious in the last weeks of the war, was over, and the world threw off the burden of horror. As in 1914 when no one knew how to start a war, so again in 1918 no one knew what was appropriate. A hysteric fit seized those who were young and knew that they could now live, while the old were silent about their anxieties. The first merely jubilant mood was expressed in an outburst of what used to be called 'mafficking', with singing and dancing in the streets. Dozens of captured German guns which had been displayed in the Mall were dragged into Trafalgar Square and burned on a gigantic bonfire. The second night was noisier than the first night and, for weeks to come, the arrival of parties of friends, demobilized from the forces, sparked off new outbursts like a succession of bank holidays or boat-race nights. Nineteen-nineteen, in the West End, was a year of repeated carnivals, with a new quality that London had not previously known. West End and East End had observed the proprieties by keeping themselves to themselves in earlier days. The 'masses' now invaded the domain of the 'classes' and soldiers with their girls danced round the fountain in Piccadilly Circus which once had been the property of Piccadilly Johnnies in evening dress. Did many make reservations like the unregarded Poet-Laureate, who wrote:

'Amid the flimsy joy of the uproarious city
My spirit on those first jubilant days of armistice
Was heavier within me, and felt a profounder fear
Than ever it knew in all the war's darkest dismay.'

The underlying anxiety felt by some perceptive persons was not, I think, general and was certainly not felt by the young. A more common view was that we could now live happily ever after in a 'land fit for heroes to live in' as the Prime Minister intended. Optimism reigned at first in government circles where the call-up of conscripts was at once stopped, the licensing restrictions were eased, reserve supplies of food were thrown on the market, and, after a few days, food-rationing was totally abolished. We supposed that the soldiers would soon return to a world of full employment at the high wartime rate of wages; and the large majority that did not understand finance accepted the word of a Cabinet Minister, Sir Eric Geddes, that any deficit in our national accounting could be covered by making Germany pay.

(2)

No contrast could be greater than that between the conclusions of the First and Second World Wars. In 1918 we had not been sure even of eventual victory till the late summer, and had seen no hope of a quick ending to the war until three or four weeks before it happened. Victory was sudden and complete and the general sensation was that of awaking from a nightmare.

In May 1945 the crisis of the war was almost two years past, and so slow was the approach to victory that enthusiasm had lost its vigour. From March to May the armies closed in on Berlin with sullen dogged fighting that produced no moment of sparkling triumph. Several days before V.E. Day the end was obvious—and we waited listlessly for a routine announcement. No one was exhilarated, since to conclude a war with Germany meant only to concentrate on a war with Japan. Experience had taught all those whose memory went back twenty years that a cessation of arms was likely to be followed by economic depression and unemployment. It was commonly foretold that social conditions would be harsher after the war, as indeed they were. We were bankrupt as a nation.

Nevertheless, it was felt that V.E. Day should be celebrated and, with memories of 1918 in my mind, I went to observe the joyful scene. As I was at an R.A.F. headquarters on V.E. Day I persuaded a very senior officer to fly me low over Central London in a light aircraft, in flat defiance of the regulations. How exciting it would be to watch the crowds and the rejoicings from the air. There was no crowd, nothing but a few loiterers in Trafalgar Square looking forlorn and miserable. Abandoning that plan we flew home and drove up to London for the evening. By ten o'clock the town was dead. Bars and restaurants had long since sold out and everyone gone home; and only Rosa Lewis at the Cavendish—very old and tired—could find us a convivial glass. The cockneys had lost the art of singing and dancing in the street. In the ensuing months, restrictions were tightened, rations were reduced, and the call-up of conscripts was maintained. The atom bomb at Hiroshima on 6th August 1945 laid such a doom upon the world that the youngest and silliest could hardly be light-hearted about the future.

(3)

On 17th March 1919, I arrived in England for demobilization, a process concluded in a few hours at a camp on Salisbury Plain, where they gave me a sheaf of papers and a first-class ticket to London. At nine in the evening, having lost my baggage, I reached Waterloo with twopence halfpenny in my pocket, which took me by Tube (with a halfpenny to spare) to the house of my old friends in South Kensington. I was not really penniless; in fact I felt rich, with an order in my wallet for a gratuity of £226. (It was rather more than I got in 1945, in depreciated currency, after a longer war, in which I reached the rank of lieutenant-colonel.)

In a general sort of way I had sometimes thought of renewing a scholastic career, broken five years ago at seventeen years old; or at least of spending my gratuity in an intellectual atmosphere while I looked about me. On learning that I might get another £250 from the Government as a university student I plumped for Oxford, to see how far £450 would take me. I was 'going out in rest' for a long time and thought it would be amusing to read some good books. While I tried to work my way into the modern world by way of Eddington, Bateson, Frazer, Marie Stopes, Bernard Shaw, Dean Inge, Bertrand Russell,

Gilbert Murray, Lytton Strachey, J. M. Keynes, Roger Fry and the Georgian Poets, I gave perfunctory attention to the academic curriculum. After I had spent all I had and all I could borrow, I supposed, I should go back to the life of action. There was the North Russian campaign where my friend Edward Holt[1] had gone, or like another of my friends (who found it rather too tough) I might be a Black-and-Tan in Ireland; or there was a man called General Critchley organizing an ex-officers' settlement in Mexico. Though well content with Oxford, indeed enchanted by the dreaming spires and all that, I could not believe it to be more than a delightful fantasy. Real life asserted itself when I got among some group of growling ex-soldiers who had no regard for the new young scholars—they were not even 'A4' boys. It was only in my last term that I thought of myself as a scholar instead of as a soldier 'on a course'. Too late, too late I came to Oxford, already post-graduate, Kitchener's Army having been the seminary where I took my first degree.

Let me bring my reminiscences to a close. For long, I lived a double life between the external world of the nineteen-twenties and the inner world which was never long out of my mind. On the one hand Oxford, an episode in western Canada, an episode in Scott Fitzgerald's Paris, and conformism—after all—for a few years as a schoolmaster; on the other, an inner glow of sensibility whenever, for an evening, I found myself in the company of ex-soldiers. Always, then, the talk went back to war experiences retailed with an ironic sense that it had been our world and ours alone. While we might criticize the generals or criticize one another we resented it when those others took the liberty of doing so. What could they know? Fortunately, perhaps, they ceased to care or consciously averted their attention from the horrific events they had not shared, and, through the nineteen-twenties, the gap between soldiers and civilians widened. I used to think that a knowledge of adult problems had been forced upon me too young and that at twenty-two I was mature. I now think quite the contrary. The 1916 fixation had caught me and stunted my mental growth, so that even ten years later I was retarded and adolescent. I could not escape from the comradeship of the trenches which had become a mental internment

1. I find I have come to the end of my book without hitherto mentioning Captain Edward Holt, M.C., my immediate senior in the battalion, who shared with me most of the experiences in France that I have described.

camp, or should I say a soldiers' home. I might as well have been in Chelsea Hospital. At last the long convalescence ended with the breaking of a barrier. The inhibition was released in the years 1929 to 1931 when society was brought to its senses by the shock of the great economic depression. The golden age of prosperity and peace again receded into a mythical future, leaving economic man to face the facts of a cold hard world. In the disillusioned nineteen-thirties the ex-soldiers at last could speak and out came tumbling the flood of wartime reminiscences in every country which had sent soldiers to the war.

19

After the War

LONG before the end of the War, Haig had produced a soldier's plan for demobilization which had been merely ignored in Whitehall, where they preferred inhuman schedules. During November and December 1918 and into January 1919, the reduction of the Army's strength by the release of selected tradesmen continued, in spite of dissatisfaction among the soldiers, and in spite of Haig's repeated protests that no provision was made for the Army of Occupation. Of his sixty divisions, an advanced force of sixteen marched forward on 17th November and crossed the Rhine into the Cologne Bridgehead on 9th December, to form an Army of Occupation which was to remain in Germany until 1929, at first under Plumer. They, too, were dwindling every week by selective demobilization and would have vanished in three months if the original plan had been carried out. Haig went home on a visit on 19th December and was received with spontaneous demonstrations of popularity which rather wiped the eye of President Wilson, then in London on an official visit. It allowed Haig an opportunity to press for more urgent attention to the claims of the fighting soldiers and for the relief of disabled men.

The great majority of British soldiers were enlisted for three years or 'the duration of the War', and though a legal commission was invoked to define what the duration of the war meant, legality was of small avail if the soldiers refused to serve. Early in January actual mutinies had broken out at several base camps, both in Britain and overseas, usually among men of the technical services. Several times Whitehall was invaded by mobs of servicemen who had seized army lorries and had driven to London to demonstrate outside the War Office. In these circumstances, when the Army was rapidly disappearing, Winston Churchill took over the War Office in January 1919. He immediately conferred with Haig and, before the end of the month, they produced a new and just system of demobilization giving priority, on a system of points, to older men, married men, and men who had served longest. At the same time Churchill raised the rates of pay for serving soldiers and offered bounties to men who would re-enlist. For example, we raised a battalion of new regulars with no difficulty from the ten dwindling units of our Division in Italy. With 70,000 new regulars and 70,000 'A4' boys Churchill enabled Haig to maintain an Army of Occupation of ten Divisions. Nevertheless, the whole strength of the Army dropped from two millions to 275,000 in 1919.

The moral problem was even greater than the manpower problem, since no one could be sure that the Army might not behave as the French Army had behaved in 1917 or—even worse—might not precipitate a social revolution. This danger was not eliminated for many months and Haig who had fought and won, like Foch, now had to steady troops who were near to mutiny, like Pétain. But the unrest in the British Armies was notably different from the French mutinies of 1917, because the serious trouble came from the rear, not from the front. I have recorded some tremors of discontent that came under my own eye and, to the best of my knowledge, no narrative account of the greater mutinies has been printed. Churchill records that in January some insubordinate transport drivers at Kempton Park attempted to set up a 'Soldiers' Council', and that on 8th February a battalion of the Guards had to be called out to protect Whitehall from a mob of soldiers who refused to join the returning leave-train at Victoria. These last were willing to go back to their units when the station staff attended to their complaints.

On 27th January a more serious outbreak occurred at the base camp at Calais, of which I have seen no printed account except that in Churchill's book. Three or four thousand men of the R.A.S.C. and the Army Ordnance Corps, that is to say men who could hardly be classed as combatants, procured arms, seized control of the camp, and defied the authorities. Haig acted with the firmness that might be expected. He recalled two fighting divisions from the forward zone under Byng, and mounted a regular operation. The mutineers were surrounded and warned that the loyal troops would open fire if they did not surrender, whereupon the mutiny collapsed. Haig seems to have proposed severe punishment under military law and was urged by Churchill to treat the mutineers leniently.

What is significant in this story is Haig's complete confidence in his own men. He judged rightly that the front-line soldiers would maintain discipline when the test came, even if they too were a little ruffled by the misconceived plan of demobilization. The fighting troops had no sympathy with the 'base wallahs' whom they regarded as little better than the profiteering munition-makers in England. The schism in the nation was between the fighting soldiers and the civilians, a psychological cleavage far too wide to be bridged by any political agitation in the back areas, and the question still to be answered was, how would the fighting troops behave after they were demobilized.

In March the Guards Division was brought home from France and paraded through London in fighting order, ostensibly to allow the Londoners to welcome their own familiar defenders, and with a secondary motive of warning the seditious that force would be met by force. I stood in Shaftesbury Avenue to watch the Guards go by, in khaki and steel helmets, while the chorus-girls from the revue then running at the Pavilion came out on the balcony to cheer, in their stage make-up and costumes. It was a celebration, and at the same time a warning that there was still a disciplined army. Throughout the spring and summer while the Peace Conference was sitting at Versailles, criticism of the Government by liberals and socialists, labour troubles, and continued unrest in the base camps, produced just the situation in which a Popular Front might have promoted an agitation to sweep away the Government.

After the signing of the Treaty of Versailles, a day of festivity, Victory Day, was announced for Saturday, 19th July, 1919. London was decorated and thronged with visitors as for a Coronation. A great camp was formed in Hyde Park for representatives of every regiment in the British Army, every Dominion, every Ally. The procession of troops bearing all their regimental colours marched nine miles through the East and West Ends of London to salute the King at Buckingham Palace. They passed through crowded streets which cheered for Foch, who flourished his British field marshal's baton, and louder—as I heard with my own ears—for Haig. No doubt we had won a victory.

The same newspapers which reported the Victory Procession discreetly mentioned in small type on back pages that on that very

Saturday, the celebrations had led to rioting between soldiers and
civilians at Glasgow, Coventry, Epsom and Luton, this last being one
of the most dangerous outbursts in modern English history though it
seems to be quite forgotten. The local soldiers' organization—or so the
meagre reports in the press imply—took offence when the town council
refused them the use of a park for their celebrations. Demonstrators in
uniform broke into the municipal buildings, dispersed the councillors,
sacked the mayor's office, and—by accident or design—burned the
Town Hall to the ground. For many hours until reinforcements of
police could be brought from London, the town of Luton was in the
hands of a riotous mob. Perhaps it was just high spirits like the conduct
of my Bolshevik train. Who was to know that this was not the first
step towards a social revolution?

Scores of old comrades' associations had sprung up, village and
parish groups, regimental associations, groups within Trade Unions,
and groups in factories and firms, some merely social, some formed for
mutual aid, and some with a political slant. No one doubted that these
associations were of great significance and might prove a steadying or a
seditious influence in the national life. Before the end of the War, two
associations of ex-soldiers had already made their influence felt at
Westminster. The National Federation of Discharged Soldiers and
Sailors (N.F.D.S.S.), with a pronounced left-wing flavour, had set
itself to fight for better pensions for disabled men. It revealed its
tendency by confining its membership to the other ranks and by refusing to admit ex-officers. Almost in opposition to the N.F.D.S.S. the
Comrades of the Great War were strongly loyalist and were encouraged by the Conservative Party organization; they were, however, far
from being reactionary and many local lodges of the Comrades were
severely critical of the Government. There was also a National Association allied to the Liberal Party, which declined in importance with
the Liberal vote, and an extremist group, the National Union of
Ex-Servicemen (N.U.X.) which failed to get much support. All the
ingredients were here for the emergence of revolutionary bands as in so
many other countries. With bad handling, the N.F.D.S.S. might have
wung to the left and turned communist; the Comrades of the Great
War might have developed into a fascist militia (though the name
'fascist' was still unknown in 1919). That they did not do so, but com
bined into the non-political British Legion, may be credited to he-

R

innate good sense of the soldiers, to the moderation and tact of the men who came to the head of these associations, and to Sir Douglas Haig who made it his last task to bring all the ex-servicemen's organizations together without distinction of rank and without political affiliations. This may yet be thought his greatest victory.

According to his biographer, Duff Cooper, Haig was invited by each of the two larger associations, the N.F.D.S.S. and the Comrades, to become President, but declined to commit himself to either until they should agree to combine. It would reduce his influence as a national leader of ex-servicemen if he committed himself to the Conservative Comrades, or to the N.F.D.S.S. which excluded officers. He devoted himself to forming an Officers' Association and to preparing the ground for a merger. The N.F.D.S.S. was persuaded to admit ex-officers in June 1919. Haig had one good card to play as C.-in-C. of the Home Forces, in the administration of large charitable funds, over £2,000,000, which he allotted in agreed proportions between the three associations, thus bringing them into negotiation. Many rivalries between local committees had to be overcome and it was not until 1921 that a constitution for the British Legion was agreed, largely through the patience and skill in negotiation of Mr. T. F. Lister of the N.F.D.S.S.

Nothing could have been more decorous than the British Legion when it had united the various groups; too decorous as some old swaddies thought. The first Armistice Day had been a carnival; the second Armistice Day, after its solemn pause at the Two Minutes' Silence which King George V was believed to have initiated, was a day of festivity again. For some years I was one of a group of friends who met, every Armistice Day, at the Café Royal for no end of a party, until we began to find ourselves out of key with the new age. Imperceptibly, the Feast-Day became a Fast-Day and one could hardly go brawling on the Sabbath. The do-gooders captured the Armistice, and the British Legion seemed to make its principal outing a day of mourning. To march to the Cenotaph was too much like attending one's own funeral, and I know many old soldiers who found it increasingly discomforting, year by year. We preferred our reunions in private with no pacifist propaganda.

Epilogue

There have been moments when, searching among disinterred shards of memory for human relics, I have wondered whether the boy I have re-discovered was anything more than a juvenile delinquent, whose characteristics were a love for ganging-up with the other boys, a craving to demonstrate his manliness, and a delight in anti-social violence. At least, I have no doubt that if I had been born the son of a German pastor, instead of being the son of an Anglican clergyman, I should have gone to war in 1914 in much the same spirit. The difference would lie in my mood when I came back, and this is what I now find most difficult to assess. There was a great deal of mental exhaustion to overcome and it was long before we adjusted ourselves to a world in which habits of violence were no longer appropriate. All the elements that produced the phenomenon of fascism in Italy and Germany were at work in the other belligerent countries, and I must explain to myself why they did not erupt in Britain too, among my contemporaries.

The secret of our confused but well-meaning approach to the problems of reconstruction was to be found in the moral justification of the war. The mood of 1914 had been exhilarating because of the rare experience of finding inclination, actual necessity, and the highest principles of conduct pointing the same way. For once in life the plain practical issue coincided with the moral issue. There was no doubt what we ought to do, and the prospect of danger and discomfort gave an additional spur. Juvenile delinquency is the frustrated response to a situation that offers no sufficient challenge for adolescent energy, and a boy like me who was ripe for mischief in April 1914 was, and thought himself, lucky when in August his errant purpose was directed towards a task that was socially acceptable. So much for the teen-age reaction. Far more important is the fact that this teen-ager found himself with the current of national opinion, joining in a spontaneous assertion of the general will. This is what Rupert Brooke meant in the series of sonnets which so accurately expressed the mood of August 1914, and which must be almost unintelligible to later generations.

In 1914, we were all of one mind excepting only those persistent individualists who manage to keep out of step in every procession. The whirligig of taste has swung so far away from the Georgian poets that one hardly dares mention them in modish circles but, till the wheel comes round and they are re-appraised by the critics, it may be necessary to remind my readers that they were progressive radicals, who threw themselves with enthusiasm into the war against German militarism. I was astonished, a year or two ago, when an able young writer who had just published a book on the Spanish troubles, gave me his opinion on the European wars of this century. 'Of course', he said with polite condescension, 'there was no moral element (Was there?) in your First World War'.

During the critical weeks of 1914, the conduct of the Germans brought about so strong a revulsion as to force the tolerant, lazy-minded British to take a moral decision. No party in the state and no pressure-group in the services wanted war with Germany, if only because we were a satisfied power with no irredentist provinces to recover, no old scores to pay off, no economic deficiencies which we could remedy by robbing our neighbours. There was nothing that we could gain by war and much that we might lose. The whole of our strategic thinking was therefore defensive and we were incapable of waging an aggressive campaign against a European power. Even our naval supremacy was maintained for the protection of commerce and, by the Declaration of London in 1911, we had expressed our intention of renouncing the use of economic blockade as a weapon. Only when the Germans blockaded us by means of the submarine campaign did we resume our traditional sea-strategy.

Why, then, did the British decide for war when they might have remained neutral and enjoyed peace for their own island? The old scare-mongering about a German invasion, while it had not induced the nation to accept military service or even to fill the ranks of the territorials, had sown a seed of doubt about German intentions, though, until some evidence appeared, the British people had remained properly sceptical. Surely the civilized Germans would not precipitate a world war in the twentieth century! When it was seen, in broad daylight, that they had launched a long-prepared attack on France and had supported it by the treacherous invasion of Belgium, entirely without provocation, the shock to British opinion was staggering, and the attempt of the German Government to justify its action on grounds of diplomatic necessity served to make their conduct look rather worse in the view of the common man. In Britain the decision for war was wholly moral, and it was taken by the people. The Liberal Government lagged behind opinion until assured that it could rely upon its own anti-militarist supporters (with few exceptions). The greater Trade Unions were for war; the *avant-garde* among the intellectuals were for war (again with few exceptions); and three million volunteers for Kitchener's Army expressed the popular response. It was dismay and indignation at German conduct that brought about this change of heart in a nation that was pacific in its habits, and most effectively in the progressive and radical section of the community. As if the invasion of Belgium had not been cause enough, the Germans added fuel to the flames by the defiant campaign of 'frightfulness' which their leaders loudly announced as their chosen method of making war.

The question of German war guilt has been much confused by idle talk about 'propaganda'. At all times, not least in 1964, the gutter-press issues a stream of absurd exaggerations which are eagerly snapped up by the sort of persons who cannot distinguish fact from rumour. I need not particularize the organs of the Press which cater for this class of readers by presenting all public affairs as a series of scandals and sensations, except to say that they have grown more reckless in the fifty years during which they have been under my observation. There was no lack of fancy in the headlines in 1914, but nothing was so horrible as the facts. It was slowly realized that the weapon of secrecy could do more harm than good, and that judicious publicity is also an effective weapon. The strength of the Ministry of Information in the later part of the war, as of the B.B.C. in the Second World War, was that it told the truth, and the truth was on our side. Meanwhile, the vulgar press continued to put out scandals and sensations which were swallowed by people who require such mental provender. The Germans also used the truth as a weapon and, in every country which they invaded, boasted that they had seized innocent hostages and massacred them to impose a reign of terror, and that they had even sacked cities by way of reprisal.

Theirs is the honour of introducing into the code of war the use of poison gas, the air bombardment of open towns, and the indiscriminate sinking of ships on the high seas. During the first year of the war these avowed actions of the German High Command repeated the shocks which had made all the liberal elements in the British nation their enemies.

Thus the First World War retained for us until the end something of the character of a crusade, and readers of history will recall that the original Crusaders failed to maintain the high principles of conduct which had first inspired them to resist Molsem aggression. Like the Crusades, the First World War revealed another aspect as a squalid series of confused episodes in which each contestant was obliged to admit that military virtues were not restricted to his party, that is to say if the term 'virtue' may be used of the qualities which soldiers respect in one another.

It is more difficult to get out of a war than to get into it. In 1917 there were three possible courses of action for a British Government; we could surrender, and neither Lloyd George at Westminster, nor my friends in Flanders, were disposed to do that; we could attempt a negotiated peace; or we could fight our way through until the German threat was destroyed. Negotiation, whether done in Woodrow Wilson's way or Trotsky's way, broke down on the intransigence of the German High Command, so that no course was open to us but to fight our way through, supposing that there might be enough wisdom in the world to re-constitute a civilized society; and at this stage I must admit to having held political opinions in 1919 that may seem indefensible in 1965. So far was I from believing the terms of the Treaty of Versailles too harsh, I thought that in some respects they were too mild. The war-guilt clauses of the Treaty should have been accompanied, I thought, by a public humiliation of the German war leaders like that which was to be inflicted, twenty-six years later, on their successors, at Nuremberg. Very soon after the Armistice, my friends and I were gloomily saying to one another that the fact of the German defeat in the field had not been given enough publicity, that the legend of a 'stab in the back' was already emerging, and that the unpunished, unrepentant German militarists would soon be threatening us again. We were lulled into security during the nineteen twenties until the appearance of the Nazi movement aroused old anxieties.

The German High Command has been consistently true to the tradition. During its first two centuries of history there was no cause so base, no leader so vile as not to win its enthusiastic support, and we old soldiers were not surprised when the General Staff aligned itself with Hitler, carrying with it those youngsters to whom the war had been nothing but an excuse for juvenile delinquency. The dilemma in which German soldiers were placed was searching, since they had gone to war in 1914, as we did, fired with enthusiasm for what they supposed a worthy cause. They had been defeated and, as their military power crumbled, thoughtful soldiers must have been assailed with doubts more harassing than lost battles. Had they deserved victory? Was not their failure a manifest blessing to the world and a concealed blessing to themselves? In short, had they not been sacrificed by unworthy leaders in a bad cause?

Within the field of politics, we had no such misgivings. For us, the horrors of war had been justified to the extent that we had liberated Belgium and the occupied provinces of France; and had destroyed the German military tyranny. No one could deny that we had started with these intentions and had done what we set out to do. If the last state of Europe was worse than the first we were not to blame. The nature of the pacifist reaction in Britain was ethical not political, and was based on the realization that the cost in blood and suffering was too high. Very well! If we must fight for liberty again, said the soldiers, let us find a less costly way of fighting, and this was the intention in 1939.

But this mode of thought widened the gap between soldiers and civilians. The war was something rejected, forgotten, by the civilians who saw it only as a disaster from which a new world was painfully emerging; and by the soldiers who saw it as an achievement, finished and tidied away. The civilians wanted to hear no more of it; the soldiers kept it to themselves to be discussed in private, like a masonic secret.

(2)

The production of books would be an easy trade if publishers could always forecast the vagaries of popular taste. I cannot say why the reading public, which was unwilling to attend to any comment on the war for about ten years after the Armistice, suddenly, in 1928 and 1929, developed an appetite for realistic expositions of trench-life, good or bad. The boom was touched off by the drums and cymbals which announced the publication in many languages of Erich Maria Remarque's *All Quiet on the Western Front*, a piece of sensational fiction chiefly notable for graphic descriptions of those bodily functions that most of us prefer to perform in private. The back-area accounts of soldiers at the base were true to life and sometimes powerfully depicted, but the nearer the characters came to the front the more did critical readers doubt whether the author had ever been there. This remains a classic example of a bad book inflated into a best-seller by the arts of publicity, not because it was forced upon the public but because its promoters correctly judged what morbid appetites just then could stomach. It appeared that dirt about the war was in demand. So gigantic a best-seller was it that scores of would-be authors[1] in every belligerent country rushed into print with revealing reminiscences, while the market was good. No one but a research worker is now likely to burrow into this pile of seasonal products, and even for the student it should be enough to work from Dr. Cyril Falls's masterly annotated list (*War Books*, 1930). The common form of this flood of print was the determination of many exhibitionists to tell the world how unhappy they had been in the Army. Book after book related a succession of disasters and discomforts with no intermission and no gleam of achievement. Every battle a defeat, every officer a nincompoop, every soldier a coward. No doubt this flood of misanthropy has engendered a myth about the First World War which has started many an enquirer on a false trail. The corrective may be applied by asking how, if the soldiers were the woebegone creatures described in the War books, did they stand against the German onslaught in March 1918 and break the Hindenburg Line in September.

This was the mood of 1929 and 1930, at a depressed moment in world affairs, a hysterical phase as well worth the attention of social scientists as the hysterical phase of 1914. The later, like the earlier, fit has had a lasting effect upon the patient so that it is as difficult now to re-enter the world as it was before the anti-war revulsion, as to re-enter the world before 1914 when war was unthinkable—or at least unthought. Perhaps now we are far enough away to see the fits of hysteria in relation to one another, at least to recall that great numbers of soldiers in 1930 indignantly repudiated the character which was foisted

1 The present writer among them.

on them by the self-pitying school. But the ear of the public was tuned in another direction. The heart of the matter is that war is a social phenomenon to be judged by its effects upon groups. To be sure it affects individuals, but only in the sense that every social event has a number of particular consequences. What the self-pitying school had to say was that they were miserable because they were misfits in the Army, the reason being that they could not share the social enthusiasm which made other men almost welcome hardships. That there should be exceptions to the normal rules of conduct is not surprising, though they tell us little except about themselves. The mass of conformists are as well worth study as the vocal handful of nonconformists. Though I shall make no effort here to assess the value of the war books of other nations, I admit that honest accounts of the soldier's life were written by German writers such as Otto Braun, Rudolf Binding and Ernst Junger. There are English war books which deserve a kindly criticism and I shall allude to three written by poets: Sassoon, Graves, and Blunden.

By chance, Siegfried Sassoon and Robert Graves found themselves serving in the same regular battalion of the Royal Welch Fusiliers. Both were commencing poets; both were exceptionally brave men; and there, but for a caprice that I shall mention presently, the resemblance ends. Sassoon, 'the fox-hunting man', was, by his own showing, a late developer who had reached the age of thirty without applying his acute and subtle intelligence to the problems of life. The war shocked him into a new dimension of thought with the consequence, not uncommon in such cases, that he fell headlong into the first heresy that he encountered, and was exploited, rather disingenuously, by the propagandists of his new cult. The pacifist press, delighted at having caught a genuine war hero, tried their best to make a conspicuous martyr of him, and Sassoon allowed himself to be offered as a sacrifice. The gesture failed because the High Command, not at all what he supposed it to be, treated him with considerate sympathy. He soon tired of the left-wing journalists who had pushed him into publicity and resumed his allegiance to the 'patient men who fight'.

'Love drove me to rebel
Love drives me back to grope with them through Hell.'

he wrote. For ten readers who know of Siegfried Sassoon's protest are there two who know that he returned to duty, performed more feats of valour, and ended the war a wounded hero, like so many others. Read his early poems again and you will find that his obsession was not so much 'anti-war' as disgust at the cleavage between the frontline soldiers and the back-area *embusqués*. He did not, of course, 'approve of the War'. Who but a half-wit could at any stage? He reluctantly came back to the common man's point of view that the honourable way out of the mess was to go forward. But Sassoon was so rare a spirit, so aloof and sensitive, as to be unable to share the emotions of the coarse-grained commonalty whom he observed with detached pity, except in moments of illumination. There are pages in his books which suggest that, like Gulliver among the Houynhnhnms, he preferred horses to human beings. The reader of his verse is almost surprised when the spark of genius flashes out in fellow-feeling, as in the poem about the column breaking into song on the march, to me the supreme revelation of the soldier's life:

> 'Everyone's voice was suddenly lifted;
> And beauty came like the setting sun:
> My heart was shaken with tears; and horror
> Drifted away . . .'

If this is not pure poetry, I know none.

How different was his loyal friend Robert Graves, the pugnacious Irishman, who could be counted on to enjoy any fight and to differ from his colleagues about the best method of conducting it. We may learn much from the fact that he ended the war an instructor in the famous 'bull-ring', the battle-training course at Rouen. But these two individualists, the secretive man who shrank from familiarity and the proud man who was determined to have his own way, shared an obsession. They were both passionately addicted to their regiment, to which they ascribed virtues it could not have possessed and advantages over all other regiments. They hated the Army; they despised their seniors; and they loved the Royal Welch Fusiliers, an irrational emotion that tells us more of the truth than any of their rationalizations. Graves, in particular, loses no opportunity of denouncing his superiors in terms which would convince us, if we believed him, that they were worthless as officers and not classifiable as gentlemen in any of the senses in which that term is used. If they had been what he says they were, the Fusiliers would have been a bad regiment, and his friend Sassoon would have been treated in quite another manner. In short, Robert Graves's book, very lively reading, tells us little about the Army and a great deal about himself. From his later writings it appears that he was as unsuccessful as I have been in saying 'Good-bye to all that'.

Edmund Blunden's *Undertones of War* is a book to be placed in another category, the only one among the many British soldiers' reminiscences that I should class as literature in its own right, a book that would be remembered and read, whatever the circumstances in which it had been written; all the others are *pièces d'occasion*. So firmly constructed, so deeply wrought out of genuine experience, so exquisitely finished is this book that it transcends circumstance and, once mastered by a reader, it can never be forgotten. Yet its devoted students are likely to be few, as the author foretells in his preface, because it is allusive and not explicit. After the wartime generation has passed away it will require a commentary and, as one of Edmund Blunden's admirers, I should be proud to think that my crude rendering of the soldiers' chorus would help some of my readers to detect his undertones.

The craze for war-books died down in 1931 and did not reappear until a generation had arisen who scarcely remembered the Second World War. By this time, we veterans of the First were so far removed from current modes of thought as to be mere relics of antiquity, buried beneath many historical strata. Not only did the pacifist mood of the early nineteen-thirties conceal our true character, but the bellicose traditions of the Spanish Civil War and of the Second World War had overlaid it with new conceptions of military ethic.

I could not join in the emotional fervour of some sections of the British people over the rights and wrongs of the Spanish Revolution. The inconsequent ferocity with which the party leaders conducted their struggle for power was traditional in Spanish history and untranslatable into English political terms. I cared little which of these corrupt gangs of thugs exterminated the other, though with perhaps a slightly greater distaste for the party that murdered priests than for the party that murdered trade-union leaders. On the other hand, British interests stood to lose more by the triumph of the fascists, since their

German allies were efficient and dangerous, than from the triumph of the 'republicans', whose Russian backers were treacherous and incompetent. Further than that I could not go, and I was satisfied when Franco neatly bilked his German friends. As for the internal state of Spain, if an outsider could judge,[1] a 'republican' triumph would have been no less bloody and a great deal more chaotic. To represent their quarrelsome combination of discredited party hacks, provincial separatists, Trotsky-ites and Anarchists as the stuff of an ideal Republic was a feat worthy of the countrymen of Don Quixote. If there was a moral element in the dismal contest in atrocity it was too much overlaid with immoral elements to engage my loyalty. But here again a man of 1914 was quite out of step. The left-wing intelligentsia, the 'Rupert Brookes' of the period, took up the cause of the Spanish 'republicans' as a new crusade; many volunteered, fought, and died; and a man can do no more. I must recall, however, that when the genuine, explicit, war against fascism broke out, a number of the Spanish crusaders took refuge in neutral countries, as if their motives had been mixed, or as if their morality were soon exhausted.

The dominant emotion in Britain in 1938 and 1939 was sheer fright. Our military weakness, our shifty diplomacy, the policy of appeasement (in the worst sense of that polluted word), mere muddle, mere cowardice, and a younger generation misguided by ten or twelve years of sentimental propaganda, had reduced the British to a state of political incoherence in which it might well have been supposed that nothing would drive them to war. Munich was the only day in my life —so far—when I have been ashamed of being British.[2] Of pretence and hypocrisy there was plenty, but I could find no moral principle at work, unless bowing to the inevitable counts as a virtue.

In the whole field of national endeavour almost nothing had been thought out for implementing the policy to which the Chamberlain Government belatedly committed us, and we should have been lost if there had not been, in one direction, a plan and a production line. Only the radio-controlled Spitfires saved us from defeat and, among government departments, only the Air Ministry comes out of the nineteen-thirties with any credit—but not much. Having won time by our defensive Battle of Britain, and having equipped ourselves with an

1. I spent one day in Barcelona in 1938! Would this make me an 'expert'?
2. Though I came near to the same sensation during the Suez incident of 1956.

effective government, we began to make war in 1941, by which time no moral choice remained to us. We were in it—sink or swim. The younger generation reacted as their fathers' sons might have been expected to react, quickly shedding the emotional fantasies that had deluded them between the Wars. Even Ribbentrop had warned Hitler that the pacifist resolution of the Oxford Union was not to be taken seriously. Teen-agers, with all their virtues and charms, have little political foresight and, when the crisis came, they were as ready as we had been to fight for King and Country.

Since the generals of the Second World War had been the majors and colonels of the First, they profited, when their turn came for high command, by the lessons of their early experience. The mistakes made in the years of defeat, 1940 and 1941, were not the same mistakes that had been made in 1915 and 1916; but the generals of 1941 again had to bear the blame for not possessing the weapons which the civilian politicians had refused to finance; this seems a constant in British military history. What the nation was spared, as a result of the foresight of the soldiers, was a repetition of the drain on our young manhood like the Somme and Passchendaele. Mistakes were plentiful, in the Second World War as in all human affairs, but for the British the price was not paid in simple bloodshed. It should not be supposed that, because we endured no massacres like that of 1st July 1916, the Second World War was more humane. There is always progress, and the sheer volume of blood spilt in the German extermination camps, in the siege of Stalingrad, in the 'conventional' bombing of Dresden, and in the atomic bombing of Hiroshima was far greater than that of any First War battle.

Time marches on; and the slippered pantaloon who writes these lines is aware that his accents are growing shrill. Perhaps he would have been wiser not to protest so much, but to let his case stand on the record of that young soldier who once sought the bubble reputation in the cannon's mouth. He has yet to explain why he renewed the search, twenty years later.

APPENDIX A

Western Front Strategy, 1914–18

The Germans had prepared strategic railways on both banks of the Rhine, with spurs leading forward to the French and Belgian frontiers. From the layout of the railways it was obvious that a main thrust would come through Cologne, Aachen and Liége. It was certain then that Belgium would be invaded. But would the Germans also invade Holland to use the Dutch strategic railways? (They did in 1939 but not in 1914.) The French staff thought not; they expected the main thrust through the Meuse valley, the shortest way to Paris. Henry Wilson disagreed and was right; he thought they would swing wider through Brussels as indeed they did, bringing Antwerp into the picture. All the newcomers to the problem (Kitchener, Roberts, Churchill) wanted to use Antwerp for taking the Germans in the flank, and even Sir John French had leanings that way; but the staff officers with secret information said it was impossible. The ships and trains and loading schedules were already prepared to bring the B.E.F. into action at Maubeuge for a campaign that would be settled in forty days. Kitchener and Haig didn't agree; they expected a long war; but the plan was already in motion and couldn't be stopped. Kitchener tried to hold back, thinking that Maubeuge was too far forward; he wanted to concentrate at Amiens but the B.E.F. actually went still farther forward to Mons.

The French plan was to advance and meet the Germans on the frontier with great strength in the centre, where French élan would drive them back against the hilly country and would there defeat them. The armies would attack everywhere so that the German advance would be thrown into confusion. This plan failed: the French could not reoccupy Alsace and though they held in the centre from Nancy to Rheims, they were overwhelmed on the left by the strength of Von Kluck's Army against which Henry Wilson had warned them. Sir John, commanding the British, and Lanrezac, commanding the French left-wing, each did very well and each fought more than one effective rear-guard action, but they quarrelled personally and co-operated badly. Lanrezac was dismissed (the penalty for having been right) and Sir John was humiliated by Kitchener who came to France and overruled him.

The Battle of the Marne and the German withdrawal to the Aisne left the whole Western Front from Soissons to Belfort—three hundred miles—much where it was to be stabilized for three years. Attention then shifted to the open flank and there followed the 'race to the sea'. The French command was now nervous about the British, who seemed to be looking over their left shoulders and thinking too much of an escape route (the policy they had to adopt in 1939). So the British were not put on the outer flank but were sandwiched between two French armies under the general control of Foch. The battle of Ypres, October–November 1914, was an allied battle and relations between the two armies were never better. In October, Kitchener and Churchill made their gallant attempt to hold the Belgian coast as far as Antwerp. Most of the detachments they landed on the coast fought their way through to link up with the B.E.F. at Ypres. By mid-October, the northern sector was stabilized from the Somme to the Channel—100 miles—completing the Western Front from Nieuport in Belgium to the Swiss frontier. It secured for Germany the industrial region of Artois and the Lorraine mines, as well as the open plains of Picardy and Champagne between the Meuse and the Somme, country whose only value was as a threat to France.

During the period of trench warfare, strategy turned on the lateral railways by which reserves and stores could be moved to a threatened sector of the front. In Champagne, the Germans were dangerously near the French lateral railway along the Marne, where a small advance would cut the French Armies in two; at Noyon they were within sixty miles of Paris; at Gommecourt Wood near Arras they were only thirty miles from the railway between Amiens and Abbeville, the main link between the British and the French.

On the other hand, the long-range objective of the allies was to breach the German lateral railway through Ostend, Roulers, Valenciennes, Maubeuge, Hirson, Sedan, and Metz, so that the German armies would be divided and could be defeated one by one. In their centre the Germans had to contend with the hilly region of the Ardennes, not rough or steep enough to prevent movement, but unprovided with railways and, in 1914, ill-provided with roads. The railway-bound armies of those days had to go round, either north about by the Meuse Valley or south about by the Moselle Valley, and if the Allies could regain control of the central sector—Sedan to Maubeuge— the Germans would be cut in two. It was only on the last day of the war that this object was achieved. (Again it may be noticed that the 1939 French armies still conceived themselves as railway-bound. The German lightning-stroke came through the supposedly impassable Ardennes by the new roads.)

In the centre the extensive Noyon salient was, for the French, part of the prize of victory. The offensives in 1915 and again in the spring of 1917 were designed to cut off the German armies in the salient from both flanks, by a British attack (with or without French help) in Artois and by a French attack in Champagne. The 1915 battles failed.

The 1916 battles were of a different character. Falkenhayn had set the pace by launching his offensive at Verdun with the deliberate intention of bringing the French armies to battle and wearing them down with repeated bombardments and assaults, a strategy of attrition not of movement. He selected Verdun as the battleground not because its capture would give him any geographical advantage but because he was convinced—and rightly—that the French would never give it up, for reasons of prestige. He would bring them to battle there, would maintain the initiative, and would destroy the French Army in the field. He did not quite succeed and failure in a battle of attrition is likely to be disastrous to the attacker.

Joffre called upon the British to draw off the pressure by opening another battle on their front which Haig—always loyal to the French alliance—accordingly did. The Battle of the Somme was again a battle of attrition. The place and time were not what Haig thought promising but were imposed upon him by Joffre. An advance on the Somme front would bring no obvious strategic benefit; it was chosen because it was thought to be a good place to bring the German Army to battle. Haig's own view was that when a breach had been effected the British armies should turn northwards and roll up the German flank since that would bring him to a real prize in the Artois industrial region; but Joffre seems not to have been much interested. He preferred to drive the Germans straight back, killing them where they stood.

Both battles, Verdun and the Somme, were partially successful in that the flower of the French Army was destroyed in one and the flower of the German Army in the other but the cost was too great. The attackers suffered heavier losses than the defenders.

The Nivelle offensive in 1917 was made irrelevant by the German withdrawal from the salient to the so-called Hindenburg Line. In Picardy they lost nothing by this withdrawal and economized by shortening and rationalizing their front. In Artois they had less ground to spare and were obliged to secure the industrial region. They therefore made a shorter withdrawal in the north and covered the flank of the Hindenburg Line by a switch, or retrenchment, known as the Wotan Line, which was to give the British much trouble.

After the Nivelle offensive of 1917, the Noyon salient having gone and the threat to Paris having receded, Haig was able to return to his own strategic objectives. His consistent view had been that an attack should be launched against the German communications in Flanders. The key-point was the railway junction of Roulers, only twelve miles from Ypres and the nearest point to the battle front on the German lateral railway. Break through to Roulers and the whole German front in Flanders must collapse, freeing the Flanders coast and allowing the British full use of their sea-power, a factor that the French underrated. Haig had been secretly preparing his Flanders attack for more than a year, both by Plumer's mining operations at Messines and by plans agreed with the Admiralty for a coastal landing. In 1915 he had been compelled while still a subordinate commander to fight other battles; in 1916 he had been diverted by Joffre from Flanders to the Somme; in early 1917 the Nivelle fiasco had drawn him into battle at Arras; it was only in the summer of that year that he could fight his own chosen battle. It was too late and the weather and the mud defeated him.

The year 1918 produced a complete reversal, when the defection of Russia enabled the Germans to bring greatly preponderant numbers to the Western Front. Ludendorff's offensives were a return to the break-through battles of 1915 and 1917. Though he succeeded in doing what Nivelle had failed to do, again, as in 1914, the fighting qualities of the British, and French, soldiers stopped him, and again, as at the Marne, the nerve of the German Higher Command failed at the decisive point. The allies were better soldiers, and Foch and Haig were better generals than their adversaries. It is nerve that wins battles and the last battle is the one that matters.

S

APPENDIX B

Statistics

I shall conclude with a few general statistics, which I offer humbly, admitting them to be inadequate.

The 'ration strength' of the B.E.F., which had been 164,000 in September 1914, rose to 600,000 by May 1915, to 1,500,000 by December 1916, and was 2,000,000 in December 1917, after which there was a decline, in the combatant rather than in the non-combatant troops. The highest figure of mouths to be fed in the Gallipoli campaign, in the autumn of 1915, was 85,000 combatants and 42,000 non-combatants (mostly in the island of Lemnos).

The total enlistment in the United Kingdom was 4,971,000, that is 22 per cent of the adult male population, of whom 3,000,000 volunteers joined the forces before conscription was introduced in April 1916. No rash deduction should be drawn from these figures since the great majority of the conscripts were called up on reaching the statutory age and many of them would have enlisted in any case.

At the end of the war, in December 1918, the distribution of the British armies was as the table on the following page.

The total casualties of the British Armies on all fronts throughout the war were: killed or died, 908,371; wounded, 2,090,212; prisoners, 191,652. The deaths in France and Flanders were 611,654 of whom 488,000 were from the United Kingdom, and 37,452 were officers. Of all British men who passed through the age group, 19 to 38, during the war years, about one in seven was killed or died on active service.

Canadian casualties in France were 207,000; Australian casualties 178,000; New Zealand casualties 45,000; Indian casualties 20,000.

U.S. casualties in France were 325,876, of whom 115,000 were killed or died.

Casualties in Gallipoli were 114,000, in Mesopotamia, 88,000; in

DISTRIBUTION OF THE BRITISH ARMIES IN 1918

	Regular and K.'s Army	Territorial	Dominion	Indian	Total
France	3 Cavalry 35 Infantry	16 Infantry	10 Infantry	—	3 Cavalry 61 Infantry
Italy	2 ,,	1 ,,	—	—	3 ,,
Egypt and Palestine	—	1 Cavalry 1 ,,	2 Cavalry	1 Cavalry 2 Infantry	4 Cavalry 3 Infantry
Salonica	4 ,,	—	—	—	4 Infantry
Mesopotamia	1 ,,	—	—	1 Cavalry 4 Infantry	1 Cavalry 5 ,,
India	—	3 ,,	—	3 Infantry	6 Infantry
U.K.	—	1 Cyclist 4 ,,	—	—	1 Cyclist 4 ,,
	3 Cavalry 42 Infantry	1 Cyclist, 1 Cavalry 25 Infantry	2 Cavalry 10 Infantry	2 Cavalry 9 Infantry	9 mounted, 90 Infantry

Egypt, 50,000; in Salonica, 27,000; in East Africa, 17,000; in Italy, 6,000; in North Russia, 800.

The first campaign of the war, from Mons to Ypres, cost us 85,000 casualties, of whom 15,000 were taken prisoner or interned in Holland. The battles of 1915, from Neuve Chapelle to Loos, cost 246,000 casualties; in the ensuing winter the drain of losses from trench warfare never sank lower than 8,000 a month (in November 1915). The figure given for the Somme period, omitting losses during the preparations in June, is 513,000, and in the severe winter of 1916–17 the monthly loss did not fall below 14,000 (in January). Arras, Messines, Passchendaele, and Cambrai cost 751,000 in 1917, including 6,000 taken prisoner in the Cambrai counter attack, the first significant figure of prisoners lost since 1914. The campaign of 1918 brought victory at a cost of 831,000, of whom 66,000 were made prisoner. The grand total for France and Flanders is 2,706,000, killed or died, wounded and prisoners. 72,000 men were wounded twice, and 11,000 three times. 573 prisoners escaped.

The Royal Navy, with a strength of 390,000, lost 32,000 dead

The Mercantile Marine lost 14,000 dead.

The R.F.C. went to France in 1914 with 109 officers, 66 aeroplanes, and 95 motor vehicles. By May 1918 their strength had risen to 1,658 pilots with 1,260 serviceable aircraft, and their casualty rate to 200 a month.

The growth of ammunition supply may be judged by the despatch to France of shells for the eighteen-pounders:

September, 1914	3,000 per month	
January, 1915	93,000 ,, ,,	
April, 1915	400,000 ,, ,,	
October, 1915	1,000,000 ,, ,,	(none yet provided by the Ministry of Munitions)
Summer of 1917	8,000,000 ,, ,,	

MAPS

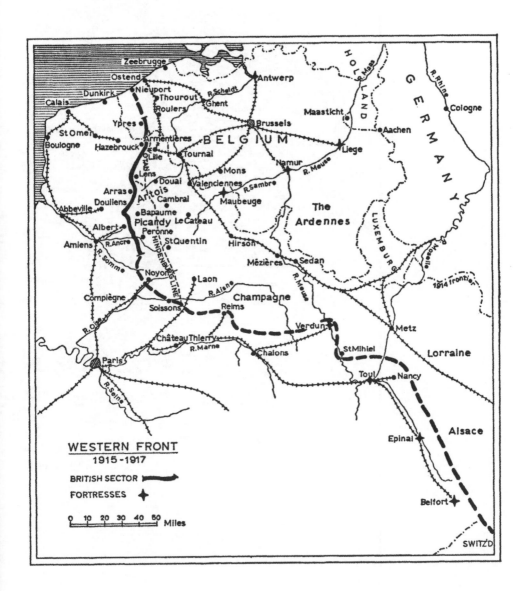

WESTERN FRONT
1915 - 1917

BRITISH SECTOR
FORTRESSES

0 10 20 30 40 50 Miles

Ostende

Bruges

°Antwerp

Dunkerque

Ghent

Belgian
Army

Calais

6th French
Army
(Degoutte)

French

Portuguese

St Omer

(Sixt v. Armin)

BRUSSELS

°Boulogne

2
(Plumer)

Portuguese

Lille

(v. Quast)

B E L

°Etaples

5
(Birdwood)

Bethune

Tourhai

Mons

Charler

Montreuil

BRITISH ARMY
(HAIG)

French Cavalry moving north

1
(Horne)

Scarpe

Douai

(Otto v. Below)

°Maubeuge
(v. der Marwitz)

Abbeville

Doullens°

3
(Byng)
Albert°

Aulnoye
(v. Hutier)

BOEHN CROWN

4 American
(Rawlinson)
Amiens

Hirson
(v. Carlowitz)

7
(v. Eberhardt)

(v. Mudra)

°Montdidier

1
(Debeney)

Laon

Rethel

Compiègne

Soissons

10
(Mangin)

Italians

Reims

Châlons

G. A. FAYOLLE

°Château-Thierry

5
(Berthelot)

4
(Gourau

PARIS

G. A. MAISTRE

F   R   A   N   C   E

Scale of Miles

0   10   20   40   60   80

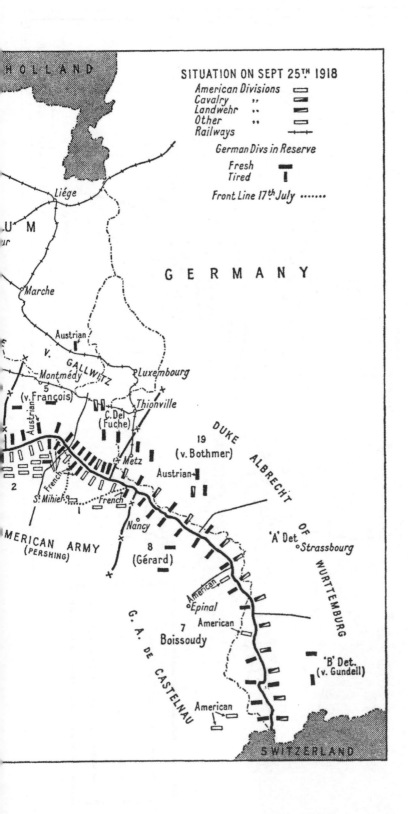

SITUATION ON SEPT 25ᵀᴴ 1918

American Divisions
Cavalry   ,,
Landwehr   ,,
Other   ,,
Railways

German Divs in Reserve

Fresh
Tired

Front Line 17ᵗʰ July ....

HOLLAND

Liége

U M

ur

Marche

GERMANY

Austrian

V.

GALLWITZ

Montmédy   Luxembourg

5
(v. François)

Thionville

Austrian

C.Del
(Fuche)

19
(v. Bothmer)

DUKE

ALBRECHT

Metz

Austrian

2

St Mihiel

French

French

Nancy

OF

'A' Det.
Strassbourg

WURTTEMBURG

MERICAN ARMY
(PERSHING)

8
(Gérard)

American
Epinal

G. A. DE CASTELNAU

American

7
Boissoudy

'B' Det.
(v. Gundell)

American

SWITZERLAND

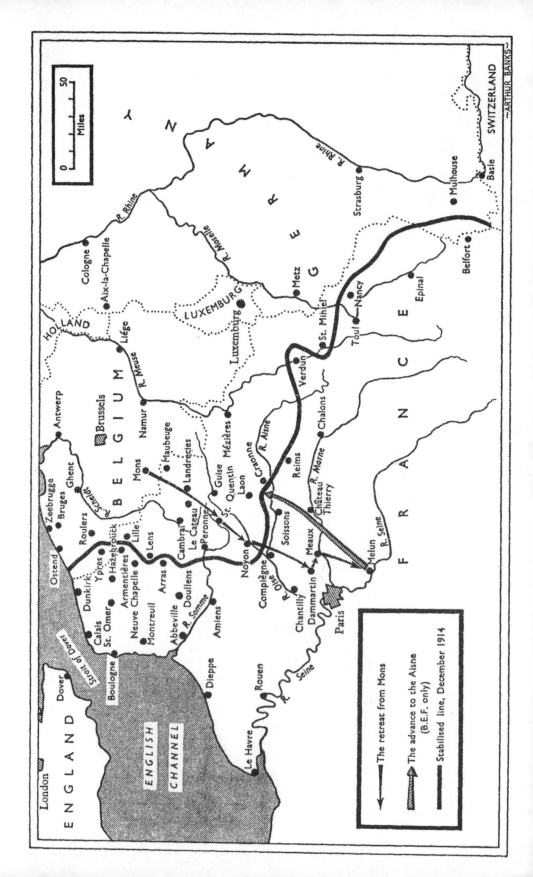

Index